Hiroo
page 17

Tokyo: An industrious city of happy, hardworking, energetic people

Last year in Japan . . .

Over fifty thousand young people lined up for hours to leave flowers at a

Prepared by *

Alex Urbansky
Andrew Watt
Astrid Klein
Dave Yarrington
Doc Agitprop
Gilles Kennedy
Gwen Robinson
Ian Kennedy
Izumi "Pina" Sekine
Jackie Mikami
Jason Atomic
Jude Brand
Kara Besher
Ken Straiton
Khristine Schaffner
Mark Dytham
Mike Kleindl
N.B.
NikNak
Phillip Musgrave
Rick Kennedy
Robbie Swinnerton
Russell Fujiwara
Stella Regalia
Steve McClure
Tim Girdler
Tim Young
Tony Trollope
Yuhei Takeuchi
Yums Hoist

With the assistance of

Kaz Hayashi
Mikie Yaginuma

Featuring photographs by

Astrid Klein
Kara Besher
Ken Straiton
Mark Dytham

And material from the archives of

Andrew Watt

Sponsored by

Sony Communication Network

* Listed alphabetically by first name. This is how the *Japan Times*, *Asahi Evening News*, *Daily Yomiuri*, and *Mainichi Daily News*, Japan's English-language newspapers, list the names of foreigners to whom the Post Office has not been able to deliver mail.

ANNUAL GUIDE TO THE CITY

2000 – 2001

by the staff of Tokyo Q

A WEEKLY ON-LINE CITY MAGAZINE

Stone Bridge Press • Berkeley, California

• • • • technique is detailed in a best-selling book on how to commit suicide.) Many of the mourners had dyed their hair • • •

Published by
Stone Bridge Press
P. O. Box 8208
Berkeley, CA 94707
☎ 510-524-8732
sbp@stonebridge.com
www.stonebridge.com

We believe that information in this book was accurate at the time of publication. You can help us by sending corrections, updates, and suggestions for inclusion in future editions of this book to the Publisher at tokyoqupdate@stonebridge.com.

Photograph on front cover by Ken Straiton.

Printed in the United States of America.

10 9 8 7 6 5 4 3 2 1
2005 2004 2003 2002 2001 2000

ISBN 1-880656-40-X

• • • • • • • flamboyantly in a style favored by Matsumoto, who was guitarist for the rock band Japan X. Police called in to •

CONTENTS

BEING AT HOME IN TOKYO 7

Finding Maps 10

NEIGHBORHOODS 13

LITTLE HOTELS 27

PERFORMANCE 33

Art Movie Houses 36
Shimokitazawa 38

NIGHTLIFE 41

Tokyo Jazz Spots 44
Key Live Music Venues 52

The Art Scene 59

For More Information 65

Tokyoscapes: Architecture 67

Architecture Galleries 68
Architecture Books and Bookstores 69

Good Tokyo Restaurants 73

Best "Old Tokyo" Restaurants 76
Best Coffee Houses 78
Best Brew Pubs 84
Yums Hoist's Five Favorites 87
Restaurants with Stylish Decor 90
Best Sidewalk Cafes 92
Cheap French Places 98
Cheap Italian Places 108
Best Wine Bars 113

Izakaya: Sake Bars 117

Izakaya Etiquette 119
A Brief Sake Glossary 122

Sento: Public Baths 129

Just Yu 133

Last Stop 139

The Tokyo Q Gang 139
Index: Where to Buy 142
Index: Where to Eat 142
Image Credits 143
About Tokyo Q 143

•••••••keep order, few of whom had any idea who Matsumoto was, said they were impressed by the docility of such a •

BEING AT HOME IN TOKYO

by Rick Kennedy

CITIES derive their character from the details. Paris: the river, the roof lines, the comfort of the benches in the parks. New York: the taxi klaxons, the narrow sky, the cloth-capped news agents with a short cigar stuck into one side of the mouth. Tokyo: the crows, the bicycles, and the ding, ding, ding of the train crossings. But somehow there seem to be more details making up Tokyo than other cities because, after all, the city is enormous. As well as tightly packed: a quarter of the population of Japan lives within fifty kilometers of Tokyo Station—that's over thirty million people. All this highly compressed diversity makes Tokyo hard to come to grips with. People new to the city seem confused, as if caught in an artillery barrage. They remark on what they later come to think of as uncharacteristic details while somehow failing to get a picture of the city as a whole.

The purpose of this little guide is to point out some really wonderful things, some of the best of what Tokyo has to offer. Consider it the little

Rick Kennedy almost always carries a little camera with him. The photos placed (more or less) randomly throughout this book are just what happened to catch his eye as he moves around this crazily photogenic city.

black book of our thirty contributors, who have collectively lived in Tokyo for 265 years. We have made no attempt to cover the city systematically. If it seems that we have spent a lot of time in Ebisu and not very much in Nerima-ku, that's an accurate perception. If it seems we don't have much to say about Tokyo's "ethnic" restaurants, that's because none happen to be on our list of absolute favorites. If you absorb the information in this little book, you will not only be extremely well informed about modern Tokyo (to the extent that your friends will pester you for suggestions on where to go and what to do), but there is a good chance that along the way you will decide that Tokyo is one of your favorite cities.

What Makes Tokyo Tokyo

Here, then, are some of the details that characterize Tokyo. Tokyoites who leave the city to reside abroad for a while know they have returned home when they come across these things again.

The fantastic tangle of electrical wires in the sky, found sculpture in the spirit of Jackson Pollock.

Cheap little French restaurants, like Pas a Pas in Yotsuya Sanchome, often better than their counterparts in Paris.

The swirling world of high-school fashion.

Quiet coffeehouses where every cup is brewed individually, and where you can take the time to read a book, or write one. A visit to Bon in Shinjuku, for instance, is an experience. You get your choice of antique, museum-quality cup and saucer and the choice of two kinds of cream. The use of sugar is not encouraged.

Homeless men supporting themselves by retrieving discarded magazines from the

•••••••large crowd of young people dressed all in black with their red-and-yellow hair standing straight up. Three •

dust bins in stations and selling them back to commuters for ¥100.

The guy with his pet crow in front of Shibuya Station, entertaining the loiterers for a few yen tossed in his hat.

Yatai street carts with their cauldron of oden stew, where customers sit on plastic beer crates and drink warm sake from chipped mugs.

Buying a bento for lunch in the basement of a department store and taking it to the park.

Sidewalk cafes, with French magazines for local color.

The underground commentary on the Rakugaki ("Scribble") Board at Yoyogi Station, where, for as long as anyone can remember, the station master has caused to be thumbtacked up every morning two old posters, blank side out, which amateur cartoonists, sometimes of startling talent, fill up by the end of the day.

The sweet lady at the post office who will show you what new commemorative stamps she has and who will, if she has time, stick them on your letters for you.

Japanese gangsters, who dress like some Platonic ideal of a Japanese gangster (white patent-leather shoes and a crisp brush cut) and sprawl on the seat to take up more than their share of space on the train, as a matter of principle.

Easy-to-park minicars with engines the size of a motorcycle's: the ideal city car.

Women in plaid uniforms bicycling house to house to deliver tiny plastic bottles of drinkable yoghurt to subscribers.

Tokyo garbagemen, with their immaculate pressed uniforms, running between pick-up spots.

Where to Buy

GROCERIES

Asian Super Store, #202, 1-1-11 Okubo, Shinjuku-ku. ☎ 03-3208-9199.
Thai shop selling vegetables, sauces, jars of bamboo shoots, and canned goods like rambutan in syrup. Intriguing canned beverages include tamarind, cane, and coconut nectar. There's also recorded Thai music to add a little authentic atmosphere to your home-cooking adventures. (Downstairs there's a supermarket where everything costs ¥100.)

Beginning the day with the six o'clock baroque concert on NHK radio.

The summer windbells and glasses of cold barley tea. And bowls of shaved ice flavored with strawberry syrup.

And ramune, old-fashioned lemonade, in a bottle sealed by a marble.

Rooftop beer halls, especially the one in Kudanshita overlooking the palace moat.

Hanabi ("flower fires" or fireworks) on the Sumida River, with the whole city gathered to watch.

Katorisenko insect coils, which give off a scent forever associated with balmy summer evenings.

Winter heating by kotatsu, with the family huddled together around the little table.

The man whose calling in life is carrying a big block of crystal-clear ice around the Ginza on the back of his old bicycle, taking orders from bars whose customers require only one perfectly sized, hand-

••• twenty-four-year-old men drove a truck over a 300-year-old wooden bridge designated a national treasure, ••••••

Finding Maps

Everyone, when they first get to Tokyo, feels threatened by the Tokyo system of assigning addresses, which seems to depend on when the address was created. They feel that they need meticulous maps if they are going to find anything. I can tell you that when you get used to it, and feel easy asking passersby questions, the problem dissolves. We didn't put maps in this book because they take up an awful lot of space that we think we can put to better use. If you're lost, just ask at the nearest police box. Directing people is the main job of the Tokyo police. And Tokyoites recognize that people new to the city have trouble getting their bearings, so they go out of their way to help. Anyway, you'll find that finding your way around is part of the adventure of living here. Discovering a new place is like finding a treasure, secret knowledge.

chiseled chunk of ice in their drinks, ice cubes being undignified.

The annual Asakusa Samba Festival, joyfully participated in by the JR Stationmasters' Samba Club, whose members wear their white summer uniforms and white gloves for the occasion.

The spectacle of six-hundred pedestrians stopped dead in their tracks outside Shibuya Station to watch an important sumo match on the huge TV monitors, then stepping off the curb en masse the second the match ends.

Nonbei Yokocho ("Drunkard's Alley") for wonderful yakitori at Tori Fuku ("Happy Bird") and companionable chatter at Enoki. For directions, ask at the police box at the Hachiko Exit of Shibuya Station, where the officer on duty gives out a set of directions to a new inquirer about every twenty seconds.

The summer high-school baseball tournament, which is televised nationally and watched by practically everyone.

The click of mahjong tiles late into the night.

Curry rice. Ramen. Gomoku soba. With a frosty mug of nama (draft) beer.

Sudare blinds of split bamboo.

Speechifying politicians at the train stations during the morning rush hour just before an election, hectoring the scurrying commuters, who do not deign to listen to a word.

The constant drone of pachinko parlors and the frenzied clamor of the barkers. With 15,000 pachinko parlors, Tokyo is the gamblingest city in the world.

Crude signs wired up to telephone poles in the nightlife neighborhoods, advertising forty minutes with a scantily dressed lady for ¥4,000.

Young children going off to school with leather backpacks, black for boys and red for girls, and yellow hats to make them more visible to motorists .

The ads for weekly magazines in the trains, giving the contents in such detail it

••••••• causing two million yen worth of damage. Their mothers hauled them down to the police station, where they were •

hardly seems necessary to buy the magazine itself.

The windows of real-estate agents plastered with floor plans of apartments for rent, each tiny room carefully colored with a different pastel.

In Tokyo, it is never necessary to buy pocket tissues. There is always someone giving them out for free.

The plangent cry of two kids assigned to stand out in front of every house on the street just before dinner and cry out "Hi no yojin"—"Beware of fire."

In June, the frantic buzz of cicadas.

Moon-viewing shoji.

Telephone etiquette that requires apologizing for being so rude as to hang up.

The earnestness of shop girls, as measured by how beautifully they can wrap purchases.

Taxi doors which open and close automatically. And taxi drivers with their white gloves and feather dusters.

The profusion of canned-drink vending machines, many times on all four corners of an intersection. Does canned coffee exist anywhere else in the world?

Bar Ber, for some reason almost always so written.

The English language used solely as decoration, without regard to meaning.

The little underground theaters in Ikebukuro, Shibuya, Ginza, and, particularly, Shimokitazawa, which provide Tokyo's equivalent of political cabaret.

Where to Buy

JAPANESE CLOTHES FOR LOUNGING AROUND AT HOME (SAMUE)

Samue is the clothing worn when performing daily chores at a Buddhist temple. Most department stores carry samue but Mitsukoshi, in Nihonbashi, has a particularly wide selection for ¥15,000 to ¥20,000. Nothing is more comfortable than lounging on tatami in samue.

Train and subway seats covered in soft velvet. "Silver Seats" set aside for oldsters and the disabled (and anyone who desperately needs some shut-eye).

The paperback book exchange shelves in Hibiya, Hongo Sanchome, and several other stations. The free shoe-polish equipment in Nezu Station.

The newspapers stacked and fanned like exotic flowers in the racks at the station kiosks, to allow them to be picked up quicker.

Hanami, the ritual viewing of the blossoming cherry, when Tokyo goes nuts.

Young people posing for the camera with a grin and a victory sign.

In the summer, neighborhood obon dancing to the same scratchy recordings year after year.

Irish pubs, with Guinness on tap.

The habit of not throwing an old chair or sofa out but taking it to the local bus stop so people can get a load off their feet.

Izakaya, little Japanese drinking places of great character, which differ from

•• arrested. It was reported that trendy young men in Osaka have taken to wearing skirts and carrying handbags as a ••••••

Where to Buy

JAPANESE CLOTHES FOR ATTENDING A STREET FESTIVAL

Ikiya, 2-32-7 Asakusa, Taito-ku.
☎ 03-3845-6326.
These clothes—light cotton upper and lowers in colorful patterns—are very comfortable. This is what you wear when you join in to carry a movable shrine through the streets, chanting and swaying. Ikiya, can fit you out on the spot for ¥3,000 to ¥5,000.

Irish pubs in that the talk is never of politics because such talk too easily turns contentious.

The snappy, solicitous drill that unfolds when you pull your car into a service station for some gas. "Can I vacuum your floor carpets for you, sir?"

Kinokuniya in Aoyama, Tokyo's most exclusive grocery store, where a white-gloved attendant runs the elevator between the first and second floors, and where there are always jeroboams of champagne on ice.

The Buck Rogers architecture of the Japanese electric fan.

The silky softness of the hinoki (Japanese cypress) counter of a sushi shop.

Sailor fountain pens, one of the best in the world and, for some reason, only available in Japan. They have remained unchanged since first produced in 1911.

The magnificent institution of the Japanese public bath, which the government thinks important enough to the general well-being to subsidize.

Shizenkyoikuen, the Institute for Nature Study in Meguro, with eighty hectares of primeval forest, where if a tree falls across a path, it is left there and the path is rerouted.

The little truck that drives around the neighborhood calling out "Green bamboo poles for sale!" The poles are for the purpose of hanging out laundry, and every once in a while, evidently, someone needs a new one.

Tokyo's parks, of which there are said to be over 7,000, some just big enough for a bench and a bush.

At the greengrocer's, apples as big as boules nestled in tissue paper.

The tradition, particularly in the older parts of town, of growing flowers and greenery in styrofoam boxes at curbside.

The tradition of some neighborhoods getting together once a month for dobu soji (cleaning the drains), after which everyone settles in for tea and rice crackers and gossip.

A visit to Tonki in Meguro for tonkatsu, a Tokyo tradition.

Arrangements of plastic flowers and tinsel up on the telephone poles in the midst of winter, just to add a bit of color.

And all the little rituals of daily living.

You will find that Tokyo is a wonderfully funky and very comfortable city, once you find your place in it. In this guide, we have tried to lead the way.

by Mike Kleindl, Rick Kennedy, Phillip Musgrave, and Andrew Watt

TOKYO'S twenty-three ku, formerly translated as "wards," now as "cities," are really too big to be thought of as neighborhoods. (Shibuya-ku has twice as many people as Amsterdam, and Shinjuku-ku, less than ten minutes away on the Yamanote Line, is two Dublins.)

No. A Tokyo neighborhood is defined by its nearest train or subway stop, with subdivisions defined by the route of the local newspaper-delivery bike and the local mailman.

Akasaka

"Red Slope." Akasaka at night is as glittery as the Ginza. Its main drag, paved with colored tiles, is trawled by highly polished limousines taking masters of industry to their assignations in expensive ryotei restaurants. Between six and seven o'clock, dozens of dazzling hostesses dressed in Dior or kimono make their way on foot from the Akasaka Mitsuke subway station to those same destinations, a voyeur's treat. In the basement of the Suntory Building, rich wine connoisseurs store their cases of Chateau d'Yquem. You are welcome to take a look.

Akihabara

"Field of Autumn Leaves." Akihabara sells 10 percent of all the electronic equipment sold in Japan. It's a mad house seven days a week. Japanese manufacturers of electronic gear treat Akihabara as a test market, carefully noting how savvy consumers react to their new products, which may not make it into mass production if they don't fly here. In Rajio Kan ("Radio Building"), the low-ceiling building that housed the original market for radio parts, grizzled specialists sell rare vacuum tubes in their original boxes, and sentimentalists can buy one of the first tape recorders ever made. On the first floor of the Yamaha Building, where the latest electronic music instruments are sold, in slack times the uniformed demonstrators are apt to break into an impromptu jam session. One of Tokyo's most famous noodle shops, Yabu Soba, where the orders are sung out to the kitchen, is here, just across the ornate bridge.

Aoyama

"Blue Mountain." Aoyama, Omotesando, and Harajuku are like sisters, with Aoyama being the most sophisticated of the three. Aoyama is quieter and less garish in her mix of chic European boutiques, art galleries, antique shops, and restaurants. Most of these are along Koto Dori, which begins just in front of Kinokuniya, Tokyo's classiest supermarket. Tokyo Blue Note, the premier jazz club, is here along with Brooks Brothers, Giorgio Armani, Max Mara, and the Blue Dog art gallery. Oseille (5-50-1 Jingumae, ☎ **03-3409-9454**) has very fine pasta, and the fish is always outstanding. A refuge from the relentless chic is the Nezu Institute of Fine Art, with its park, tea houses, and ponds, perhaps the best place in the city to see the autumn maples.

Where to Buy

BAMBOO BASKETS

Mr. Bunseki, who dresses in comfortable blue-cotton Edo-style homewear, makes beautiful baskets and vases to order from old smoked bamboo he finds in country houses about to be torn down. He will invariably pour you a cup of tea. His shop is in Sendagi, off Yanaka Ginza shopping street. Everyone knows where he is.

Asakusa

"Low Grass." Asakusa is home to Senso-ji temple, Tokyo's only generally agreed on tourist attraction. It's also where you can find a public bath with a stage bathers can mount après bath to sing a song or perform a classical dance; an off-Ginza Kabuki theater; a street market for used clothes, where it is possible to buy a single shoe; a multi-story off-track betting parlor; and a venerable striptease theater. Asakusa is the site in May of the Sanja Matsuri, the largest street festival in Japan, which draws a million revelers, and in autumn the Asakusa Samba Festival.

Asakusa merchants can't decide whether the area sells better as a quaint old Tokyo center of commercial activity of a scarcely believable diversity or a modern, chromium-and-neon city center, so Asakusa's identity is confused and in the grip of constant change. In Tokyo, such confusion is the sign of a neighborhood that's *alive*.

Daikanyama

"Magistrate's Mountain." Daikanyama, two minutes out of Shibuya on the Tokyu Line, is, along with Den-en-chofu on the same line, a thoroughly classy neighborhood (most Tokyo neighborhoods being an indiscriminate mixture of class and the mundane). The Danish and Malaysian embassies are here, on tree-lined Kyu Yamate Dori. Jun Ashida, the fashion designer, has his base here, as does the Tokyo branch of Le Cordon Bleu, the famous cooking school. There's Hillside Terrace, one of Tokyo's first architecturally aware shopping malls, and its extension, Hillside West, a few hundred meters up on the other side of the avenue, both designed by Fumihiko Maki. Cafe Michelangelo, one of the city's best sidewalk cafes, is here. The private houses are large, and fancy foreign motorcars abound.

Den-en-chofu

"Chofu Town in the Style of the European Countryside." Den-en-chofu was laid out in 1918 by the Tokyu Corporation, which just happens to own the rail line that goes through the town. Go out the South Exit of the station, and you'll come to a little plaza with streets going off in five directions through one of Tokyo's flushest neighborhoods—the houses are large and well built, some in traditional style with classic Japanese gardens, some with a northern European design, and some by Japanese architects whose work appears regularly in the architectural magazines. The families heading Japanese industry live here, as do the foreign presidents of joint venture companies. There's a lovely little park with a pond and hundreds of cherry trees.

Go out the North Exit of the station, and down the gentle slope to the left you'll find C'est La Vie, a fine little French restaurant, which must maintain high standards because the residents of Den-en-chofu visit France regularly.

Ebisu

Ebisu (the name of the happy Chinese god of prosperity) is a favorite area of the lively, young, fashionable crowd, who come for the sleek restaurants, bars, and shops selling foreign style as seen in advertisements. A series of moving sidewalks take you from the station to Ebisu Garden Place, for which the venerable Ebisu Brewery was torn down. New also are the Tokyo Photography Museum and a faux French chateau housing a restaurant with first-class credentials, which, however, few visit. Some consider Ebisu Garden a showplace of what-the-hell eclectic modern Tokyo, while others consider it a missed opportunity for Tokyo to make its own architectural statement.

Ekota

"Picture of an Old Field." Ekota is three stops out of Ikebukuro on the Seibu Ikebukuro Line. When times were rough, it was the site of some fierce battles, but it is

•• 24 percent of the Sapporo police force were told they were too fat to run after and catch a crook. A teacher told ••••••

now a quiet residential neighborhood. We include it here just because we like the place. There is a fine little coffee shop named Poor House, which serves a good plate of curry and whose proprietor, Mr. Minowa, closes down every March so he can visit Bali. Not far away is Tokyo's only Nepalese restaurant, Swatantra, run by the genial Mr. Takase, who speaks fluent Nepali. There are two nice little jazz clubs—Pineapple County (☎ **03-3994-0456**) and Buddy (☎ **03-3953-1152**). Another reason we like Ekota is because the priest at Sengen Temple is very quick to offer visitors a cup of tea.

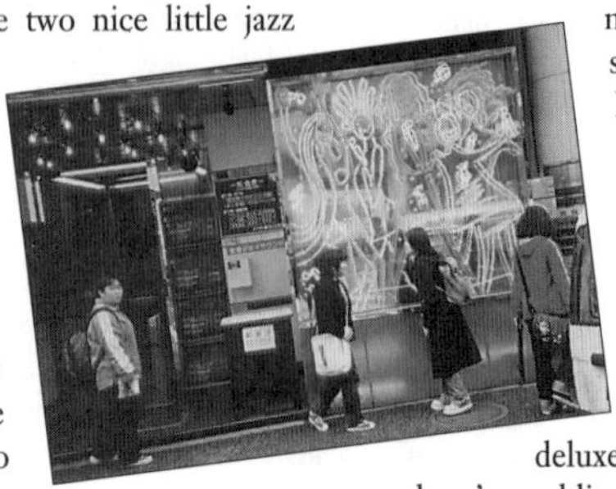

Ginza

"Silver Mint." There are dozens of Ginzas in Tokyo, and hundreds more in small towns throughout the country. "Ginza" is simply the name given the most prominent shopping street in the area. Certainly this Ginza at the Ginza subway station is the most glittering shopping area in Japan—and maybe in the world.

All of Tokyo's famous department stores have a presence in Ginza, where many of them began. Every major Japanese business has an office in Ginza, as do foreign firms if they want to be taken seriously.

Ginza is also a major entertainment center, with many buildings having four hostess bars on every floor. The Kabuki theater is here, as is the immense new Tokyo International Forum with its four concert halls.

Most things cost more in Ginza than anywhere else, and the Kyukyodo incense store has for many years occupied Japan's most expensive real estate. Maruzen, the Ginza's bookstore (although it is in adjacent Nihonbashi), has a Gutenberg Bible on display.

On Sundays, Ginza Dori is closed to traffic and shops put out seats in the middle of the avenue for strollers to take their ease. For all of Ginza's glitter, there are lots of narrow alleyways with cozy little shops and companionable drinking places. Three doors down from Kyubei, perhaps Tokyo's top sushi restaurant (where the deluxe course goes for ¥30,000) there's a public bath (entry ¥385). There is a working rice field in Ginza.

Gotanda

"Five Rice Fields." Sony has its headquarters in Gotanda, on the site of the first Sony building, which was a wooden barracks. Kani Hokken Hall, a major concert hall, is on the west side of the station. The two modern buildings constituting the Tokyo Design Center, full of furniture displays, have an interesting design-oriented bookstore on the first floor. Not far from the station is the atmospheric yoshoku restaurant, Bistro F. Nearer Sony is Franklin Avenue, serving Tokyo's best hamburgers and where it is possible to eat in a little garden, and Ne Quittez Pas, where a former Olympic boxer turns out some of Tokyo's most creative dishes, like watermelon soup. The Hara Museum of Contemporary Art is worth a visit, and you can have lunch in the museum's garden,

•••••••the Diet that in his high school in Hiroshima, students read comic books in class with their feet on the desk and •

too. In Gotenyama, the wealthy resid area, live the parents of Empress Mi as do a vast number of attractive mistr for whom there is a profusion of je shops, which would otherwise seem place.

Harajuku

"Field House." Harajuku has a spl sonality. One half is seen on the called Takeshita Dori, where tee come from all over the country to themselves in the most outlandis they can find. And the other half is the stately boulevard called Omot which runs parallel to Takeshita D which likes to think of itself as Champs-Elysées. On Omotesando, there are shops like Paul Stuart and Ralph Lauren and Hanae Mori (in the basement of whose building there are some wonderful antique shops and on the top floor a restaurant, Le Papillon, which serves a magnificent Sunday brunch).

Hiroo

"Open Space." Hiroo is known as a "gaijin ghetto," a neighborhood where foreigners live in huge, expensive high-rise apartments. All the shoes in the shoe shops seem oversized, and the ads in the Hiroo subway station are for schools that teach Japanese.

Hiroo is also host to one of Tokyo's most landscaped parks, Arisugawa Park, with its pond and stream and waterfall.

Hongo

"Book Country." Hongo is where you'll find the main campus of Tokyo University. The campus itself is a scruffy place, with some buildings being downright slums and, of course, because of this, much beloved by the students. But the university's presence here has spawned a lot of used bookstores, laid-back little drinking places, and several majestic Japanese inns—a rarity in Tokyo, alas.

Iidabashi

"Bridge Over the Rice Field." Iidabashi was one of the few parts of Tokyo that was not leveled during the war. (Uguisudani, "Nightingale Valley," is another.) The main street, Kagurazaka, leads up to Bishamon-ten, a fine old temple where the geisha of this old entertainment area come to pray in the early evening. Across the street from the temple, down an alley graced with weeping

• bicycle down the hallways. A survey by the *Asahi Shimbun* found that 67 percent of the electorate have a deep •••••••

-ku.

items such as
hand-warming
o ¥100,000), illus-
od novels (¥5,000),
, and low reading stands.
nono design stencils (¥500 to
) make fine lampshades. Open
n weekends—the owner spends the
weekdays scouring the countryside.

willows, is Iseto, an atmospheric place to drink a flask or two.

Ikebukuro

"Pond Bag." Ikebukuro is one of the four most bustling stops on the Yamanote Line, the other three being Shibuya, Shinjuku, and Ueno. It's the sleaziest of these, full of massage parlors and basement dives. Two of the largest department stores in the world are here, Seibu and Tobu, as well as the huge Geijutsu Gekijo concert hall with its 100-meter-long escalator.

Ikebukuro has a lively and varied street life. It's a playground for the ordinary thirty-something guy with not a lot of money to spend.

Jiyugaoka

"Free Hill." The stylish young come to Jiyugaoka buy their LL Bean boots and Eddie Bauer sweaters and maybe a little Swedish something for the apartment. Then they go to one of Jiyugaoka's fashionable little Italian restaurants and drink aka wain (red wine). Jiyugaoka has something of the feel of Harvard Square.

Kamakura

"Sickle Warehouse." While not strictly part of Tokyo, Kamakura is considered a "bedroom" town for Tokyo and Yokohama. The one-hour commute to Tokyo Station is not much longer than a crosstown train ride on the Yamanote Line, but the spiritual distance is much, much further. More than 800 years ago, Kamakura was the capital of Japan and thus enjoyed all the luxuries required by an emperor. With over eighty-five temples and shrines, and a multitude of parks, monuments, and museums, it is possible to spend weeks here and not see everything. Unlike Kyoto, though, everything is close together so you can take in many of the best places in a day.

The sights of Kamakura don't have a "tourist attraction" feel to them. They retain the spiritual power they've always had. It is often said that the Japanese are not a religious people, but seeing the locals and sightseers who come every day to pray, to light candles, and to wish for good luck, such a comment seems absurd. One of the best ways to see the city is to rent a bicycle at the station and pick up a map sold at any kiosk. These places should be on any "must see" list: the Great Buddha, Hase Kannon, Komyo-ji with its two gardens, Kakuon-ji in autumn, Zuisen-ji in any season, Zeni-arai Benten, Meigetsu-in in

••••••distrust of politicians. When asked what they wanted most from their elected officials, most people saic

June, Hikoku-in "Bamboo Temple," Engaku-ji, and Kencho-ji.

Near the station, Komachi Dori is crowded with interesting shops and restaurants selling sembei, washi paper, bamboo baskets, pottery, antiques, cheap souvenirs, and food of every kind. In the summer, Kamakura has a resort feel with its beaches filled cheek to oiled cheek with windsurfers, families, office ladies, and oldsters. The fireworks display at the beach during Bon season is not to be missed.

Kanda Jinbocho

"God's Field, Jinbo's Town." Kanda Jinbocho is the spiritual home for collectors of antiquarian (or simply used) books, magazines, postcards, and other paper collectibles. Expect the unexpected. Pick up a numbered map at almost any of the 125 bookstores and browse away. Particularly notable stores: Isseido (☎ **03-3292-0071**, #31 on map), Kitazawa Shoten (☎ **03-3263-0011**, #88), Ogawa Tosho (☎ **03-3262-0908**, #89), Oshima Shoten (☎ **03-3237-3559**, #83), Subun-so (☎ **03-3292-7877**, #119), and Yagushi Shoten for books on movies (☎ **03-3261-57708**, #81).

Kichijoji

"Temple of the God of Happiness." Behind Tokyu Department Store and bordered by Nakamichi shopping street on one side and Tokyu Dori on the other is Kichijoji, a shopping, strolling, dining area unlike any other in Tokyo. Within the environs of these twelve tiny blocks are bistros, restaurants, coffee shops, boutiques, flower stalls, izakaya, antique shops, gourmet food shops, a button emporium, and a Bohemian glass store. Spend the day wandering through the tiny streets, then seek out Aki (☎ **0422-21-1353**, 2-14-9 Honcho), a wonderful little izakaya frequented by writers. A fine jazz club, Sometime (☎ **0422-21-6336**, 1-11-31 Honcho), is a few minutes from the station. A bit farther from the station is Tokyo's only branch of Kansai's Kintetsu Department Store, which is worth visiting for the selection of Kansai food in the basement and the French cafe on the second floor for the city's best hot chocolate.

Koenji

"Tall Round Temple." Koenji is a major stop on the Chuo Line. A kilometer-long shopping mall (shotengai) with a brightly lit Tex-Mex place at the end, and nearer the station the Yonchome Cafe, which looks like Rick's Cafe Americaine in Casablanca but whose menu is an exact replica of one you'd find in an American roadside diner.

But the real reason to check out Koenji is that it is home to six live blues houses: Jirokichi (☎ **03-3339-2727**), T's Saloon (☎ **03-3318-5737**), Penguin House (☎ **03-3330-6294**), Mickey (☎ **03-3330-3678**), Oil City (☎ **03-5306-5053**), and Inaoza (☎ **03-3336-4480**).

Meguro

"Black Eye." Meguro has two things worth noting, and they are right next to each other. About 500 meters from the station, you'll come across the Teien Art Museum,

"decisiveness." Noting that the Japanese diet is changing in ways that would have been unimaginable a few

built in 1933 by a French architect as the residence of Prince Asaka and Princess Nobuko, daughter of Emperor Meiji. It's a beautiful old art-deco pile, full of Lalique glass and period furniture.

Adjacent is Shizenkyoikuen, or the National Institute for Nature Study, which is a vast virgin primeval forest, untouched except for a discreet planked walkway. Amazing to find such a thing in the middle of one of the most densely populated cities in the world!

On the other side of the station is Tonki, the tonkatsu restaurant, where the Japanese values of precision, politeness, cleanliness, and efficiency are continuously on display. Tonki is a Tokyo institution.

Mejiro

"White Eye." Mejiro has a tree-lined main street, Mejiro Dori, which accommodates good used-book stores, antique shops, little art galleries, and an old sake shop that also sells fine wine. People are well dressed, and you'll see more kimono worn here than in most neighborhoods. Every Christmas, local maidens pull on their white gloves and give a handbell concert in the church.

Former Prime Minister Kakuei Tanaka, perhaps Japan's most powerful political figure of the postwar era, lived on Meiji Dori in a huge mansion. The local university is Gakushuin, The Peers' University.

Worth noting are Tanakaya, a delicatessen with a fine selection of beers of the world, brandies, malt whiskies, and chocolates (turn left on Meiji Dori after leaving the station, and walk 10 meters) and Restaurant Beaux Arts, a charming, inexpensive French restaurant in an artist's loft over one of the city's finest frame shops—500 or so meters farther along Meiji Dori.

Musashi Koganei

"Small Gold Well in Musashi." The reason to come to Musashi Koganei is to visit the Edo-Tokyo Open Air Architectural Museum, which has the wonderful traditional house of a high-ranking politician, with a lovely garden that you can wander though. And there's a public bath of the era, a sake shop, a farm house, a police box, a candy store, and other buildings—all carefully maintained. In the museum's little gift shop are items you would find in a shop in Tokyo 100 years ago.

Nezu, Sendagi, Yanaka

"Water's Edge," "Cutting 1,000 Trees," and "Middle of the Valley." Nezu, Sendagi, Yanaka are three neighborhoods one stop away from each other on the Chiyoda Line. They got through the war unscathed, and together they give the best picture of what life must have been like in Old Tokyo. There are still many two-story wooden buildings, the shopkeepers seem to know all their customers by name, and local craftsmen still make things like bath buckets of cedar, not because they are beautiful but because that is how a bath bucket should be made. Young foreign scholars of Japanese language and literature install themselves in the area because it has an easy pace and a traditional feel,

•••••••years ago—more bread, less rice; more meat, less fish; and a dramatic rise in the consumption of wine, cheese,

because it's still relatively cheap (although rents are creeping up), and because it's easy to get to the neighborhoods where people carry briefcases to work.

Ningyocho

"Town of Dolls." Ningyocho is a charming neighborhood with more than its share of shops selling traditional things, like kimono and all its accoutrements, samisen and koto, and things for tea and flower arranging. Window shopping in Ningyocho will put you in mind of a quiet meal at a traditional restaurant, and here Ningyocho can oblige you, too.

Nishi-Ogikubo

"West Hollow of Reeds." At Nishiogi, pick up from the police box at the station a free map showing the couple dozen antique shops in the area. The shops are not the sleek and expensive shops you'll find in central Tokyo, but more relaxed affairs (they don't open much before noon) presided over by young people with an eye for design. You could pick up, say, a set of glasses of the type used in Japanese drinking places in the 1920s for ¥500 apiece.

Ochanomizu

"Water for Tea." Ochanomizu is home to the wonderful Yama no Ue ("Hilltop") Hotel, with its literary associations, and the street running down to Jimbocho, lined with stores selling banjos, guitars, trumpets and ukeleles to aspiring musicians.

Odaiba

"Fortifications." Odaiba is the closest thing Tokyo has to a Buck Roger's style spaceport and, as such, is another example of Tokyo's penchant for garish architecture. Other than the futuristic buildings, the main attraction of Odaiba for the hordes of high school students who throng there is that it is a man-made island. There is an amusement park, convention centers, a shopping mall, a few fountains and newly planted trees, and an elevated train that whizzes around the whole complex. The train ride out is interesting for the views of the Rainbow Bridge and the Port of Tokyo. Much more fun, though, would be to take the water taxi from Hamamatsucho. Television dramas are filmed in Odaiba for the dramatic background of the Tokyo skyline and the feeling of open space.

Where to Buy

WRAPPING MATERIALS

Tsutsumu Factory, 137-15 Udagawacho, Shibuya-ku. ☎ 03-5478-1330.

Want to take someone's breath away with a beautifully wrapped present? Tsutsumu will let you choose just the right box, just the right paper with just the right pattern, and let you pick out just the right ribbon from a couple hundred possibilities.

Roppongi

"Six Trees." Everyone will tell you Roppongi has gone to the dogs. It's true: Roppongi has more than its share of rowdy bars and discos; there are drugs to be had; on the weekends the shaven-headed U.S. military comes here to prowl; and at the end of an evening, which here is six in the morning, the streets are littered.

But there are good things, too. Roppongi apartments tend to be large (thus expensive), which appeals to the foreign element. Wave, run by Seibu department store, is one of the city's best record stores, and Aoyama Book Center one of its best book-

and pasta—the government decided to abandon its insistence that the nation always be able to feed itself

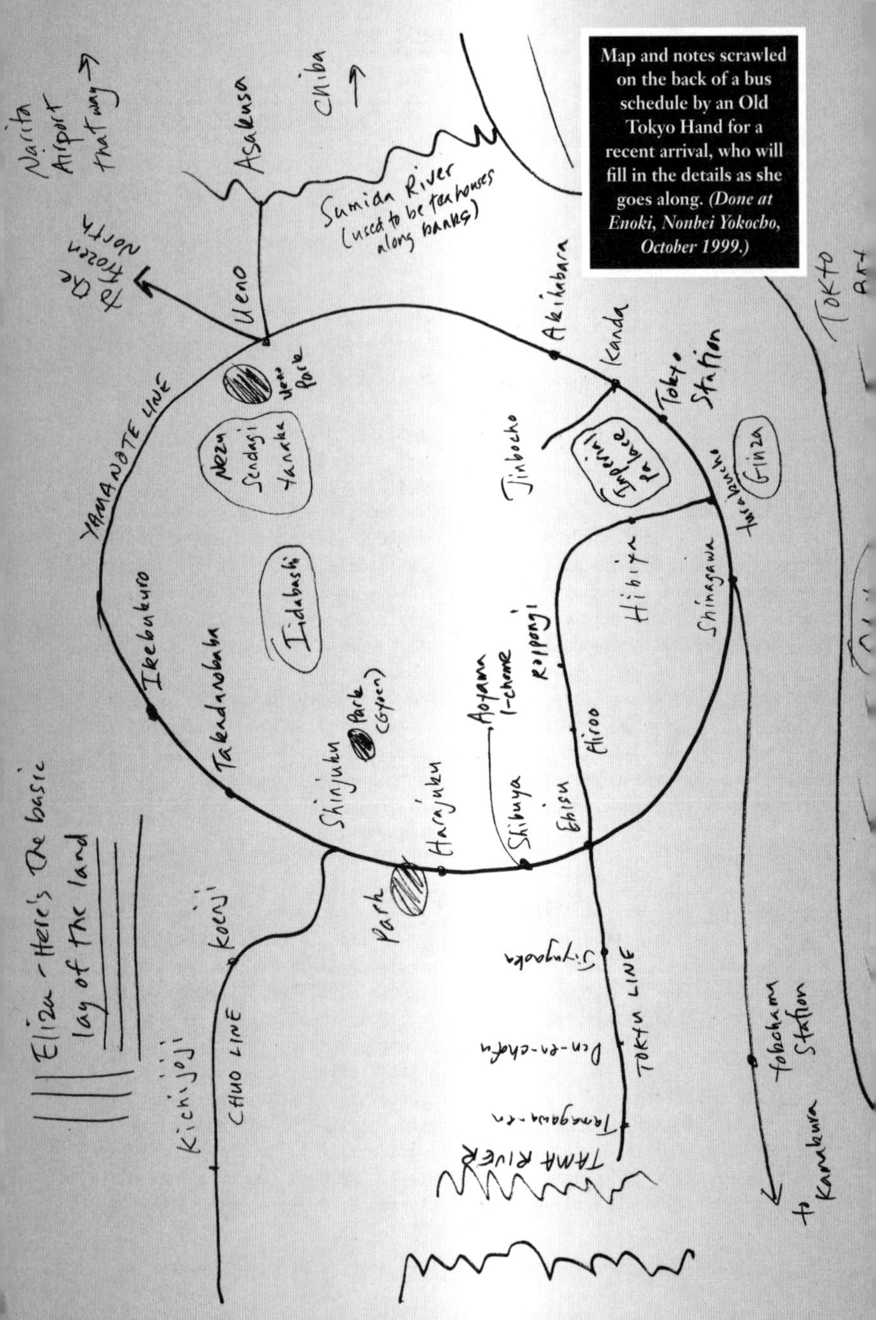

Map and notes scrawled on the back of a bus schedule by an Old Tokyo Hand for a recent arrival, who will fill in the details as she goes along. *(Done at Enoki, Nonbei Yokocho, October 1999.)*

Here's a basic rundown:

UENO: Plain + unvarnished. Around here you hear "zuzu ben" northern dialect.

ASAKUSA: Tokyo's spiritual home – built around busy Sensoji (ca. 8th century!)

CHIBA: A peninsula to the east. Tokyo's New Jersey?

AKIHABARA: Quiet, relaxing, sweet music by Mozart – not!

KANDA: Pretty sleazy. Head up to Jinbocho for used book shops.

TOKYO: The station, I mean. Not much happening...

SHINAGAWA: Or here. Tokyo + Shinagawa are both big train stops, and trains are what move the city!

ODAIBA: Great view of Tokyo as a harbor city. Crowded. Take the water taxi from Asakusa.

YOKOHAMA: A suburb, but also J's 2nd largest city.

KAMAKURA: Ancient former capital. Artists live here. Good kite flying!

GINZA: Ignore the smell of money here. Back alleys are full of surprises.

HIBIYA: Closer to the Palace than the map shows. Breakfast at Les Saisons, then go sit in the park.

ROPPONGI: Sex, drugs, + bad rock 'n roll.

EBISU: Smart, stylish people live here. Ignore the fake French chateau.

AOYAMA 1-CHOME: Tokyo's Madison Ave. Consumers on parade.

SHIBUYA: Near the station, a teenage sex menagerie. Nice walk up tree-lined Dogenzaka to Aoyama.

HARAJUKU: Takeshita-dori for teenage fashion, and Omotesando for sort of European feeling.

SHINJUKU: Vibrant! West side big buildings feels like Brasilia. East side with big park is peaceful.

NEZU, SENDAGI, YANAKA: Remnants of Old Tokyo.

IIDABASHI: Walk up from Kagurazaka. Go to Iseto for drinks.

TAKADANOBABA: Home to Waseda U – cheap student eats + movies.

JIYUGAOKA: Giant suburban mall packs 'em in.

DEN-EN-CHOFU: Classiest residential area. Go to C'est La Vie restaurant.

TAMAGAWA-EN: Grassy riverbank where Tokyo picnics.

IKEBUKURO: Major drinking + eating zone. No pretensions.

KOENJI: Lots of jazz boites north of station.

KICHIJOJI: Western Tokyo's hot spot. Nakamichi St is a maze of funk + fashion. Not too expensive. A good place to live!

Oh, Eliza, you're going to have a fine time!

stores. The Axis Building, improbably run by Bridgestone, the tire manufacturer, is a showcase of the best of Japanese design—take a look at Nuno in the basement for a display of extraordinary fabrics.

Roppongi also has a number of fine places to dine, most notably Vincent, a superlative (and expensive) French restaurant.

Ryogoku

"Both Countries." Ryogoku is home to the National Sumo Stadium and a number of sumo stables. Ryogoku is where to come to see huge mountains of men doing all the ordinary things—riding a bicycle, making a telephone call, sucking on a popsicle—all the while dressed in traditional yukata with their hair in topknots. Chanko nabe, great cauldrons of fish stew, which sumotori favor to keep their weight up, are featured by a number of restaurants in the area.

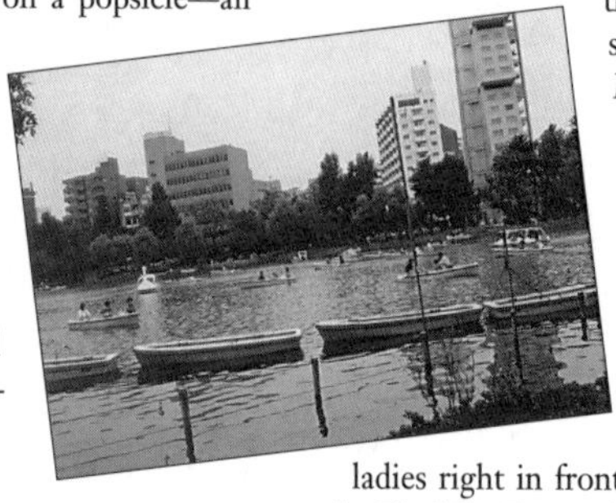

Sangenjaya

"Three Tea Houses." Sangenjaya is another place name we cannot resist. Notable here is the new Carrot Tower, from whose top floor bar you can look out across Tokyo and see in the distance the tall buildings of both Shibuya and Shinjuku, the rest of the city at their feet. It is like being able to take in at a glance two redwood forests separated by ten miles. An amazing urban landscape, which suggests that Tokyo has a lot of growing to do.

Shibuya

"Astringent Valley." Let's try to put this in perspective. Shibuya is not a neighborhood. It's a city of 800,000 people, with all the diversity that figure suggests. In Shibuya, there are elegant areas with restaurants the Crown Prince takes the Crown Princess to for lunch. There's the Bunkamura ("Culture Village") complex that regularly displays art borrowed from the world's great museums, and which has in its basement what it imagines is a replica of Les Deux Magots cafe in Paris. Shibuya is where NHK has its headquarters.

But Shibuya is also home to Nonbei Yokocho ("Drunkards' Alley"), with its collection of charmingly ramshackle little drinking places. Next to Nonbei Yokocho, there are people sleeping rough in Miyashita Park.

The area around Shibuya Station attracts some of the scruffier elements of Japanese youth, who spend their evenings propositioning young ladies right in front of the police box at the Hachiko Exit, a famous meeting place. An observer has called these youth, tanned in winter and invariably sporting long black coats, Karasu ("Crows").

Shimokitazawa

"Lower Northern Marsh." The people who were born in Shimokita (the popular name) and the people who come here coexist quite happily. Though small compared to other Tokyo neighborhoods, Shimokita has something to offer all generations, from young to old, like cheap and simple clothes shops, casual restaurants, izakaya, old coffee shops, food markets, traditional tea shops, senbei vendors, and

•••••••without resorting to imports. Nissan, known for its cars and trucks, and Ishikawajima-Harima Heavy Industries, antique shops. During the day, the place teems with grunge-clad teens heading for the Rock 'n Roll Diner and its tasty burgers. Evenings are quieter, with couples on their way to the inexpensive eateries on the narrow side streets. One of the Cozzolino brothers, Angelo, has two restaurants here: Il Cantuccio and La Befana.

Shimokita is a center of underground theater. Honda Gekijo ("Honda Theater") is the most polished of the theaters in the area, and Za Suzunari ("The Jam-packed") is probably the liveliest.

Shinbashi

"New Bridge." Shinbashi was the first train station in Tokyo. The idea was not to put a station where Tokyo Station is now because that would be too near the Imperial Palace, in case the foreigners living in Yokohama somehow got it into their heads to get on the train in Yokohama and storm the palace. Now Shinbashi is one of Tokyo's great areas for those little drinking places that are so necessary for people to get a genuine understanding of each other. The area around Karasumori Jinja is particularly lively.

Shinjuku

"New Dwellings." There is probably more going on in Shinjuku than in any other place on this list. The bustle seems built-in, and around the station decibel-measuring devices are at risk. In many ways, Shinjuku is the engine of Tokyo. Shinjuku Station, with its four built-in department stores, is the busiest in the world, with 1.5 million commuters scurrying through it every day. Tokyo's Star-Wars town hall is here, as is Kabukicho, Ground Zero of Japan's rampaging cabaret industry, and Golden Gai (now sadly threatened by developers), the apotheosis of a neighborhood, with alleys only as wide as your outstretched arms, lined with tiny drinking places, each with its own distinctive character. Near the station, there's also Omoide Yokocho, an area of little drinking spots, which can barely restrain its natural exuberance. Shinjuku has taken over from Marunouchi near Tokyo Station the role of the city's business center.

Shinjuku Gyoen Park (admission ¥200), with its French, English, and Japanese gardens, is where the Prime Minister holds his annual garden party and is one of the most elegant places in Tokyo to view the blossoming cherry. Shinjuku boasts one of Tokyo's two opera houses, and on the west side of the station a dozen skyscrapers create a Manhattan-like landscape. One of Tokyo's most polished hotels, the Park Hyatt, is here, and the view from the bar on the top floor looking out over the city sometimes includes Fuji. Next door is the Conran shop, where young Tokyoites are learning how to make their apartments look as though they're in London.

Shin-Okubo

"New Hollow." One stop out of Shinjuku, Shin-Okubo is where lots of people from other Asian countries live and work. Some wonderful Korean restaurants are here. The newsstands carry papers from all over Asia. It can get rough late at night, though.

Takadanobaba

"Takada's Horse Place." Waseda University, up Waseda Dori from the station, has made Baba Tokyo's liveliest student town. Lots of used book stores, a couple of good movie theaters (the Shochiku and Cinema ACT), cheap eateries like La Dinette (nice after a bath at Seikai-yu, where the mural over the bath is of Mount Blanc), and a range of tiny theaters for student productions. Biblos, on the fifth floor of the Horindo bookshop across from the station, has an excellent collection of Penguins and foreign magazines, and it's pleasant to adjourn to Ben's Cafe nearby for a leisurely read and a very good cafe latte.

The Waseda jazz band sometimes serenades revelers tumbling out of the station late at night. The weekend before Christmas, churchgoers from the local Korean churches parade up and down Waseda Dori singing carols and lighting their way with candles.

At the easternmost tip of Toyama Park is the highest point in the twenty-three wards of Tokyo—Hakoneyama.

Tamagawa-en

"Tama River Garden." There's nothing much going on in Tamagawa-en itself, except a tennis club for the well-heeled. But from the station, it's only a short stroll to the grassy west bank of the river—a fine spot for a picnic. The Tama is Tokyo's finest river, gradually getting cleaner, with the carp coming back and a bird sanctuary at its mouth. Creaky rowboats for rent.

Ueno

"Upper Field." Ueno is where the trains come in from the north, so there is a rustic feel about the area and lots of regional restaurants, where people wear caps saying things like "Komatsu Bulldozer." Ueno Park is the most popular place to view the blossoming of the cherry and is the site of the National Museum of Western Art, the Tokyo National Museum, and the Tokyo Metropolitan Fine Art Museum. Shinobazu Pond is graced by thousands of waterlilies and has so far fought off the initiative to put a parking garage under it. Everybody recognizes that Ueno is where to buy used motorcycles and Buddhist altars, and there is a profusion of small wholesalers dealing in dolls, fans, hats, rubber boots, balloons, and party hats. Ameyokocho ("American Alley") is where you can get almost anything at a discount, and the street action is pure Tokyo theater.

Yokohama

"Next to the Bay." Though Yokohama with its three million people is right next door to Tokyo, it has a different feel to it. Walk from the station to Yamashita Park on the waterfront (the route is clearly marked), and you'll get the feeling you are in pre-war Lisbon—that is, until you look out on Minato Mirai at the new construction going on, including Japan's highest building.

••••••*Gendai* reported that during the Birmingham Summit, when President Clinton and Prime Minister Tony Blair •

by Alex Urbansky

TOKYO has many fine hotels: international blockbusters like the Imperial, the New Otani, and the Okura, and a number of smaller but highly polished new hotels like the Seiyo in the Ginza and the Park Hyatt in Shinjuku. It is an experience to stay at any of them. But they are expensive. As it happens, though, there are a number of quite fine second-level hotels, which, because of their greater intimacy and their lower prices, are preferred by many people who know Tokyo well. Here is a generous baker's dozen of them, ranging from the classy Fairmont and Yama no Ue hotels to the extremely cheap but perfectly fine New Koyo, together with some further ideas on where to stay.

Arimax Hotel

Kamiyamacho, Shibuya-ku. ☎ ***03-5454-1122****. Singles from ¥18,000, doubles from ¥23,000. Nearest station:* SHIBUYA.

The Arimax is the most expensive hotel on this list. It seems to have mod-

Where to Buy

BUTTERFLIES

Shiga Insect Shop, Aoyama. Azure-winged butterflies from Peru, Brazilian tiger moths, stag beetles the size of a lemon. Need a particular centipede to complete your collection? For over forty years Shiga-san has been satisfying the needs of fanatic lepidopterists. He carries the finest bamboo-handled nets, neat little packets of mounting pins, gold-framed display boxes, killing jars, and hundreds of jewel-like insects in his two glass display cases. Drop buy to pick up the current issue of *The Butterfly Weekly* for ¥300.

eled itself after one of the cozy little hotels of London, with impeccable service and the subdued atmosphere of a gentleman's club. In a quiet backwater near NHK.

Asia Kaikan

8-10-32 Akasaka, Minato-ku. ☎ ***03-3402-6111****. Singles from ¥7,500. Six-minute walk from* AOYAMA ITCHOME *Station.*
In a quiet cul-de-sac, this spic-and-span hotel caters particularly to the Asian traveler.

Creston Hotel

10-8 Kamiyamacho, Shibuya-ku. ☎ ***03-3481-5800****. 53 rooms. Singles ¥13,000 to ¥15,000. Nearest station:* SHIBUYA.
Practically in the shadow of NHK, this little hotel is much favored by foreign rock stars. Shibuya is the gathering spot of teenagers on the prowl, where Tokyo's youth culture is on continuous display. The hotel is located in a relatively quiet backwater, however.

Fairmont Hotel

2-1-17 Kudan-Minami , Chiyoda-ku. ☎ ***03-3262-1151****. Singles ¥11,000 to ¥13,000. Nearest subway stop:* KUDANSHITA *(700 meters away, not far from the Indian Embassy).*
Located off a leafy promenade overlooking the Imperial moat and near Jinbocho, where there are about 125 bookshops. Hanada, a fine shop selling easy-to-afford pottery where you can have a cup of tea, is just around the corner on Yasukuni Dori. Nearby is the Budokan, Tokyo's Madison Square Garden, and the Yasukuni Shrine, with its whiff of militarism. Within easy distance of the Marunouchi business district. An airport limousine stop.

Hotel Bellclassic

3-33-6 Otsuka, Toshima-ku. ☎ ***03-5950-1200****. Singles ¥14,000. Nearest station:* OTSUKA *(go out the South Exit, turn right, and you'll see the hotel looming before you, 100 meters up the hill).*
Otsuka is an obscure part of town, noted mostly for being one of the stops on Tokyo's last trolley line. Still, this very large new hotel is spotless and run with a kind of maniac efficiency, and you are only fourteen minutes from Shinjuku on the Yamanote Line.

Hotel Kojimachi Kaikan

2-4-3 Hirakawacho, Chiyoda-ku. ☎ ***03-3265-5361****. The nicely appointed single rooms go for ¥9,817. Three-minute walk from* KOJIMACHI *Station on the Yurakucho Line.*
Just a year old, this fifteen-story hotel in an elegant neighborhood has five restaurants and a public bath on the top floor.

Marunouchi Hotel

1-6-3 Marunouchi, Chiyoda-ku. ☎ ***03-3215-***

2151. Singles begin at ¥13,000. An easy walk from the Marunouchi exits of TOKYO *Station, with the Imperial Palace five minutes away.*
Think of this hotel as being in Tokyo's Wall Street area. The Marunouchi, founded in 1924 and recently renovated, is a perfect example of a highly polished small Tokyo hotel, with select Japanese antiques on display; a French, Chinese, and traditional Japanese restaurant; and a cozy bar.

New Koyo Economy Hotel

2-26-13 Nihonzutsumi, Taito-ku. ☎ ***03-3873-0343****. Singles from a scarcely believable ¥2,500. Turn left out of Exit 2 of* MINOWA *Station on the Hibiya Line, and walk ten minutes.*
Communal kitchen and separate shower. They have both Western- and Japanese-style rooms, but take the Japanese.

Olympic Inn

Three locations: Nishi-Shinjuku (☎ ***03-3375-5050****), Shibuya (☎* ***03-3469-5050****), and Kanda (☎* ***03-5256-5050****). Singles ¥8,000 to ¥10,000. Doubles from ¥11,000.*
Well-run, immaculate pocket hotels. The lobby will have just two leather armchairs, but everything will be cared for, including breakfast and the morning paper. Simple, but all anyone could wish for.

Richmond Hotel

3-5-14 Mejiro, Toshima-ku. ☎ ***03-3565-4111****. Singles from ¥9,800. Exit* MEJIRO *Station, turn left, and it's a minute down Mejiro Dori.*
Mejiro is a classy part of town, with Tanakaya, one of Tokyo's best delicatessens, and the wonderful Beaux-Arts restaurant over a frame shop, both on tree-lined Mejiro Dori, along with antique shops, used-book shops, art galleries, and

•• stately, grandmotherly dance style seen at neighborhood summer bon odori festivals. Hashimoto's staff was said ••••••

in the other direction, Gakshuin (Peers') University.

Shiba Daimon Hotel

2-3-6 Shiba-koen, Minato-ku. ☎ ***03-3431-3716****. Singles begin at ¥8,100. Ten minutes from* HAMAMATSUCHO *Station.*
Near Daimon ("Big Gate") off Hibiya Park, and a short stroll to the Grotto Bar of the atmospheric restaurant Crescent.

Shibuya City Hotel

1-1 Maruyamacho, Shibuya. ☎ ***03-5489-1010****. Singles from ¥9,000. Right across from the entrance to Bunkamura, eight minutes from* SHIBUYA *Station.*
The headquarters hotel in another small chain of immaculate pocket-sized hotels. A branch, the **Nishi-Shinjuku Hotel** at 7-14-14 Nishi-Shinjuku (☎ **03-5389-1010**), has slightly lower rates.

Shibuya Toba Hotel

3-1 Udagawacho, Shibuya-ku. ☎ ***03-3476-0111****. Singles from ¥12,000. A ten-minute walk from* SHIBUYA *Station.*
A fine little hotel up Koen Dori on the way to NHK.

Takanawa Tobu Hotel

4-7-6 Takanawa, Minato-ku. ☎ ***03-3447-0111****. Singles from ¥13,000. Nearest station:* SHINAGAWA.
An elegant little hostelerie.

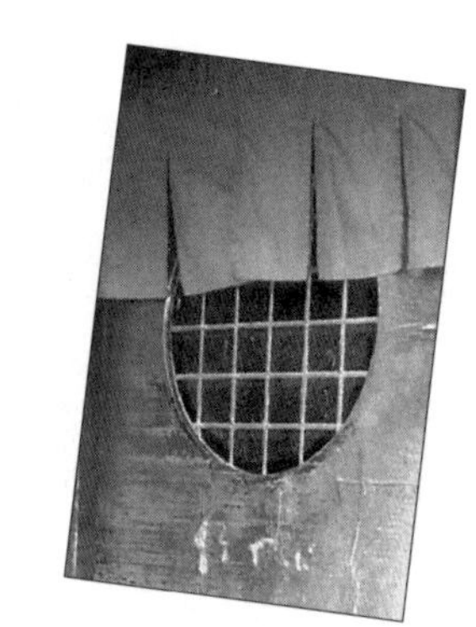

Tokyo Station Hotel

1-9-1 Marunouchi, Chiyoda-ku. ☎ ***03-3231-2511****. Singles from ¥10,000.*
An eccentric but characterful choice. The hotel was the cat's meow in 1850 and hasn't changed since. Horse-driven carriages can pull up outside, and a charming faded gentility reigns.

•••••••to be too embarrassed to watch. In Kyushi a taxi driver threw sixty ¥10,000 bills off a bridge onto a busy highway •

Where to Buy

COMBS

Yonoya Comb Shop, Denpoin Street, 1-37-10 Asakusa, Taito-ku. ☎ 03-3844-1755.
A wide variety of handmade boxwood combs, with teeth cut by hand, are guaranteed never to snag the hair. A tiny shop run by two sweet ladies of a certain age, who, although they speak little English, seem to know exactly what their customers want. It is sad to think that when they go, the shop will close.

Vila Fontanu Nihonbashi

1-7-6 Nihonbashi Honcho, Chuo-ku. *☎ **03-3242-3370**. Singles from ¥7,800. Four-minute walk from* MITSUKOSHIMAE *on the Hanzomon or Ginza Line.*
Smack in the middle of the Ginza, with nice bathrooms and very clean.

Yama no Ue ("Hilltop") Hotel

*1-1 Surugadai, Chiyoda-ku. ☎ **03-3293-2311**. Singles from ¥15,000. A skip and a jump from* TOKYO *Station and the Ginza.*
Tokyo's equivalent of New York's Algonquin, the famous literary hotel. Mishima holed up here to write his last novels. Has a fine little French restaurant and a little bar off the lobby where a precision martini can be had. Just down the slope is the Jinbocho book district.

Business Hotels

One cut below the above hotels is a category of no-nonsense, perfectly clean, but stripped-down "business hotels." Business hotels are cheap but no place to meet anyone for dinner. There will be one or more business hotels within walking distance of almost every stop on the Yamanote Line, their rooftop neon signs clearly visible from the station exits.

Sunroute Hotels is the largest chain of business hotels in Japan, with four in the center of Tokyo: **Sunroute Asakasa** (☎ **03-3847-1511**) at 1-8-5 Kaminarimon, a one-minute walk from Tawaramachi Station. Singles from ¥7,800. **Sunroute Ikebukuro** (☎ **03-3980-1911**) at 1-39-4 Higashi-Ikebukuro, a two-minute walk from the East Exit of Ikebukuro Station. Singles from ¥9,000. **Sunroute Tokyo** (☎ **03-3375-3211**) at 2-3-1 Yoyogi, a three-minute walk from the South Exit of Shinjuku Station. Singles from ¥12,500. **Sunroute Shibuya** (☎ **03-3464-6411**) at 1-11 Nanpeidaicho, a five-minute walk from the South Exit of Shibuya Station. Singles from ¥6,700 without bath; from ¥10,000 with bath.

The Japan City Hotel Association (☎ **03-3258-1090**) at 43 Higashi-Matsushita-cho, Kanda, Chiyoda-ku, Tokyo 101-0042, has a booklet listing sixty-nine business hotels in Tokyo with singles for as little as ¥5,500.

Tsukasa ("Su Casa") has clean and efficient rooms for rent by the month, ¥97,000 for singles, ¥119,000 for doubles, and ¥225,000 for triples, in Yokohama,

because he was unhappy over his share of the family inheritance. In the ensuing vehicular chaos, police managed

Where to Buy

NIGHTINGALE DROPPINGS

Geisha used chalky nightingale droppings to whiten their faces and necks. Packets are available in one of the stores in the Nakamise shopping arcade leading up to Sensoji temple in Asakusa.

Kawasaki, and six locations in Tokyo. Call **03-3440-0111** for more information.

Some other reasonably priced options to be considered are staying at a Japanese inn, such as the ten-room **Sawanoya** (☎ **03-3833-2251**) at 2-3-11 Yanaka, Taito-ku, near Nezu Station , for ¥4500 to ¥5000, well known for taking care of bumbling foreigners; **Fukudaya** (☎ **03-3467-5833**) at 4-5-9 Aobadai, Meguro-ku, for ¥7,000, reached by leaving the South Exit of Shibuya Station and boarding the Tokyu bus for Wakabayashi Orikaeshijo and getting off at the second stop—Aobadai Yonchome; **Katsutaro** (☎ **03-3821-9808**) at 4-16-8 Ikenohata, Taito-ku, a fifteen-minute walk from the Shinobazu Exit of Ueno Station, for ¥4,500; and **Ryokan Asakusa Shigetsu,** run by Katsuo Tobita, who is in touch with the ryokan scene in Tokyo generally (☎ **03-3843-2345**, fax 03-3843-2348).

Hearty foreigners looking for a place to stay for a few months favor old wooden apartments. They have tatami, television, and air conditioners but are otherwise fairly primitive. It's an adventure, though, and they are cheap—say around ¥70,000 a month. **Sakura House** (☎ **03-5330-5250**) is a real-estate agency specializing in these old apartments.

Still another possibility is to tuck yourself into a "capsule hotel," the nearest of which the police box at any station on the Yamanote Line will be able to direct you to. A capsule hotel is a Tokyo invention. It is essentially a bed with a TV set and a fan in a box. You can't sit up in the bed, it is so space efficient, but capsule hotels can cost as little as ¥3,000.

Another Tokyo institution is the "foreigners' house," which are roomy old private houses in undistinguished suburbs that rent small rooms to foreigners for as long as they want. Many are the foreigners who have set up house in a foreigners' house while they get their bearings. The atmosphere tends to be similar to that of a fraternity house. Foreigners' houses regularly advertise in the *Tokyo Journal*, an English-language monthly of tattered reputation.

If worse comes to worse, you could present yourself at a love hotel in one of the city's many carousing districts. These hotels have rooms designed to be rented by the hour and tend to be decorated by someone with an inflamed imagination (chromium trapezes, for example). If the hotel hasn't been able to rent a room out for the night, they will often let it go cheaply in the early hours of the morning to someone who just wants a little shut-eye.

PERFORMANCE

by Gilles Kennedy

TOKYO: cosmopolitan city with a thespian twist. Where else could you see avant-garde dance in an old bathhouse threatened with the wrecker's ball, participate in a contemporary dance interpretation of the Kama Sutra in Yushima Seido, the country's only Confucian temple, or watch Noh at night, lit by monstrous flaming torches in a shrine so sacred it is otherwise off-limits?

Tokyo is a magnet that celebrates the traditional Japanese performing arts and attracts and thrives on the marginal. Going to the theater here poses few linguistic obstacles, such is the focus on imagery and mime. A visit to the national theaters showing Noh, Kabuki, Bunraku, and the other traditional performing arts is obligatory for any understanding of the culture, but insight and enrichment are also to be found at the small venues promoting avant-garde work in drama, dance, performance art, and the world-famous dance form of Butoh.

With so many Tokyoites living an hour or more commute from the cen-

Where to Buy

UKELELES

Ring Guitars, 3-1 Yotsuya, Shinjuku-ku. ☎ 03-3351-4845.

Ring Guitars has a wall of ukeleles, which in Japan are a highly exotic instrument. A beautiful Martin Kamaka model from the 1920s goes for ¥120,000.

ter, things start early, and just like the trains, punctuality is assured. Get your tickets from the venues themselves, ticket outlets such as Pia, CNN Playguide, and Ticket Saison, or convenience stores. Some venues offer a same-day discount for big-item productions, but tickets are generally purchased weeks in advance at a slightly reduced price. For discounts on the day, arrive early at the box office and show your student ID if you have one— "jeans" seats, often cushions enviably close to the stage action, are usually priced about ¥2,000 — but the imported and big-item productions can set price ceilings at the high ¥20,000 level. Wheelchair access at the newer venues is assured, and patrons at other places have been known to get a lift on the ramps for stage sets, at the back of the theater. Audience concentration and near-total silence is a given, often followed by thunderous applause and the odd, slightly tentative "Bravo!" Since there is no specific theater for dance and ballet, check performance listings for productions at halls that do double duty for concerts and musicals. And don't forget the often hilarious sit-down comedy storytelling rakugo, gag-heavy manzai, and magic tricks to be found in the Ueno area at Suzumoto Engeijo and Honmokutei, the only rakugo theater left with the original tatami seating.

BASTIONS OF TRADITION

Kabuki-za

4-12-15 Ginza, Chuo-ku. ☎ ***03-3541-3131***. HIGASHI-GINZA *Station on the Hibiya Line.*

This stunning architectural landmark dates from 1889 and was rebuilt in 1925. The ultimate in theatrical flexibility, you can take in a packed lunch to performances (or buy one on the premises), slip out for a break, or just take a quick nap when the pace slackens off. Buy tickets for the entire day or just a single act—ask for a hitomaku. English earphone interpretation available and also a synopsis of the action. Programs change the first week of the month, so the stage lies fallow for some days in preparation.

Kokuritsu Gekijo (National Theatre)

4-1 Hayabusacho, Chuo-ku. ☎ ***03-3265-7411***. NAGATACHO *Station on the Yurakucho Line.*

The traditional performing arts hold sway here, with a large hall seating 1,746 for Kabuki and Bunraku and a smaller hall with 630 seats for traditional vaudeville shows and other delights. Don't be put off by the log cabin appearance in concrete.

Kokuritsu Nogaku-do (National Noh Theatre)

4-18-1 Sendagaya, Shibuya-ku. ☎ ***03-3423-1331***. SENDAGAYA *Station on the JR Sobu Line.*

An extraordinary example of nature and the performing arts cooperating in restful harmony. Near-daily programme of one Noh and one Kyogen play on a cypress wood stage amidst elegant gardens—curtain times are early.

Shin Kokuritsu Gekijo (New National Theatre)

1-1-1- Honmachi, Shibuya-ku. ☎ ***03-5351-3011***. HATSUDAI *Station on the Keio Line.*

Gleaming complex of opera house, one large and one small theater hosting the best in drama, ballet, and dance, with acclaimed new productions of foreign and Japanese opera.

MUSIC

Casals Hall

1-6 Surugadai Kanda, Chiyoda-ku. ☎ ***03-3291-2525***. OCHANOMIZU *Station on the JR Chuo Line.*

Named for the famed cellist, to promote chamber music and contemporary compositions for more intimate ensembles. Centered in a lively university area of town, it also holds lectures, symposia, and the Festival of New American Music Interlink every autumn. Musical souvenirs on sale are of questionable taste.

Orchard Hall

2-24-1 Dogenzaka, Shibuya-ku. ☎ ***03-3477-9150***. SHIBUYA *Station on the JR Yamanote Line. http://www.nihon.or.jp/Bunkamura/*

The Bunkamura (Culture Village) complex beside the swish headquarters of Tokyu Department Store is major dress-up land, especially when the hall puts on its own productions of opera, ballet, and orchestral performances. Base for the Japanese leg of the Mostly Mozart Festival and Tokyo Philharmonic Orchestra. Bunkamura also houses Theatre Cocoon (☎ **03-3477-9999**), a small hall reserved for contemporary productions of dance, film, and music.

Suntory Hall

1-13-1 Akasaka, Minato-ku. ☎ ***03-3584-9999***. TAMEIKE-SANNO *Station on the Ginza Line.*

The revolutionary leader of the classical music scene in Tokyo, Suntory holds competitions, dishes out awards, is a prime talent spotter locally and an impressive importer of overseas orchestras and soloists. Great organ, some free lunchtime concerts, and a generous plaza named after Herbert von Karajan, in Gothic script, no less.

Tokyo Opera City Concert Hall: Takemitsu Memorial

3-20-2 Nishi-Shinjuku, Shinjuku-ku.

• were evacuated so a World War II bomb could be defused. The Health and Welfare Ministry, alarmed at the ••••••

Art Movie Houses

Gone is the Tokyo where you could see classic films all day and all night. The juggernaut of multiplex theaters is shutting small movie houses down, but a few stalwart places still show films from, say, Iceland, Iran, and Mongolia. To save several hundred yen, search out the discount ticket shops such as Ticket Pia and Ticket Saison and Shinjuku Matsutake Playguide (☎ 03-3354-1993) in the narrow alley behind the original Kinokuniya bookstore. These shops sell tickets for the theaters in their neighborhoods. Several of the theaters listed below run late shows, which for some perverse reason means 9 pm.

Cinema Shimokitazawa (Shimokitazawa)
☎ *03-5452-1400. Five minutes from the station.*
One more reason to visit Shimokita. A new "small" theater with a hip retro look. Runs carefully selected films.

Cine Saison (Shibuya)
☎ *03-3770-1721. 6F of the Prime Building.*
Mainly old French films. Often runs late shows.

Eurospace 1 & 2 (Shibuya)
☎ *03-3461-021. Take the South Exit from the station. Theater is in the Higashi-Takefuji Building.*
The most far-out theater in Tokyo. Films (especially small ones) play here that are shown nowhere else in Tokyo. Often runs late shows.

Cine Amuse (Shibuya)
☎ *03-3496-2888. Across from Tokyu Department Store main building.*
Mainly independent films from Japan, America, and Europe.

Le Cinema (Shibuya)
☎ *03-3477-9264. In Tokyu Bunkamura 6F.*
Shows mostly French films. Has a little cocktail bar in the foyer.

Space Part 3 (Shibuya)
☎ *03-3477-5905. In Parco Part III, 8F.*

Chanter Cine (Ginza)
☎ *03-3591-1151. Near Hibiya Station.*

☎ ***03-5353-0770.*** HATSUDAI *Station on the Keio Line. http://www.nttprintec.co.jp/TOCCF*
A top venue for classical and contemporary music, boasting an exemplary dedication to premieres of Japanese and other modern composers, and promoting new compositions through its Next Millennium Composition Award, judged by Dutilleux, Ligeti, and Berio. Check out the "music wall" beside the steps leading up to the venue.

MUSICALS

Takarazuka

1,000 Days Gekijo. ☎ ***03-5251-2001.***
The all-female company's temporary venue is near Yurakucho Station while the massive 2,546-seat Takarazuka theater opposite the Imperial Hotel in Hibiya is under reconstruction. Schlock, glitter, glamour and feather boas excite the dedication and loyalty associated with rock fans—hang out around the theater after performances to catch a whiff of the frenzy. Spectacle all the

Cine La Sept (Ginza)
☎ *03-3212-3761. Near Yurakucho Central Exit.*

Cinema Square Tokyu (Shinjuku)
☎ *03-3202-1189. In Kabukicho, Tokyu Milano Building 3F.*
Minor European and Asian films.

Cine Switch 1 & 2 (Ginza)
☎ *03-356-0707. Near Yonchome crossing behind Wako Department Store.*
Mostly European films.

Cinema Milano (Shinjuku)
☎ *03-3202-1189. In Kabukicho, Tokyu Milano Building 4F.*

Cinema Qualite (Shinjuku)
☎ *03-3354-5670. In Musashino-kan Building 3F.*
Classic foreign and Hollywood films. Today's independent films.

Box Higashi-Nakano (Nakano)
☎ *03-5389-6780. In Porepore-za Building.*
Specializes in films that are shown nowhere else in Tokyo.

Yebisu Garden Cinema (Ebisu)
☎ *03-5420-6161. In Ebisu Garden Place.*
Another cinema specializing in films seen nowhere else in the city. Very comfortable seats.

Cine Vivant (Roppongi)
☎ *03-3403-6061. Near Azabu police station.*

Haiyu-za Talkie Night (Roppongi)
☎ 03-3401-4073. In the Haiyu-za theater.
Specializes in cult films and often runs late shows.

Iwanami Hall (Jinbocho)
☎ *03-3262-5252. Iwanami Building 10F.*
Often shows Asian films.

Waseda Shochiku (Takadanobaba)
☎ *03-3200-8968. Three minutes from Waseda Exit.*
Usually shows double features of current films but several weeks after initial opening date.

way, even as noted by James Michener in his novel *Sayonara*. Curtain times are super early, and "matinees" can start as early as 11 am.

MAINSTREAM

Aoyama Gekijo

5-53-1 Jingumae, Shibuya-ku. ☎ ***03-3797-5678.*** OMOTESANDO *Station on the Chiyoda Line.*
With 1,200 capacity, Aoyama puts on some ritzy shows, musicals, drama, and the Aoyama Ballet Festival in August and Aoyama Drama Festival in September-November. As it is in Kodomo no Shiro, or the National Children's Castle, there is plenty planned for children. Aoyama Enkei Gekijo is an intimate theater in the round, which shows innovative dance and plays.

Haiyuza Gekijo

4-9-2 Roppongi, Minato-ku. ☎ ***03-3470-2880.*** ROPPONGI *Station on the Hibiya Line.*
The actor's theater, home to many great Japanese stars and flush with auditions, readings, and rehearsals on any given day.

Shimokitazawa

Although Tokyo has no theater district as such, the area around Shimokitazawa Station in Setagaya-ku on the Inokashira and Odakyu lines is blossoming as home to small theaters showing established and avant-garde plays in a youth-geared shopping and dining paradise, where you can spend a reasonable amount on theater tickets and repair to great clubs and bars afterward. The drama diet is provided largely by young stage-smiths writing non-stop, slang-filled dialogue and jokes. **Geki Shogekijo** (☎ 03-3466-0020) is right beside the train tracks, sandwiched between the older stalwarts **Za Suzunari**, 1-45-15 Kitazawa (☎ 03-3469-0511), old granddaddy **Honda Gekijo** at 2-10-15 Kitazawa (☎ 03-3468-0030), and **Off Off Theatre**, at 2-11-8 Kitazawa (☎ 03-3424-3755). **Shimokitazawa Ekimae Gekijo** at 2-11-8 Kitazawa (☎ 03-3414-0019), **Shimokitazawa Gallery Gekijo** (☎ 03-3466-0020), and **Shimokitazawa Sho Gekijo** (☎ 03-3466-0020) are getting reputations for short runs of good new writing.

Ginza Saison Gekijo

1-11-1 Ginza, Chuo-ku. ☎ ***03-5353-0555***. KYOBASHI *Station on the Ginza Line.*

This luxury 774-seater works closely with the Saison Foundation for the Performing Arts to bring in productions by national theaters overseas and to present the Japanese premieres of the Butoh company Sankaijuku, star onnagata performer Bando Tamasaburo, the Royal Shakespeare Company, Leningrad Maly Drama Theatre, Comedie Francaise, etc. Get there early—small, slow lifts up to the theater, no stair access.

Parco Theatre

15-1 Udagawacho, Shibuya-ku. ☎ ***03-3477-5858***. SHIBUYA *Station on the JR Yamanote Line.*

Plays that appeal to the youth-populated streets of Shibuya, guaranteed to attract the crowds, with some imports such as Philippe Genty and modernized Kabuki.

Setagaya Public Theatre

4-1-1 Taishido, Setagaya-ku. ☎ ***03-5432-1525***. SANGENJAYA *Station on the Shin-Tamagawa Line.*

Director Hiroshi Takahagi and Artistic Director Makoto Sato ensure visionary programming at Tokyo's most innovative theater, including a Brecht series, contemporary plays and reworkings of the Japanese and other classics, dance, and occasionally the traditional performing arts. The adjacent Theatre Tram is named for the small train line that runs just beside it and shows modern dance and contemporary drama. Almost always something decent going on.

Theater X (cai)

2-10-14 Ryogoku, Sumida-ku. ☎ ***03-5624-1181***. RYOGOKU *Station on the JR Sobu Line.*

East Tokyo's happening performance venue, hosting socially critical drama, dance, concerts, and small festivals with excellent credentials in east European works, presided over by Producer Misako Ueda.

Tokyo Geijutsu Gekijo

1-8-1 Nishi-Ikebukuro, Toshima-ku. ☎ ***03-***

5391-2111. IKEBUKURO *Station on the JR Yamanote Line.*
Active publicly administered halls, the more interesting being the small performance spaces at basement level.

Tokyo Globe

3-1-2 Hyakunincho, Shinjuku-ku. ☎ ***03-3360-1151***. SHIN-OKUBO *Station on the JR Yamanote Line.*
Charming, dusty pink re-creation by architect Arata Isozaki of the original Shakespearean theater in London. Always reliable for top-flight imported productions—often, of course, Shakespeare—local performances, and a spring festival supporting new works. Gallery seats are available for reasonable prices—just don't get stuck behind a pillar with obliterated sight lines.

Where to Buy

MAGIC TRICKS

Magic Land, 3-5-2 Kayabacho, Chuo-ku. ☎ *03-3666-4749.*
Signed photos of every major magician in the world line the walls of this small, crowded shop. Silks, cards, balloons, gags, videos, close-up magic, and illusions are here somewhere under this or that stack of boxes. With his ponytail and beard, Ton-san looks more like a biker than the exceptional artist he is. He has illustrated countless magic books and his original tricks are used worldwide. Mama-san (no one calls her anything else) lives behind the counter and will demonstrate any of the tricks for you. Free coffee.

CONTEMPORARY

Asbestoskan

1-6-17 Nakamachi, Meguro-ku. ☎ ***03-3793-3164***. MEGURO *Station on the JR Yamanote Line.*
The Holy Grail for Butoh lovers is presided over by Akiko Motofuji, widow of Tatsumi Hijikata, the founder with Kazuo Ohno of the theatrical dance form of Butoh. Workshops, film showings, occasional performances, and thorough archives currently being copied for the library at the Theatre Museum at Waseda University.

Die Pratze

2-12 Nishi-Gokencho, Shinjuku-ku. ☎ ***03-3235-7074***. KAGURAZAKA *Station on the Tozai Line.*
Playwright and Director Shigeo Makabe's base is home to his alternative theater group, OM2. It shows performance, film, eclectic collaborations, and the Bikkuri House-fu Engeki Festival in March–April.

Kokusai Koryu Forum (Japan Foundation Forum)

2-17-22 Akasaka, Minato-ku. ☎ ***03-5562-3892***. TAMEIKE-SANNO *Station on the Ginza Line.*
Showcase for the work of the Japan Foundation, it presents many theater and dance collaborations between Japanese companies and groups from other Asian countries, often with impressive art exhibits in the large foyer.

• • television sets in Tokyo alone were tuned to the Japan-Croatia soccer match, which Japan lost 0-1 to bring • • • • • •

Komaba Agora Gekijo

1-11-13 Komaba, Meguro-ku. ☎ ***03-3467-2743***. KOMABA TODAI-MAE *Station on the Inokashira Line.*

A real gem, across the train tracks from the Todai University campus, with a tremendous regimen of spirited theatrical experiments, the January–March Dai-Sekimatsu Engeki-ten Festival of Contemporary Theater and Dance, and the biennial January–February Nikkan Dance Festival of solo works from South Korea and Japan. Base of Seinendan Theatre Company, under Director Oriza Hirata, and Japan Playwrights' Association. Arrive early, exchange your ticket for a token for your seat, and proceed inside, removing your shoes, on a first-come, first-get-squashed-in basis. Alternatively, have the sardine experience in the upstairs balcony.

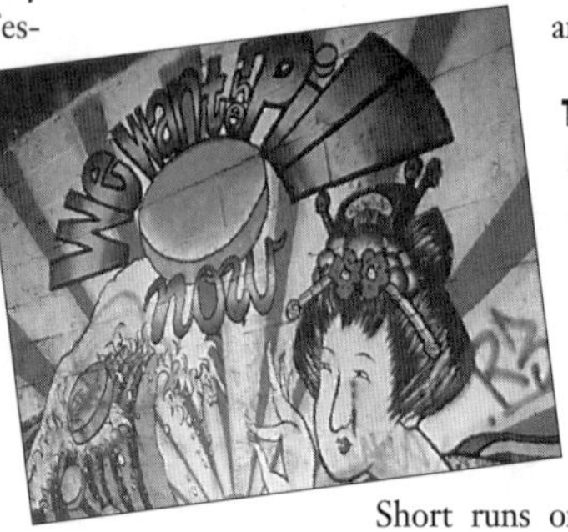

Plan B

4-26-20 Yayoicho, Nakano-ku. ☎ ***03-3384-2051***. NAKANO FUJIMICHO *Station on the Marunouchi Line. http://www.adguard.co.jp/artcamp/planb/*

Radical tiny performance space, particularly for Butoh in the mold of the great Min Tanaka, with solo dance, poetry, music, comedy, and conceptual work. Operational base for the annual summer Hakushu Artcamp, west of Tokyo. Stay around after the performance ends for some snacks and a drink with the cast and technicians.

Session House

100-58 Yaraicho, Shinjuku-ku. ☎ ***03-3266-0461***. KAGURAZAKA *Station on the Tozai Line.*

Fast becoming the undisputed space for new modern dance projects, with one of the best notice boards for upcoming performances, workshops, and collaborative works.

Terpsichore

3-49-15 Nakano, Nakano-ku. ☎ ***03-3383-3719***. NAKANO *Station on the Chuo Line.*

Few Butoh dancers have not debuted an early work at this Muse-inspired space. Short runs only of beginners, dance groups, old Butoh hands directing young dancers, lectures, and conferences. Friendly, dedicated staff and open invitations to mingle after shows to meet the performers. Exchange your ticket at the door, queue outside, place shoes in the bag provided, and sit cheek-to-jowl just inches from the feet of the performers as the trains rumble by outside.

Tiny Alice

2-13-6 Shinjuku, Shinjuku-ku. ☎ ***03-3354-7307***. SHINJUKU SANCHOME *Station on the Marunouchi Line.*

Underground theater hosting eclectic July–October festival, headed by Hiroko Nishimura, of modern drama from Japan and overseas with emphasis on collaborations with Asian directors and companies.

••••••Japan's first appearance in the World Cup finals to an abrupt end. Japanese fans impressed many in France with

NIGHTLIFE

by Jude "Sister Chill" Brand

SINCE Japan's economic bubble burst, the number of bars in Tokyo has quadrupled. As some of our better-traveled and more independently minded denizens realized they'd have to hunker down, they decided to have some fun in the process and, so, open a bar. There are now hundreds of funky, characterful bars scattered throughout Tokyo. Many of my favorites thrive in a far-flung corner of the suburbs. No chain stores or pubs are listed—they're easy enough to find. Instead, I offer you a hitlist of my top-40 all-time favorites. Kanpai!

3-2-8

PIONEER PARTY DUNGEON

Kotsu Anzen Center Building B1F, 3-24-20 Nishi-Azabu, Minato-ku. ☎ ***03-3401-4968****. Open from 8 pm till 4 am Monday to Thursday, till 5 am on Friday and Saturday, and till 3 am on Sunday. Entry ¥2,000 with two drinks.*

A simple neon arc plunges down a bare concrete wall at the Kasumicho intersection in Nishi-Azabu. The stairs below lead to 3-2-8 (or "san-ni-pa," as it is read in Japanese), a DJ bar of some twenty years standing. It rarely gets going before midnight. Sometimes you'll find a bare handful of regulars at the bar—art students, hardcore forty-somethings, or anyone who likes living on the edge. Other nights you'll walk into a wall of people. The music runs from soul to house.

Acaraje, Acarje Tropicana

RELIABLE LATIN JOINT

ACARAJE

Emerodo Building B1F, 1-8-19 Nishi-Azabu, Minato-ku. ☎ ***03-3401-0973***. *Open from 9 pm till 1 am Monday to Thursday, and till 2 am Friday and Saturday. Closed Sundays and holidays. Cover charge ¥2,000 with one drink.*

ACARAJE TROPICANA

Edge Building B2F, 1-1-1 Nishi-Azabu, Minato-ku. ☎ ***03-3479-4690***. *Open for dinner from 6 pm till 10 pm and for drinks till 3 am Tuesday to Thursday, till 5 am Friday and Saturday, and from 7 pm till 3 am Sunday. Closed Mondays. No cover charge.*

As with the original Acaraje, Tropicana combines three essential party ingredients: Latin people, Latin music, and unpretentiousness. It is a place to dance (classes held every Sunday), play foosball, or tuck into a tasty meal and watch Carnival or World Cup videos. Of course, they make an excellent margarita. Crowded on weekends, so a cover is charged. The menu is reliable and the staff down-to-earth. The original Acaraje caters more to a Japanese crowd. A visit to either is usually worth the hangover.

Aman (et Cha)

SUMPTUOUS MILLIONAIRE'S HIDEAWAY

AMAN

2-3-20-2F Jiyugaoka, Meguro-ku. ☎ ***03-3721-9680***. *Open from 7 pm till 4 am every day. ¥600 table charge includes oshibori (hot towel) and otsumami (snack); ¥1,500 cover on live nights; drinks around ¥1,000.*

CHA—SALON DE THE

Open for tea and cakes from 11 am till 6 pm every day.

Aman is sumptuous—sleek teak paneling surrounding beautifully crafted lounges and chairs, illuminated in the center by a pair of elegantly sculpted metal candlestands. Aspidistra crowd a skylit patio lined with low benches and cushions. Shuichi Kosaka stopped designing bars and restaurants for other people when he opened Aman. He imports his tea from Europe, his whiskey from Scotland, and his cigars from the Dominican Republic. A jazz or classical ensemble performs once a month. Italian sportswear is de rigueur any time.

Art Cube

THE INCREDIBLE SHRINKING BAR

Fujiya Building 1F, 1-3-9 Kami-Meguro, Meguro-ku. ☎ ***03-3760-3172***. *Open any time between 7 and 10 pm till 2 or 3 am, or whenever, every day. No holidays. Entry ¥1,000 (NOT including a drink).*

Art Cube is Tokyo's tiniest bar—it seats six, and has done so for more than twenty years. The interior is warmly lit, inescapably cozy, and incredibly uncluttered. A

Where to Buy

ROCK CONCERT VIDEOS

Airs, 7-16-1 Nishi-Shinjuku, Shinjuku-ku. ☎ 03-3366-0903.

Even the most jaded of rock fans will be excited to walk the aisles of this busy shop. Stars who have come here before you have autographed their photos, which manage to look the other way as you examine their bootleg concert videos. Artists from Abba to Zappa fill the shelves and you can take a look on a VCR before buying. Official releases are upstairs. Music fans will also want to explore the other small music shops in the area specializing in genre, collectibles, bootlegs and imports.

massive structural pillar divides an already cupboard-sized space into two cubicles. The master must squeeze behind the pillar to serve either side. Art posters hang where possible. One night the master played the entire sound track from Bagdad Cafe, but you may bring your own CDs, too. Mita-san, who hosts the graveyard shift, is a ponderer and a philosopher. Customers are mostly insomniacs or hostesses on their way home from work.

Balzac

AMBIENT LOUNGE

4-4-7-101 Aobadai, Meguro-ku. ☎ ***03-3468-6400****. Open from 9 pm till 3 am Wednesday to Sunday. Closed Tuesdays. ¥500 table charge includes snack; drinks ¥800.*

Balzac is a curious establishment tacked onto the car park of a residential highrise near Shibuya. Even though a sign glows reassuringly on the street, it looks like private property. Inside, space has been maximized through minimalism—unadorned white walls surround; beige matting slips underfoot. Furnishings are sparse and simple—two wicker chairs hug a candle by the window; pairs of low-slung black leather armchairs and couches tuck in at coffee tables. Well-dressed office workers sip cocktails early in the evening, and a raggle-taggle crew of baby DJs tend to accumulate 'round midnight. Music is an eclectic mix of old ska and ambient. Watch out for their events.

Bodeguita

CUBAN NIGHTSPOT THAT HOPS

New Life Ebisu Building 2F, 1-7-8 Ebisu, Shibuya-ku. ☎ ***03-3715-7721****. Bar open from 6 till 12 pm and kitchen till 11:30 pm Monday to Saturday. Closed Sundays and holidays. No cover charge.*

Claustrophobics beware—this place gets so crowded on the weekends you literally can't get in. Tokyo's down-home Latin community flocks here to wiggle and wobble the salsa, samba, and merengue—you name it (and the customers usually can). Unattached juanitas will be cavalierly asked to dance by unattached hombres, who otherwise tend to brood. During the week, Japanese businessmen come to knock back beer, and young Latin couples come to eat (the decor is strictly ristorante); otherwise it's empty. Cheaper than a ticket to Havana and just as much fun.

Budoya

TOKYO WINE SALOON

Shoei Building 5F, 3-10 Kajicho, Chiyoda-ku. ☎ ***03-3254-0637****. Open from 5 till 11:30 pm Monday to Saturday, closed Sundays and holidays. ¥500 table charge includes snack; drinks from ¥600.*

Budoya is a pit stop of long standing in

"Nip-pon, Nip-pon" throughout the match. A Swiss missionary resident in Japan sued his Japanese brokerage firm

Tokyo Jazz Spots

Tokyo has always loved jazz, from the shops catering to aficionados who treasure vinyl LPs and vacuum tubes like rare jewels to the coffeeshops where you can request your favorite turntable cartridge and speakers, for maximum acoustic pleasure, with your java. The places listed below are some of our favorites.

JAZZ CLUBS
These places feature mostly Japanese musicians, with live performances every evening.

Blue
NYK Building B1, 6-2-9 Minami-Aoyama, Minato-ku. ☎ 03-3797-1591.
Open from 9 pm. Groups like U.F.O., Jazz Brothers.

Sometime
Iseya B1, 1-11-31 Honmachi, Kichijoji (two minutes from North Exit). ☎ 0422-21-6336.
Open from 7 pm. Cover ¥1,200, drinks from ¥400.

Body & Soul
Anis Building B1, 6-13-9 Minami-Aoyama, Minato-ku (seven minutes from Omotesando Station). ☎ 03-5466-3348.
Open from 8:30 pm. Cover ¥3,500, drinks from ¥600.

Pit Inn
Accord Shinjuku B1, 2-12-4 Shinjuku (ten minutes from East Exit of Shinjuku Station). ☎ 03-3354-2024.
Open from 12:30 pm. Cover ¥1,300 with one drink. From 7:30 pm, cover ¥3,000 with one drink.

Pit Inn
Shimeshoji Building B1, 3-17-7 Roppongi, Minato-ku (eight minutes from Roppongi Station). ☎ 03-3585-1063.
Open from 7:30 pm. Cover ¥3,500 with one drink.

Someday
Ichibangai Building B1, 1-10-7 Hyakunincho, Shinjuku-ku (one minute from Shin-Okubo JR Station). ☎ 03-3364-2518. http://someday.net /index.html.
Open from 7:30 pm. Cover ¥2,800, drinks from ¥500. Jazz and Latin jazz

LIVE HOUSES
While these are not strictly jazz clubs, they sometimes feature live jazz.
You often have to buy advance tickets for these venues.

Sabas Tokyo
2-8-2 Jingumae, Shibuya. ☎ 03-5411-3335.
Mainly bossa nova (e.g., Tonhino Horta). If you like, you can have a Brazilian dinner while listening to music.

Club Quattro
32-13-4F Udagawacho, Shibuya-ku (just across from the Beam Building). ☎ 03-3477-8750.
Smaller than Liquid Room, usually all standing. Sade and Cesaria Evora have been featured here. A great little place.

Kanda. Early evenings, salaried employees sit cheek-to-elbow in every corner—the air thick with smoke, background jazz barely discernable above raucous chatter. But late evening belongs to old cronies of Ken—an old Silk Road hippie who developed a taste for wine in Europe and decided to open a wine "salon" (though "saloon" is a better description). Photographers and potters, performers and creators drift in to eat and drink the house red. Flyers for off-off Meiji Dori performances yellow on the notice board. Someone occasionally grabs a guitar.

Cacciatora

NEO-BEATNIK CHICKEN SHACK

1-9-12-B1F Ebisu-Minami, Shibuya-ku. ☎ ***03-3715-8218****. Open for lunch from 11:30 am till 2 pm Monday to Friday, and for dinner from 6 till 12 pm through Saturday. Closed for lunch holidays and Sundays. Open 3 till 10 pm last Sunday of month. No cover charge; cover charge last Sunday ¥2,000 includes one drink and one snack.*

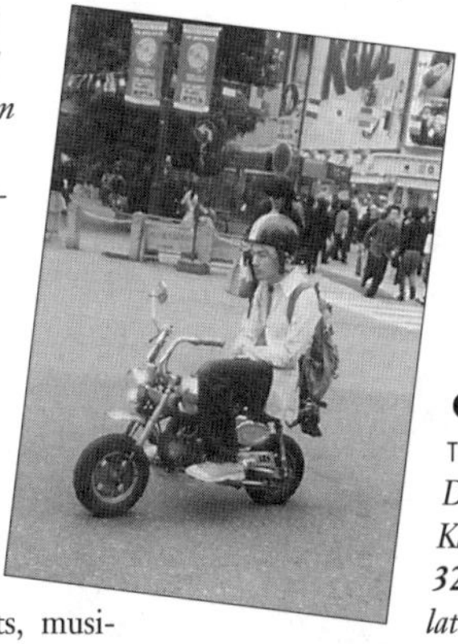

Cacciatora is a neo-beatnik bar—a rallying point for local graphic designers, artists, musicians, etc. If it's creative, someone in the room does it for a living. Moriki-san, the owner and a former muralist, has a talent for attracting interesting people. He hung up his brush when he met Ueno Hirosuke, an illustrator and the man behind Cacciatora's interior graphics. Ueno's work has a breezy pop-industrial feel. Young bloods wear tie-dyed flares; experienced dudes wear ad agency chino. Chicken Cacciatora is on the menu.

Cafe Mogambo

ADULT AND UNFUSSY

Osawa Building 1F, 6-1-7 Roppongi, Minato-ku. ☎ ***03-3403-4833****. Open from 6 pm till 5 am Monday to Saturday; closed Sundays. No cover charge; beer ¥800; spirits ¥1,000.*

Cafe Mogambo felt like a comfy old glove from the day it opened, with drinkers nodding orders and fielding calls from the pay phone. The interior thumbs its nose at style, with a lackluster collection of Asian knickknacks melding unobtrusively enough with bamboo-covered walls. An oval bar sits in the center, and stand-and-lean counters hug the walls. Nigel, the owner, is an old Asia hand with a sixth sense for scouting good staff. A down-home cross section of foreigners claim Mogambo's as their own. Beware the bell: ring it and you buy all present a drink. Hundreds of Polaroids eulogize those who have done so.

Cafe Ole Bar

THE UNITED STATES THEREOF...

Dai 2 Metro Building 1F, 2-38-2 Kabukicho, Shinjuku-ku. ☎ ***03-3200-2349****. Open from 8 pm till late(ish) every night. No cover charge; beer and shots ¥600, cocktails ¥800.*

Cafe Ole Bar whiffs of a Mexican bordertown, though in this case (and appropriately) it's holed up in the back blocks of Kabukicho, Tokyo's red-light district. Here, strangers are acknowledged with a nod, regulars greeted with a slap on the back and a shot. Laser toys flicker electric red across the ceiling. Tear sheets from an antique car calendar cover a disused vent. Furnishings are slapdash. Sometimes you'll find yourself alone with your MTV; other times you'll walk into a wild, raging party pumped up with "dirty" (as Miguel likes to call them) techno-Latin mixes.

•• Telecommunications, alarmed at young people's spurning of conventional mail in favor of e-mail, said it is ••••••

Where to Buy

BAZOOKAS

Sam's Militaria, 1-32-4 Higashi-Ikebukuro, Toshima-ku. ☎ *03-3971-4935.* President Sam Motojima should be able to fit you right up.

Castillo

RETRO DANCE DIVE

Daini Aoi Building 1F, 6-1-8 Roppongi, Minato-ku. ☎ ***03-3475-1629.*** *Open from 7 pm till 6 am Sunday to Thursday and from 6 pm till 6 am Friday and Saturday. No cover charge.*

Castillo has a mirror ball—it's that sort of place: a bit retro, a bit weird. The DJs spin disco and soul chart classics from the '70s to early '80s, with a dash of new wave. It's a multi-denominational archival revival—the way radio would have been then. Dexi's Midnight Runners led to J. Giles Band led to something from KC and the Sunshine Band led to The Cure, before the mirror ball slipped down a few cogs for a slow song. No one is particularly cool, nor do they seem to care.

Ça Va, Ça Va

WHISKEY BAR FOR CONNOISSEURS

Gomeikan Building B1F, 3-3-9 Shinjuku, Shinjuku-ku. ☎ ***03-3353-4650.*** *Open from 6:30 pm till 3 am every day. No holidays. Table charge ¥1,000; cheapest blended whiskey ¥800; cheapest single malt ¥1,100.*

It is rare to stumble upon a good bar in Tokyo, especially one for serious whiskey connoisseurs, but I did. Ça Va, Ça Va is hidden between two greasy spoons on a grotty back street in Shinjuku. The menu lists over 100 malt Scotch whiskeys according to highland region, which cost anywhere from ¥1,100 to ¥6,000 a shot. The bartenders are discreet of action and unobtrusively attentive. Lighting is delicately arranged so that, after having served a customer, a half-step back they disappear into shadow (as all good bartenders should).

Club Dragon (ex Rude)

WARM LEATHERETTE IN TOKYO'S TENDERLOIN

Accord Building B2F, 2-12-4 Shinjuku, Shinjuku-ku. ☎ ***03-3341-0606.*** *Open from 8 pm till late, Monday to Saturday, closed Sundays and holidays. Cover charge ¥1,000 includes one drink; ¥2,000 for women on Fridays; men only on Saturdays.*

Rude is history. It moved out of its closet to become Club Dragon, a bigger and better venue in Shinjuku's gay Nichome district. Some things are the same—it's still massively popular, Ken-chan still struts his stuff in a pair of leather chaps, and, if you're in for the late shift, the body boys'll be there—only now they do strip-trapeze acts from chains hung over the dance floor. The music is anywhere from just this side of techno to just that side of disco.

Corubar's

RUM IN THE SUBURBS

5-12-3 Okusawa, Setagaya-ku. ☎ ***03-5701-2377.*** *Open from 7 pm till 4 am every night. No cover charge; beer and cocktails from ¥500.*

Corubar's is yet another gem tucked away in the backblocks of Jiyugaoka (Okusawa, to be exact). Inoue-san, the master, looks like a streetwise Buddha, with his shaven head, T-shirt chic, and propensity for hunching into deep belly laughs. He loves Coruba rum, hence the name. He also loves Latin and blues tunes. The bartender prefers rock and ska. During the week, small groups of locals pop in for a late-night drink at the long laquered bar or climb in at one of the tall tables. Black light flickers here and there. It's comfortable and cool. On the weekend it usually hops.

E Cafe

LOVE AND PEACE RETREAT

Sato Building 2F, 1-13-5 Ebisu-Nishi, Shibuya-ku. ☎ ***03-5458-9368****. Open from 8 pm till 2 am Monday to Thursday, later on Friday and Saturday, closed Sundays. Table charge ¥500 includes snack; canned beer ¥600; mixed drinks ¥800.*

The sheer plate glass windows of E Cafe's second-story perch overlook a shrine nestled among an oasis of tall leafy trees. Yuko-san, the quietly chic proprietress, has handpicked an assortment of antiques to create her self-styled "love and peace chill-out space." Her prize: a '40s dentist's chair, complete with fully functioning hydraulics and instrument stand. Unless a DJ friend drops by, Yuko spins an ethereal mix of ambient and house. This is where Tokyo's fringe generation comes to contemplate the universe, in the treehouse retreat by the temple.

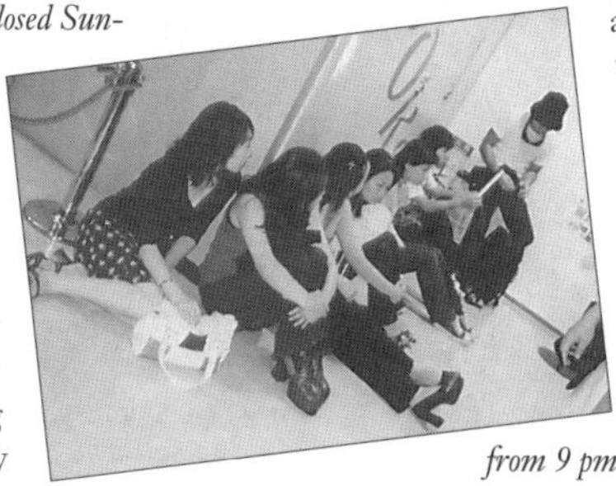

Edge End

UK INDIES LOUNGE

Nono Building 2F, 1-17-12 Dogenzaka, Shibuya-ku. ☎ ***03-5458-6385****. Open every night from 6 till 12 pm (unless Oasis is in town). Entry ¥800 includes one drink; events ¥2,000 includes two drinks.*

When Endo-san's small pizza delivery business in sleepy-town Saitama got squashed by the big boys, he decided to pursue his passion—UK indies music. He rented a former karaoke snack bar but did not have the money to redecorate. Little crushed-velvet seats pull in at low tables. Mirrored walls are hidden by rough corrugated cardboard, now covered in signatures by Ben Folds Five, Mazarine Street, and Echobelly. All the DJs who spin are babies, most of whom Endo-san met jostling in the audience at concerts. They still go to school, too, so he usually closes 'round midnight.

Endorphine

ROCK GROTTO

1-31-9-2F Jiyugaoka, Meguro-ku. ☎ ***03-5701-1510****. Open from 9 pm till 4 am Monday to Thursday till 6 am Friday and Saturday, closed Sundays. Music charge ¥500; beer from ¥600; mixed drinks from ¥700.*

Endorphine is shrouded in darkness. A long heavy-wood bar fronts a dozen log stools. Beyond, a Medusa's head of wax tendrils overflowing from a candle, frozen in time like the Led Zepplin poster on the wall above. Old twelve-inch rock albums occupy a third of the space behind the bar; a menagerie of figurines another third. The theme is '70s rock, but anything goes.

• found that 26 percent of men and 40 percent of women want to change their jobs, even though there are now ••••••

It sometimes gets busy, but usually you will be one of a handful of drinkers, perhaps chatting to the master in 4/4 time, as a young biker sips beer waiting for a girlfriend.

Enjoy! House

ASIA MEETS THE 70S

2-9-9-2F Ebisu-Nishi, Shibuya-ku. ☎ ***03-5489-1591****. Open from 1 pm till 1 am Monday to Thursday, till 3 am Friday and Saturday. No cover charge; drinks from ¥500.*

Beyond the incense haze that leads to Enjoy! House awaits a riot of color and imagery. The walls are covered in anything a thumbtack can hold captive—Hindu deity posters, Coca-Cola balloons, fairy lights. Lace, tinsel, fur, and sequins drape alcoves. A candle flickers in a skull. Senses thus assaulted, Goh-san, the master, seems at home—big bugeye shades, zebra beret sprouting an Afro, medallions jingling. He traveled to New York via Nepal, and this is the result. A kaleidoscope of cultures woven into a crazy Casbah. DJs spin on the weekend, otherwise it's funk, uncut.

Fellow

TRIBAL TRIANGLE

Hayakawa Building B1F, 1-6-10 Dogenzaka, Shibuya-ku. ☎ ***03-5458-2010****. Open from 8 pm till 2 am or later Monday to Saturday, closed Sundays and holidays. Table charge ¥300 includes snack.*

Fellow was conceived by an architect, but the integrity of the original design—dark peach-colored walls contrasting with a triangular stainless steel bar—has been lost in the jumble of ethnic bric-a-brac that has accumulated in five years. Omochi-san, the manager, is the culprit. He wears his hair long, prefers cheesecloth to milled cotton, and sports a necklace not a necktie. The music slips from UA to The Fugees to obscure tribal beats, but often as not you'll find the customers—mostly cool thirty-something design professionals who've followed Omochi from club to bar—and the staff glued to the TV.

2626 (Flo Flo)

MAGICAL MYSTERY BAR

2-8-5 Ebisu-Nishi, Shibuya-ku. ☎ ***03-3770-2626****. Open from 8 pm till 5 am Monday to Saturday, closed Sundays and holidays. Table charge ¥500 before 12 pm, ¥700 after 12 pm, drinks from ¥800.*

On the street, a red lamp barely illuminates a board that reads "2626" (pronounced "flo flo"). An identical red glow emanates from the end of a two-foot-wide no-man's-land between buildings. The magic begins as one sidles down to enter. The master is a classically trained guitarist, who serves drinks between genre flipping CDs—Billie Holiday, Pink Floyd, Okinawan folk songs. If in the mood, he'll pick up a guitar or shamisen. The clientele is as mixed as the music, but one thing is understood—one must wait till he's finished playing to order.

GB

WHERE THE BOYS ARE

Business Hotel T Building B1F, 2-12-3 Shin-

juku, Shinjuku-ku. ☎ ***03-3352-8972****. Open from 8 pm till 2 am Monday to Thursday, till 2:30 am Friday, till 3 am Saturday, and till 1:30 am Sunday. No cover charge.*

GB is strictly men only, who flock here most nights. A spacious central bar serves about twenty stools, beyond which men stand and lean and watch. All eyes face each other and the door. The lighting is deftly arranged. The clientele is mostly young Japanese boys who come to flirt with expats. Muscle boys clench and pose but usually head elsewhere. GB is great for newbies as most of the staff and customers speak English—Tokyo's best foreigner-friendly gay singles bar. Though a bit of a cliché with residents, this is where the boys are.

George's

SOUL HEAVEN

7-55-9 Roppongi, Minato-ku. ☎ ***03-3405-9049****. Open whenever George is ready till 7 am every morning. No cover charge; beer ¥1,000 ; jukebox ¥200 a tune.*

George's is a soul bar. From the hand-scripted neon outside, flickering through greasy nicotine-stained windows, to the black eyeliner and slash-of-red lipstick style of the mama, it's a classic. The jukebox is stacked with old Bakelite 45s, featuring some of the best soul singles ever pressed (Etta James, Willie Jackson, mandatory JB), selected from the 20,000-plus stockpile the mama has stashed. Barely ten feet wide and fifteen barstools deep, the walls and ceiling are covered in yellowing pictures signed by Motown greats—the less stained, the more recent the visit. You never know who might be there. Unless you like hotel lobbies, George's is a must.

Gonbe

SOUL IN THE SUBURBS

2-1-18 Nakamachi, Setagaya-ku. ☎ ***03-3702-9458****. Usually open by 10 pm till 1:30 am or later, Monday to Saturday, closed Sundays. No table charge; drinks from ¥500.*

Gonbe is secreted away in Todoroki, an up-market residential suburb—a strange location for a cool, late-night bar. Kin-chan, the master, spins everything from silk-stocking smooth soul through to free-your-mind funk, from his 1,000-strong CD collection. A small bar holds up a corner, and low tables and chairs clutter the rest. A few album covers circle the ceiling (he buys them for the sexy covers), and black light bounces off knickknacks. All Gonbe's customers live nearby—a few old boys drop by, but the bulk are savvy twenty- to thirty-somethings who sip Bombay gin and speak perfect English.

Hot Rod Cafe

HARLEYS IN A BARN (WITH THEIR ENGINES RUNNING)

145 Saedocho, Suzuki-ku, Yokohama. ☎ ***045-935-7477****. Only open Fridays and Saturdays from 10:00 pm till 4:00 am. No charge; beer ¥800.*

A biker haunt where you park your hog at the bar? Yes, in an area where identical factories stretch for miles. The directions?

Look for a drink machine next to an eel restaurant. But they work. This warehouse is pumped up on bass and awash in black light. A bar hugs a corner. A half-dozen T-birds and Corvettes glower on the far side. And between, a sea of Harleys. Everyone rides in: lone Japanese, army-dudes in Rising Sun colors; even the woolly headed bartender jumped on a Harley to go home. Beware the bike count, when everyone cranks their engines.

Inaoiza

HALFWAY HOUSE FOR SPACE PIRATES

Sunny Mansion #202, 2-38-16 Kita-Koenji, Suginami-ku. ☎ ***03-3336-4480****. Open from 7 pm till 2 am Wednesday to Monday, closed Tuesdays. Music charge ¥1,500 ; no cover after 11 pm; beer ¥600.*

Inaoiza bills itself as a live house, though I think of it as a halfway house for space pirates hitchhiking the galaxy. Shibata-san, the master, used to play guitar but decided a bar would be more fun. The interior is small, dark, and cramped, and looks like it was built from a shipwreck—fishing net here, masthead there, and wooden planks everywhere. The "stage" is a raised area from where patrons are shooed before showtime. Early, customers are usually friends of the band; later, leggy young girls prop up the bar waiting for space pirates.

Kinswomyn

ONE FOR THE GIRLS

Daiichi Tenka Building 3F, 2-15-10 Shinjuku, Shinjuku-ku. ☎ ***03-3354-8720****. Open from 7 pm till 3 am Monday to Saturday, closed Sundays and holidays. No cover charge; drinks ¥700.*

. . . or womyn, I should say, and womyn only—no men evens the score with the boys' bars. Kinswomyn is Tokyo's first cool lesbian bar (old-guard hangouts are still prohibitively expensive). Tara-chan, the mama, sunglasses propped on head, looks you straight in the eye and smiles as she takes your order. The interior is carpeted, low-ceilinged, and softly lit. A central semi-circular bar serves a dozen-plus stools. Old-guard lesbians (detectable by their butch-fem posturing) occasionally drop by, but for the most part it's a hip relaxed crowd. Camisoles are as common as tennis shoes.

Mix

INDUSTRIAL-STRENGTH BUNKER

Sanwa Jitsugyo Building B1F, 3-16-19 Kita-Aoyama, Minato-ku. ☎ ***03-3797-1313****. Open from 7 pm till 5 am every night. Entry ¥2,000 with two drinks; no charge on Sunday.*

Truly hip Tokyo clubbers have always shunned Roppongi in favor of Aoyama or Nishi-Azabu next door, and one of the coolest alternatives is Mix. The interior is pure Tank Girl chic. The clientele as cool as its concrete. This is where the DJs from other clubs hang out. The music is mostly reggae, but, as the name suggests, it's a mixed bag (soul, hip hop, funk). Mix is one long skinny room. The entrance is in the middle, the bar on the right, and dancefloor on the left—a crippling layout when it gets packed on the weekend. Weeknights are best.

New Sazae

DIVE THAT WON'T SAY DIE

Ishikawa Building 2F, 2-18-5 Shinjuku, Shinjuku-ku. ☎ ***03-3354-1745****. Open from 10 pm till 5 am Sunday to Thursday, till 6 am on Friday and Saturday. First drink ¥1,000; ¥600 to ¥800 after that.*

I know of only two people who made it to the original Sazae in the '60s. In 2000, the "new" one doesn't look like budging—its murky depths littered with tables and chairs (legs wobbly, upholstery repaired with tape), graffiti-covered walls started from scratch every decade or so, a couple of game machines aglow in a corner. Heavy curtains ensure that no light invades. Customers range from transvestites in frocks through hard-nosed bleached blondes to sullen-faced voyeurs. All who enter lose a night in their life (and most of the next day).

Nigiro

UP-MARKET YATAI

No fixed address. ☎ *090-8947-8448 or 090-5215-0011. Open from 8 pm till 2 am every day, but best to call. Drinks ¥400, except glass wine ¥600.*

Yatai, by definition, are constantly on the move. But with Sakai-san always at the helm and a hardcore following, Nigiro always promises excellent food and a warm bonhomie. The handmade linguine in basilico sauce is dreamlike in its delicacy. The customers are everyone from fifty-something couples to twenty-something graphic designers and DJs. At Nigiro's core is the usual yatai cart, though relatively chic and comfortable, with a counter of thick lacquered wood; shutters extending into a red formica cross defining the ceiling; heavy plastic sheeting draped on top; and kerosene heaters, kettles atop, simmering warmly in winter. Nigiro, as you will learn, is "origin" spelled backward.

Where to Buy

GOGGLES

Honorary, 3-9 Sakuragaoka, Shibuya-ku. ☎ 03-3496-3461.

Honorary is where you go to buy anything associated with Vespa motorscooters. They have a selection of several dozen types of goggles, many of them wonderful old antiques that beg to be worn with a leather helmet and a long silk scarf.

The Old Blind Cat

SMOKIN' JAZZ DEN

Konwa Center Building B2F, 3-26-3 Shinjuku, Shinjuku-ku. ☎ ***03-3354-9354****. Open from 6 pm till midnight Monday to Saturday, closed Sundays and holidays. Charge ¥200 before 8 pm, ¥500 after with snacks.*

Steep stairs drop one on the Old Cat's doormat, where thirty years of nicotine-enhanced jazz appreciation has congealed into a soupy layer. A bar runs through it, and a half-dozen cramped booths line the wall opposite. The mama hands you a menu and an ashtray the size of a wagon wheel. Drinks are

• • practice which had hitherto been discouraged out of concern for the environment. It was reported that due to the • • • • • •

Key Live Music Venues

Tokyo Dome (aka Big Egg)
1-3 Koraku, Bunkyo-ku. ☎ 03-5800-9999.
Cavernous (60,000 capacity), acoustically challenged venue designed for baseball games, not concerts.

Budokan
Kitanomaru-Koen, Chiyoda-ku. ☎ 03-3216-5100.
A somewhat funky venue that can rather uncomfortably hold 14,130 people. Main function of the venerable Budokan is to serve as an arena for traditional martial arts competitions. The Beatles played the hall in 1966, and artists such as Cheap Trick and Bob Dylan have recorded live albums there. Big problem: no alcohol sold on premises.

NHK Hall
2-2-1 Jinnan, Shibuya-ku. ☎ 03-3465-1751.
The nationwide TV/radio network's main concert hall often features great bands, Japanese and foreign, just before they move on to larger venues such as the Budokan.

Nakano Sun Plaza Hall
4-1-1 Nakano, Nakano-ku. ☎ 03-3388-1151.
Has a capacity of 2,222 and is known for its announcements instructing concert-goers not to stand up, dance, take pictures, make recordings, exchange stock market tips, shoot the artists, or do anything else that might conceivably disturb the performance.

Kan'i Hoken Hall
8-4-13 Nishi-Gotanda, Shinagawa-ku. ☎ 03-3490-5111.
Bland, acoustically less than wonderful run-of-the-mill concert hall.

Club Quattro Shibuya
Quattro by Parco 5F, 32-13 Udagawa-cho, Shibuya-ku. ☎ 03-3477-8750.
Mid-sized (1,000 capacity), this is one of the best places in Shibuya to hear live music. Crowded, smoky, and noisy, but the sense of immediacy of seeing top-notch Japanese and foreign acts in such an intimate setting is worth it.

On Air East
2-14-9 Dogenzaka, Shibuya-ku. ☎ 03-3476-8787.
Another well-known, mid-sized Shibuya concert venue, in the heart of the love hotel district. Usually packed to the gills with punters (no seats provided, as a rule).

Suntory. The playlist includes Marlena Shaw taunting "Run Away Little Boy" and Gene Harris schmoozing "In the Wee Small Hours of the Morning." Japanese writer Haruki Murakami worked in a record store next door in high school. Now, middle-aged businessmen in suits cluster at booths, intellectuals lurch solo into the bar.

Paranoia Cafe

HELL-HOLE BAR

Victory Building 3F, 4-12-5 Roppongi, Minato-ku. ***☎ 03-5411-8018****. Open from 7 pm till 2 am Monday to Thursday till 4 am Friday and Saturday. Entry ¥1,000, events ¥4,000.*

Outside, a giant eyeball malevolently glares down. The stairs up are shrouded in dark-

•••••••intense price competition brought about by the deregulation of the nation's gasoline market, gasoline in some

On Air West
2-3 Maruyamacho, Shibuya-ku. ☎ 03-5458-4646.
Smaller cousin of On Air East just across the street. Features Japanese and foreign acts tending to be more obscure/cultish than those appearing at On Air East.

Shibuya Kokaido
1-1 Udagawacho, Shibuya-ku. ☎ 03-3463-1211.
For some reason, this garden-variety, ward government–run hall tends to bring out the best in all sorts of performers.

Orchard Hall
2-24-1 Dogenzaka, Shibuya-ku. ☎ 03-3477-9150.
Beautiful classical concert hall in the Bunkamura complex that is sometimes used for pop/rock concerts.

Koseinenkin Kaikan
5-3-1 Shinjuku, Shinjuku-ku. ☎ 03-3356-1111.
Another mid-sized hall, comfy without being classy.

Liquid Room
7F Humax Pavilion, 1-20-1 Kabukicho, Shinjuku-ku. ☎ 03-3200-6831.
Shinjuku's version of On Air East, in the heart of the sleazy Kabukicho district. Lots of techno and other cutting-edge stuff.

Akasaka Blitz
TBS Square, 5-3-6 Akasaka, Minato-ku. ☎ 03-3224-0567.
Mid-sized, variable-format (seats or all standing, depending on the show) venue often used by major record labels for "showcase" gigs by big-name domestic acts that normally play bigger halls.

Ebisu Garden Hall
Ebisu Garden Place, 1-13-2 Mita, Meguro-ku. ☎ 03-5424-0111.

Tokyo International Forum
3-5-1 Marunouchi, Chiyoda-ku. ☎ 03-5221-9000.
Nice and new, and in the heart of Tokyo.

Tokyo Bay NK Hall
Tokyo Bay, 1-8 Maihama, Urayasu-shi, Chiba. ☎ 0473-55-7000.
Inconveniently located out near Disneyland.

Club Cittá Kawasaki
4 Ogawacho, Kawasaki-ku, Kawasaki-shi. ☎ 044-246-8888.
The gritty, down-home vibe of Kawasaki makes Cittá a great place to rock 'n' roll the evening away.

ness. Inside, the walls are a sea of screaming faces. The roof is infested with unblinking eyeballs. One corner houses a prison cell complete with lockable gate. Pets Dog-foot and Eye-hand perch unleashed on the bar. Horror movies play nonstop. Heavy metal screeches from speakers. But what else when Screaming Mad George opens a bar—a Japanese special-effects expert with a convincing and decidedly grizzly way with latex? Drinks are a little expensive, but worth it for the wacky interior. By contrast, the customers seem quite drab.

People's Bar

SOULFUL OASIS

Dai 36 Togensha Building B1F, 4-5-9 Rop-

parts of the country was selling for as little as ¥77 a liter, about one-third the price of an equivalent volume of

Velfarre
7-14-22 Roppongi, Minato-ku. ☎ *03-3402-8000.*
Primarily a disco run by the Avex record label, Velfarre also hosts various live acts, mainly of the dance/techno ilk.

Blue Note Tokyo
Raika Building, 6-3-16 Minami-Aoyama, Minato-ku. ☎ *03-5485-0088.*
Classy and pricey place to check out top jazz acts visiting Japan.

Club CAY
Aoyama Spiral B1, 5-6-23 Minami-Aoyama, Minato-ku. ☎ *03-3498-5790.*
Great basement space that specializes in rootsy "ethnic" music from Japan and abroad.

Heaven's Door
Keio Hallo Building B1, 1-33-19 Sangenjaya, Setagaya-ku. ☎ *03-3410-9581.*
Not a good place for those concerned about potential hearing loss.

Shinjuku Loft
Daini Mizota Building B1, 7-5-10 Nishi-Shinjuku, Shinjuku-ku. ☎ *03-3365-0698.*
Great place to check out new Japanese musical talent. Loud!

Crocodile Shibuya
Sekiguchi Building B1, 6-18-8 Jingumae, Shibuya-ku. ☎ *03-3499-5205.*
Good hard-rocking live house with a friendly vibe.

Milk
Roob6, 1-13-3 Ebisu-Nishi, Shibuya-ku. ☎ *03-5458-2826.*
The Korova milk bar from *A Clockwork Orange* with a hard-core soundtrack instead of Ludwig Van. Great layout, featuring all sorts of different rooms in which to ensconce oneself.

Eggman Shibuya
1-6-8 Jinnan, Shibuya-ku. ☎ *03-3496-1561.*
Good place to see Japanese bands just before they hit it big.

Club Que
5-29-15 B1 Daizawa, Setagaya-ku. ☎ *03-5481-4141.*
Typical concrete bunker-type Tokyo live house, featuring up-and-coming indies bands in studenty/hip Shimokitazawa.

—compiled by Steve McClure

pongi, Minato-ku. ☎ ***03-3479-4898****. Open from 9 pm till 5 am Monday to Thursday, till 7 am Friday and Saturday, and till 2 am on Sunday and holidays. No cover charge.*
People's Bar is an oasis. Raj, the master, is as open and friendly as anyone hosting a broom closet-sized bar can be, and has been careful to nurture his clientele away from the mayhem that typifies Roppongi. He recently opened Bombay Cafe to cater to late-night eats, too. Raj bills People's as a soul bar, but DJs spin across the board: soul, funk, hip-hop, reggae, and even R&B. It does get packed on weekends, but otherwise it's a relaxed group of brothers who drop by to pick up a good vibe or soul mate.

Poor

NEW-AGE CHILLING ZONE
Menar Jingumae Building 4F, 1-8-5 Jingumae, Shibuya-ku. ☎ ***03-5411-0246****. Open from 7 pm till 2 am Monday to Saturday, closed Sundays. ¥500 table charge; drinks from ¥600.*

••••••Coca Cola. The government urged everyone to wear a hat when out in the mid-day sun. Eighty police searched the

Poor has no sign and no elevator. Four flights lead to a cave-like entry, beyond which a tunnel runs left and right. Each side houses a bar backed by a puzzle of hand-made shelves painted in primaries with contrasting organic touches. No angle is 90 degrees. To the left, an assortment of cushioned corners beckon intimate conversation; to the right a large table adrift in a bamboo forest caters to larger groups. Candles flicker everywhere. It is managed by three quietly hip Japanese boys, whose DJ friends drop by with drum 'n' bass and ambient tapes. Otherwise, they mostly play reggae.

Pousse Cafe

RELAXED ROOFTOP PERCH

AQ Building 3F, 2-15-22 Jiyugaoka, Meguro-ku. ☎ ***03-5701-1588.*** *Open from midday till 6 pm for tea, till 3 am for drinks, closed Wednesdays. No cover charge; glass wine ¥600; beer from ¥700; mixed drinks from ¥800.*

Kotaro-san, also called Mark, wanted to create a relaxed environment where one could order by simply pushing one's glass forward—hence Pousse Cafe. The interior is simple yet stylish. The service is sensitive. A counter fronts eight stools. Tables hug the stucco wall opposite, beyond which are more tables on a bamboo terrace. Wine bottles sit neatly racked. Pousse sometimes hosts concerts by Morgan Fisher; otherwise the playlist runs from opera through jazz. Mostly Japanese couples stop by for an after-dinner drink. Mark recently handed Pousse over to Katsu-san, the manager.

Pub Elvis

KARAOKE WITH THE KING

Tack Eleven Building 2F, 2-19-7 Takadanobaba, Shinjuku-ku. ☎ ***03-3232-0073.*** *Open from 7 pm till 2 am Monday to Saturday, closed Sundays and holidays. Cover charge around ¥1,000; ¥300 music charge on Tuesday; karaoke ¥200 per tune; 20% service charge after midnight.*

Opposite Takadanobaba Station, amidst the clatter and din of ramshackle izakaya and their roseate patrons, is a pub dedicated to The King. Though Elvis's ghost might not be impressed—it is a rather shabby little karaoke joint. The interior is littered with Elvis posters and paraphernalia. A small bandstand lies ready in back, mikes and spotlights poised. A thick Elvis songbook is on standby, some lyrics handwritten on scraps of paper. A '50s-theme band plays every Tuesday. Elvis impersonator alert any night.

Rolling Stone

HARD PLACE THAT ROCKS

Ebichu Building B1F, 3-2-7 Shinjuku, Shinjuku-ku. ☎ ***03-3354-7347.*** *Open from 6 pm till 4:15 am Monday to Friday, till 5 am Saturday and Sunday. Table charge weekdays ¥200 before midnight, ¥500 thereafter; weekends, men ¥2,000 with two drinks, women ¥1,500 ditto.*

Take a last gasp of fresh air before descending into this dive. Rolling Stone is about music—rock played loud at decibels that deny conversation. And it's about life-

••• country around Sayama, Saitama prefecture, for four days before finally running to ground a 3.6-meter python •••••

style—hardcore and metal subculturalists come to sit and look mean, and sometimes pick a fight. The battered interior is papered in Stones posters. Don't be fooled by the miniskirted waitresses—I've seen them muscle drunken GIs up the stairs without any visible strain on their manicures. Best avoid weekends.

Where to Buy

ARCHERY EQUIPMENT

Asahi Kyugu, 2-19-31 Nishi-Sugamo, Toshima-ku. ☎ 03-3971-2046.

This shop carries both highly technical western equipment and the elegant, simple, and very expensive Japanese equipment. It is to be expected that Japanese customers invariably are attracted to Western equipment and Westerners to Japanese.

Salsa Caribe

RADIO BAGOTA IN A BARN

Reine Roppongi Building 2F, 5-3-4 Roppongi, Minato-ku. ☎ ***03-3746-0244/0246****. Open from 6 pm till 5 am every day. Entry ¥1,500 with one drink on Friday and Saturday, otherwise no charge.*

Salsa Caribe, like a Latin bar anywhere the world over, attracts a brotherhood of extroverts who love to dance. Most of Caribe's customers are Peruvian or Columbian, the latter country's top-40 dance charts pumped nonstop through the club's speakers. The interior is barn-meets-dancehall: one big multicolored box with a bar down one side and edged with benches. Weekends usually hop, but remember: Latin dance etiquette rules—any hombre may ask any juanita to dance; if she accepts, he will politely thank her afterward and quietly accept "no" to a second dance, if so rebuffed.

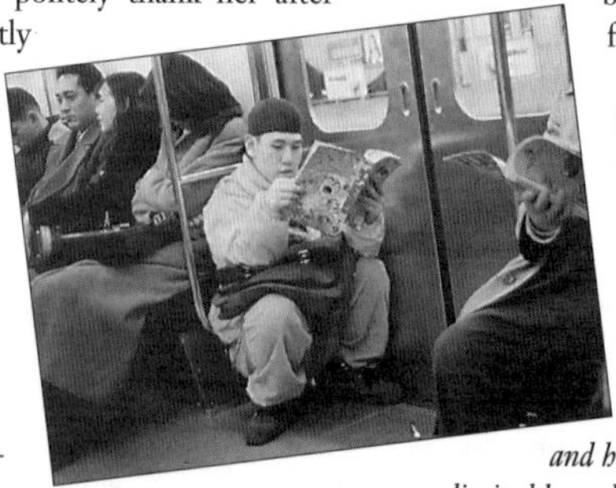

Salsa Sudada

JUMPING LATIN REFUGE

La Pallette Building 3F, 7-13-8 Roppongi, Minato-ku. ☎ ***03-5474-8806****. Open every day from 6 pm till 6 am, no holidays. Charge ¥1,500 with one drink, on weekends only.*

Salsa Sudada took a year to get a toehold in Tokyo's Latin scene, housed as it is in a bubble-era building, which is so well soundproofed that not a whiff of the block party beyond is evident till the third floor. There, you can feel the cooka-racha. A bar runs its length. Opposite, half a dozen tables front a mural—a colorful splash depicting a couple dancing barefoot on a beach, which aptly sets the tone. A friendly fifty-fifty mix of Latinos and locals come to dance—but what else in a Latin bar, besides a tussle or two at foosball?

Smash Hits

ENKA-FREE ZONE

M2 Hiroo Building B1F, 5-2-26 Hiroo, Shibuya-ku. ☎ ***03-3444-0432****. Open from 8 pm till 3 am Monday to Saturday, from 7 pm till midnight Sundays and holidays. Charge ¥3,000 with unlimited karaoke and one drink.*

Karaoke is inescapable in Japan. If you would rather belt out a tune in English

•••••••that had slithered off when its owner let it outside for a spot of sunbathing. Pet iguanas, said to become more ••

than wade through a tearjerker in Japanese, then Smash Hits is for you. The songbook boasts over 8,000 titles in English, including blues, rock, and top-40 favorites. Warning: with tiered seating overlooking the stage, it is not for the jelly-kneed, but remember, you can always request the mike at your seat. Mostly local crooners hit it midweek (they also boast 10,000 titles in Japanese), but the weekend draws more foreigners (only the English song list is available).

Sonne

THE MIDNIGHT SUN

Jiyugaoka Depato 2F, 1-28-8-3 Jiyugaoka, Meguro-ku. ☎ ***03-3718-8884****. Open from 7(ish) till 3(ish) every night. No charge; draft beer ¥800; mixed drinks with fresh juice ¥1,000; otherwise ¥800.*

Sonne is located in the rambling two-story row of establishments collectively known as Jiyugaoka Depato. Come midnight, like most other shotengai, the street in front is dotted with small gangs of teenagers and solitary drunks. Sonne's door is always open—but not to them. Rie and Reo have other plans. Together they stripped the interior to bare concrete and installed a solid wood bar. Rie decorated with baskets of fruit and wine, and Reo added his 1000-strong record collection. Photographers sit next to philosophers, and rock 'n' roll Johnnys next to young misses sensitive to the phases of the moon.

Tableaux Lounge

SMOKING JACKETS AND JAZZ

Sunroser Daikanyama Building B1F, 11-6 Sarugakucho, Shibuya-ku. ☎ ***03-5489-2202****. Open from 6 pm till 4 am every night. Music charge ¥1,000 plus ¥2,000 minimum order per person; drinks around ¥1,000; cigars ¥700–¥6,000.*

Tableaux Lounge is everything you'd expect from an offshoot of the flagship restaurant of the Hasegawa empire—sunken sitting room with an open fireplace, books in shelves towering to the ceiling, high-backed leather couches and chairs cradling tables lit by a single candle, a pianist perched at a baby grand delivering tinkling jazz lullabies. Of course it's expensive, but that doesn't stop it filling up most nights with ad-agency hotshots, brokers and embassy nobs, who crowd three at a time into the humidor to ogle and stroke cigars.

Tantra

SCENES FROM THE KAMA SUTRA

Address and phone number withheld. Discretion assured. Open every night from 8 pm till late. Table charge ¥1,000; drinks around ¥1,000.

According to my dictionary, "tantra" means "each of a class of Hindu or Buddhist mystical and magical writings." What it doesn't tell you the bartender will: specifically, seeking happiness through sex. One must heft through heavy metal doors to enter. A bronze Hindi temptress awaits. Beyond, a spacious concrete room is arranged with low furnishings and lighting. Stone slabs depicting scenes from the

active in hot weather, escaped from their owners in Tokyo, Yokohama, Kofu and Matsuyama. A wild monkey came

Kama Sutra lean against walls. Pillars stand sentinel at the entrance of two curtained alcoves (one for couples, the other for groups). Figurines in lotus position meditate either side of the bar. The music is opera or ambient. One does not pop in alone.

Uluru 125

AUSSIE WINE CAVE

3-22-6 Jingumae, Shibuya-ku. ☎ ***03-3406-0125****. Open from 6 pm till midnight Monday to Saturday, closed Sundays and Golden Week. No charge; bottle ¥3,500–¥35,000; glass ¥800.*

Uluru is the Aboriginal name for Ayer's Rock, through which the 125th line of longitude runs before swinging north to Japan. The entrance to Uluru 125 is a misshapen attempt at the Rock. The interior is cozy and a successful blend of modern and earthy touches. The menu reads like a who's-who of Australian wine families and regions—Penfolds, Barossa, Brown Brothers, Eden, Jamieson's Run. A cabernet sauvignon of the latter is what hooked the owner, who still keeps a day job even though he just opened an Australian restaurant. The clientele are either young with money or Aussie wine mavens.

(Milligram) Under Line

JAZZ UNDER THE TRACKS

3-29-70 Shibuya, Shibuya-ku. ☎ ***03-5458-2366****. Open from 6 pm till 3 am Monday to Friday till later on Saturday, closed Sundays. No charge; beer ¥800, mixed drinks ¥600.*

Under Line is tucked under the JR Yamanote tracks next to Shibuya Station. No one seems to notice when trains thunder overhead, as they sit and groove to the mama's collection of jazz. Two Japanese women, Michi and Gera (together "MG"), hence Milligram, secured the space. They ripped out the back wall to expose the foundations of the Yamanote Line. A plate-glass window overlooks the lane in front. A huge leather sofa somehow jams into the interior along with a bar and DJ booth. Customers are mostly Japanese, but a few fringe-dwelling foreigners have also dug in.

Vision Network

TOKYO'S ALTERNATIVE EDGE

5-47-6 Jingumae, Shibuya-ku. ☎ ***03-3407-6863****; fax: 03-3400-5060. Las Chicas:* ☎ **03-3407-6865**. *Open from 11 am till 11 pm every day. Email: vnetwork@mb.tokyo.infoweb.or.jp.*

Vision Network is an ever-evolving scene. The cornerstone of the company's philosophy is channeling one of life's most ephemeral commodities—youth, its culture and energy. Las Chicas is the focal point—a cafe that started in a corner and has grown to engulf the ground floor. The rest of the building is in constant flux. The current configuration includes a bar (Chrome), an event space, a radio station (radio:on), a members club (Tokyo Salon), a beauty salon, a hideaway bar (Nude), and a funky T-shirt shop. A couple of terminals are also available for surfing the net (free if you're waiting for a table).

•••••• down of the steaming mountains to run wild in the streets of Osaka stealing fruit and laundry hung out to dry, but

by Kara Besher

A TOKYO art scene does exist, despite rumors to the contrary. You won't find it in a particular area, nor is there any bohemian cafe or salon where artists and other creative types hang out, discussing color theory and Zen over tiny vials of rice wine. It's a hidden and dispersed series of mini-events, temporal and elusive, like much of Tokyo culture.

Uncovering it is a reward in itself. Visual expression sometimes gives the most revealing clues as to what is really going on beneath the surface, in a country where restraint is considered a high virtue. Nobody can seem to agree on the attributes of Japanese art; most often cited are issues of reverence vs. disregard for nature, imitation vs. mastery, art vs. craft, refined beauty vs. unadulterated kitsch—the debate is endless. Or put it all out of mind, simply open your eyes, and absorb.

Nowadays, many major international exhibitions make a stop in Tokyo. New York City's Museum of Modern Art, The Barnes Collection, Musée d'Orsay, and the Picasso Museum all staged blockbuster exhibitions in recent years, and Mona Lisa herself paid a much-heralded visit in 1979. These shows tend to draw huge crowds of eager amateur aficionados, and a five-hour weekend waiting line is not uncommon. Take your choice, but here, frankly, the wisest choice is Japanese art.

Whether it is the hallucinatory visions of the indigenous Jomon (inventors of pottery thousands of years before anywhere else in the world), the idealism of the Nara period, the delicate musings of the Fujiwara, the muscular Kamakura era, the grand and confident Edo period, the rather self-conscious Meiji, or the wild techno-pop rantings of today's young artists, opportunities for viewing excellent examples of Japanese art abound. Be it painting, ceramics, ukiyoe prints, scrolls, folding screens, tea ceremony utensils, Buddhist bronzes, or Zen calligraphy, you can see it all here.

This said, Tokyo remains essentially a modern city, emerging as it did from the ashes of WWII firebombing, which left little behind. Home to the country's National Museum, Tokyo is also the undisputed heart center of contemporary Japanese culture. If you long for ancient artifacts, you had best take your penlight and mini telescopular monocle (essential tools of the temple-art enthusiast) down Kyoto and Nara way. Here in Tokyo, tucked in amongst the frenetic buzz and urban sprawl, you'll find the boldest modern expressions of cutting-edge architecture and fashion, art and artifice.

Scarcity of urban space and the lack of a real market for contemporary art have forced artists and gallerists alike into making some hard compromises. The artist typically has a day job and either uses a corner of a modest apartment as an improvised studio or lives far out of the city. Studio visits are unheard-of. Considered a sacrilege most anywhere else, many Tokyo galleries regularly rent out their smallish spaces to individual artists on a weekly basis, at a sum of approximately three to five thousand U.S. dollars for a five-day exhibition. Moreover, the artist often foots the bill for framing, transport, printing of announcements, postage, and opening reception, and is expected to be present at the gallery as much as possible for the duration of the show. Be careful when commenting on the work displayed; the artist is often lurking about. A distinction is made between rental shows and exhibitions that the gallery plans and executes in-house; these are called "kikaku-ten." Some galleries with particularly high production standards or an impressive clientele enjoy sufficient competition to book them that the quality remains uniformly high. Other galleries rely on what might be thought of as a succession of "vanity" shows to survive.

Museums in Japan emphasize rotating displays of parts of their collection, seldom showing everything at once. Unlike their Western counterparts, where you can expect to see the same painting reassuring-

a pet crocodile escaping from its owner in Kyoto was soon apprehended. In Ito, Shizuoka prefecture, two-hundred

ly anchored to the same wall over the years, Japanese museums tend to bring certain artworks out for a limited time only, keeping them reverently stored in special boxes in the meantime. Public artwork display traditionally takes seasonal cues as a point of departure, in the same way that a home tokonoma alcove aesthetically reflects the seasons. For example, the Nezu Museum only shows its Ogata Korin Iris folding screen, a designated National Treasure, once a year in springtime, precisely when the irises are in full bloom throughout the parks of the city.

Although justifiably described as conservative, the Japanese art scene has been showing signs of invigoration in recent years. In March of 1995, the gargantuan Museum of Contemporary Art, Tokyo was established near the waterfront area in Kiba, Tokyo, promising greater recognition for living Japanese artists. Tacit censorship over art with a political message, especially that which touches upon Japan's wartime activities and the emperor system, and not so tacit official police bans on nude images—all these are being relaxed. Tokyo auction houses are undergoing deregulation, opening themselves to non-trade participants. Magazines have been publishing overseas auction results, undermining a secondary market that had been kept artificially high by unscrupulous dealers. A handful of young, determined gallerists are creating a healthier market by actively promoting and nurturing selected emerging artists, and popularizing a commitment to the month-long exhibition. The Ginza district, considered Tokyo's gallery center, is seeing the effects of rapid decentralization. Lured by cheaper rents and fresher audiences, galleries are spreading to other parts of the city. New laws relating to the establishment of non-profit foundations have made it easier for grassroots cultural organizations to get a deserved foothold, and artist cooperatives are springing up.

Nevertheless, the Tokyo art world is characterized by a certain lack of sophistication that is alternately frustrating and endearing. Unlike the cold and antiseptic New York gallery cube, with its predictably white walls, clockwork machinations, and killer marketing techniques, they haven't quite gotten things down to a science here yet. All the choices haven't been made for you in Tokyo's art world, and the excitement of discovery somehow always seems imminent. There's a kind of haphazard way that

Where to Buy

ART SUPPLIES

Ito-ya, 6F and 7F, 2-7-15 Ginza, Chuo-ku. ☎ 03-3561-8311.

This store, like Tokyu Hands, caters to the Japanese love of gadgets and is particularly strong on things having to do with writing and keeping diaries and other records. A good place to buy bushugi bukuro—the highly decorative envelopes used on ceremonial occasions.

people took part in a race down the river in wooden washtubs. The number of Japanese tourists venturing abroad

things happen, and art is found in the most unlikely places. You can come across a memorable exhibition on the top floor of a department store, in a boutique (Issey Miyake, Comme des Garçons, Kosuke Tsumura, and Shiseido all have their respective art spaces), and at various utilities/television/beer/insurance company headquarters. Forced to be innovative, Tokyo galleries have been fashioned from a variety of spaces: a converted rubber factory, a candy factory, a rice market, a bathhouse. Shoestring microgalleries are found in four-story walk-ups among hostess clubs, down deep in the bowels of an office building, and occasionally in private homes.

Contemporary Art Walks

To help navigate this seemingly chaotic mess of art venues, below are several suggested routes that will help you maximize your art-viewing time. There are a number of places that, although not mentioned here because of their location, may merit a trip on their own depending on the exhibition. These include Setagaya Art Museum, the Hara Museum of Contemporary Art, P-3 Art and Environment, and a few others. Some planning is involved; checking your route on a map and confirming schedules beforehand is strongly advised. Most museums are closed on Mondays; galleries are usually closed on Sundays and Mondays; and department-store spaces' closing days vary. Call for details.

The Ginza

The main advantage of gallery-hopping in the Ginza is its concentration: over three-hundred galleries within a ten-square-block radius. Once oriented, it is possible to peruse a number of places in a short time. On Monday evenings, generally between 5 and 7 PM, many rental galleries stage mini opening receptions with the artist present and refreshments served. Certain museum curators can be seen tackling ten or twelve galleries in an evening. Alternatively, a Tuesday through Saturday afternoon walk is also good. Note: indiscriminate gallery blitzing is only recommended for the most dedicated enthusiast; the selection is decidedly hit-or-miss. For those willing to give it a try, one loop-shaped route is:

Starting from the main Ginza intersection, walk south toward Matsuzakaya from the Nissan dealership; halfway down the block on the eighth floor, above the Body Shop, is Gallery Natsuka, a typical rental gallery with some good artists shown, including Saburo Ota. From there, exit left, continue walking down Ginza Dori; a couple blocks down on your right will be the Ginza Art Space, located in the basement of the Shiseido Building and producing a number of longer shows with established international and domestic artists, who have a knack for making the most incredible chameleon-like use of every foot of their somewhat limited space.

Continue walking in a southerly direction, cross Ginza Dori, and turn left along the street just before the overpass. Shortly you will see a fish tank; turn left again, and a few paces up there will be a sign for Gallery Q, a funky little basement gallery that has the distinction of sometimes showing artists from other parts of Asia such as Korea, Taiwan and Mongolia. If you keep walking up the street, on the left side on street level you will encounter Kamakura Gallery, a dignified space specializing in minimal and conceptual art. Walking back up to the main intersection, turn right at Mitsukoshi Department Store and walk two blocks, taking a left at the corner. A couple blocks up on the right will be a placard for Gallery Kobayashi, a selective rental gallery that has shown Tadashi Kawamata and Emiko Kasahara. Up farther on the same street are Gallery K, Gallery Gen, and Gallery Humanite around the corner—all are sometimes worth a look. You will come to the end of the road roughly at Hotel Seiyo; take a left and cross Ginza Dori. Going left on this big boulevard a few paces, you will see Gallery Koyanagi, a well-run establishment that produces month-long shows with artists who tend toward a subtle touch: Hiroshi Sugimoto, Rei Naito, and Yoshihiro Suda. From there, toward Hibiya, try not to miss Satani Gallery, a major force in Tokyo's art world since 1978, with an initial focus on artists like Max Ernst and Duchamp; nowadays they are more likely to be showing artists like Yasumasa Morimura, Shigeo Toya, and Araki. Then on to Gallery Gan, with its immaculate mountings of contemporary art. End your day with the cutting-edge Nagamine Projects, located in a dingy unmarked narrow walk-up around the corner.

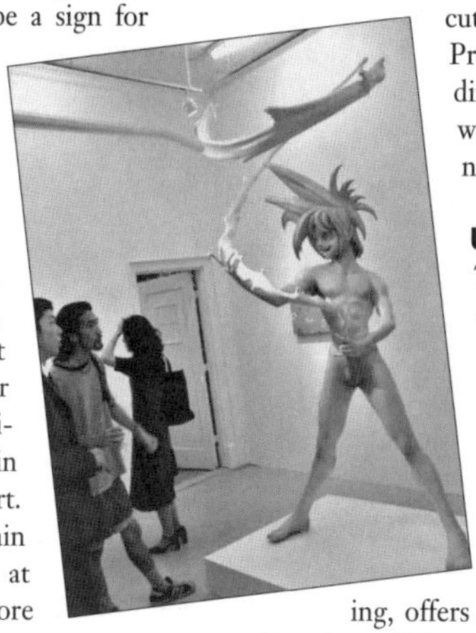

Ueno/Nippori

This route entails a lot of walking and is perfect for a full-day outing, especially if the weather is fine. The area just north of Ueno, having largely escaped the effects of WWII firebombing, offers an eclectic contrast of old and new Tokyo.

From Ueno JR Station, you can select from among several museums in Ueno Park; these are open early, from 9:30 or 10 am. Tokyo National Museum is also located here, with its large selection of ancient Japanese art. After a morning museum visit, traverse the road through the park, which passes by Geidai (Tokyo University of Fine Arts), and continue walking roughly straight into the narrow alley, which will indicate that you are entering an older section of town. In about ten minutes, you should find yourself in front of SKAI the Bathhouse, a former eighteenth-century public bath facility where an open, high-ceilinged space perfectly accommodates the large-scale exhibitions produced there: artists such as Masato Nakamura, Takashi Murakami, and David Tremlett. The Asakura Choso Memorial Museum is recommended when visiting the Nippori/

difficult to arouse, went to the polls in record numbers to vote for just about anybody but candidates

Yanaka district for the first time. Although Asakura's sculpture is decidedly run-of-the-mill academic, his charming former residence combines the best of Japanese and Western elements with its gentleman's atelier and Japanese garden. Expect to get pleasantly lost while wandering the crooked narrow streets here, lined with ramshackle houses, temples, and cemeteries, many surviving from the Edo period. If you're up for more art hunting, also nearby are Artforum Yanaka, a rental gallery, and Casa, a privately-run alternative space with infrequent shows and a mission to foster new perspectives within Japan's art world. Finally, a bit out-of-the-way, on the Akihabara side of Ueno Station, is the new and noteworthy artist cooperative command N. Spearheaded by artist Masato Nakamura, the tiny exhibition space belies an organizational dynamo; you just may encounter a lively discussion or one of many artist "powwows" conducted regularly in the basement here.

Kiba/Monzen-Nakacho

This mainly indoor route is perfect for a rainy full day or afternoon.

From Kiba Station, the Museum of Contemporary Art, Tokyo (aka MOT) is a short taxi ride or a fifteen-minute walk on the far end of Kiba Park. With over 33,500 square meters of space, MOT is the largest structure for the display of art in all of Japan. Several huge exhibition halls serve as venues for temporary exhibitions as well as their permanent collection, which offers a brief introduction to post–WWII Japanese art. The museum also houses a good art library with over 65,000 books and periodicals, video booths, an electronic database, and a high-vision theater. There is a noisy little museum cafe and a restaurant, plus a gift shop in the long lobby atrium.

After you are done exploring MOT, take a one- or two-click taxi ride or the subway to Monzen-Nakacho and locate the historic Shokuryo Building, a former rice market that now encompasses three art galleries. On the third floor, the non-profit Sagacho Exhibit Space, run by the amiable Kazuko Koike, remains one of the most consistently interesting spaces in town. Artists who have shown in its large stone-floored space include Anselm Kiefer, Yasumasa Morimura, and Tracey Emin. In the main exhibition area, reminders of the building's past—sheaths of rice—can be seen in decorative relief detailing. On the second floor is Tomio Koyama Gallery, a fun little commercial gallery that concentrates on Japanese pop artists like Yoshitomo Nara and Takashi Murakami. The most recent addition to the Shokuryo Building is the Taro Nasu Gallery, where you are likely to see smart shows of young European photographers.

•••••••representing Prime Minister Hashimoto's Liberal Democratic party. The LDP didn't win a single seat in Tokyo

For More Information

RESOURCES

Weekly listings of museum and gallery exhibits are found in *The Japan Times* newspaper's Saturday edition; magazines often have some information. On the Internet, Tokyo Q's "Art Scene" (www. tokyoq.com) offers a selection updated weekly. The Museum of Contemporary Art, Setagaya Museum, and the Tokyo Metropolitan Museum of Art all have art libraries within their facilities.

The Japan Foundation has recently opened a new reference room for exhibition catalogues. Bookstores with an emphasis on art include Nadiff and Maruzen; out-of-print editions can be found in the Jinbocho book district. Reference books include *Tokyo Museums* by Flannigan and *Tokyo Contemporary Art Guide*, the latter only available through the Japan-Netherlands Institute.

ADDRESSES

AKI-EX Gallery
Minami-Aoyama Cityhouse, 5-4-44 Minami-Aoyama, Minato-ku. ☎ 03-3499-4254.

Artforum Yanaka
6-4-7 Yanaka, Taito-ku. ☎ 03-3824-0804.

Asakura Choso Memorial Museum
7-18-10 Yanaka, Taito-ku. ☎ 03-3821-4549.

Casa
7-18-17 Yanaka, Taito-ku. ☎ 03-5685-1170.

command N
1-2-3 Ueno, Taito-ku. ☎ 03-5812-7506.

G Art Gallery
Ginza 18 Building B1, 2-5-18 Ginza, Chuo-ku. ☎ 03-3562-5858.

Gallery Gan
7-2-22 Ginza, Chuo-ku. ☎ 03-3573-6555.

Gallery Gen
Ginza-ichi Building 3F, 1-10-19 Ginza, Chuo-ku. ☎ 03-3561-6869.

Ginza Artspace
The Ginza Building B1, 7-8-10 Ginza, Chuo-ku. ☎ 03-3571-7741.

Hillside Gallery
Hillside Terrace A, 29-18 Sarugakucho, Shibuya-ku. ☎ 03-3476-4795.

Gallery Humanite Tokyo
Ginza Premier Building 4F, 1-8-2 Ginza, Chuo-ku. ☎ 03-3564-4350.

ICC Tokyo Opera
City Tower 4F, 3-20-2 Nishi-Shinjuku, Shinjuku-ku. ☎ 03-5353-0800.

Gallery Idea
Kyodo Biru Shin-Aoyama 2F, 5-9-15 Minami-Aoyama, Minato-ku. ☎ 03-3406-3721.

Gallery K
Dai 2 Ginryoku Building 3F, 1-9-6 Ginza, Chuo-ku. ☎ 03-3563-4578.

Kamakura Gallery
Hirakata Building 1F, 7-10-8 Ginza, Chuo-ku. ☎ 03-3574-8307.

Gallery Kobayashi
Yamato Building B1, 3-8-12 Ginza,

Chuo-ku. ☎ *03-3561-0515.*

Gallery Koyanagi
Koyanagi Building 1F, 1-7-5 Ginza, Chuo-ku. ☎ *03-3561-1896.*

Las Chicas Cafe
5-47-6 Jingumae, Shibuya-ku. ☎ *03-3407-6865.*

Mizuma Art Gallery
5-46-13 Jingumae, Shibuya-ku. ☎ *03-3499-0226.*

Nadiff
4-9-8 Jingumae, Shibuya-ku. ☎ *03-3403-8814.*

Nagamine Projects
Nan-oh Building 4F, 7-2-17 Ginza, Chuo-ku. ☎ *03-3575-5775.*

Gallery Natsuka
Ginza Plaza Building 8F, 5-8-17 Ginza, Chuo-ku. ☎ *03-3571-0715.*

Nikon Salon, Ginza
Matsushima Eyeglass Store, 3F, 3-5-6 Ginza, Chuo-ku. ☎ *03-3562-5756.*

Ota Fine Arts
2-8-11 Ebisu-Nishi, Shibuya-ku. ☎ *03-3780-0911.*

P-House
1-29-9 Ebisu-Nishi, Shibuya-ku. ☎ *03-5458-3359.*

Gallery Q
8-10-7 Ginza, Chuo-ku. ☎ *03-3573-2808.*

Museum of Contemporary Art, Tokyo
4-1-1 Miyoshi, Koto-ku. ☎ *03-5245-4111.*

Rontgen Kunstraum
Twin Minami-Aoyama Building, 3-14-13 Minami-Aoyama, Minato-ku. ☎ *03-3401-1466.*

Sagacho, Taro Nasu Gallery, Tomio Koyama Gallery
Shokuryo Building 2F and 3F, 1-8-13 Saga, Eito-ku. ☎ *03-3630-7759.*

Satani Gallery
Dai 2 Asahi Building B1, 4-2-6 Ginza, Chuo-ku. ☎ *03-3564-6733.*

SCAI the Bathhouse
6-1-23 Yanaka, Taito-ku. ☎ *03-3821-1144.*

Spiral Garden
Spiral Building 1F, 5-6-23 Minami-Aoyama, Minato-ku. ☎ *03-5468-1244.*

Toki Art Space
3-42-5 Jingumae, Shibuya-ku. ☎ *03-3479-0332.*

Tokyo National Museum
Ueno Park. ☎ *03-3272-8600.*

Wako Works of Art
4F, Wako Art Salon
6F, Wako Hall
Wako Department Store, 4-5-11 Ginza, Chuo-ku. ☎ *03-3562-2111.*

Watari-um Museum of Contemporary Art
3-7-6 Jingumae, Shibuya-ku. ☎ *03-3402-3001.*

Zeit Foto Salon
Yagicho Building 5F, 1-7-2 Nihonbashi-Muromachi, Chuo-ku, 03-3246-1370.

••••••• visibly shattered Hashimoto announced his resignation. A new high-tech Godzilla film, made by Sony in

Tokyoscapes: Architecture

by Mark Dytham and Astrid Klein

THE city is an architect's dream. The excesses of the bubble economy have proved to an extreme that this is a city with no visual planning laws. As long as a building meets all the statutory regulations for zoning, floor area, and shadow lines, it can look like anything: a Japanese flag or a motorbike morphed with a cockroach.

So why, then, at first glance does the city look gray, dull, and monotonous? Step forward the huge "Super Gene Cons," the massive general contractors who design and build over 95 percent of Tokyo. In many cases the designs, albeit cleanly detailed and efficient, are the lowest common denominator in terms of design.

But it is the other 5 percent that makes this city special. Clients who want something different from Day One tend to employ just an architect, not a construction company. Unlike the West, where architecture is seen somewhat as a service industry, here, because of the split between construction companies, the architect is seen as the sensei, the teacher, and what he says

Architecture Galleries

TN Probe
5-14-35 Roppongi, Minato-ku. ☎ 03-3505-8800, fax 03-3505-8810. Open 11 am to 7 pm, Monday–Saturday only when there is an exhibit. http://www.mmstudio.miinet.or.jp/tnprobe/
Excellent exhibitions, usually one-man shows, with many exhibits touring under the auspices of MoMA.

Gallery MA
TOTO Nogizaka Bldg 3F, 1-24-3 Minami-Aoyama, Minato-ku. ☎ 03-3595-9689, fax 03-3595-9450. Open 11 am to 7 pm. Tuesday–Saturday only when there is an exhibit.
One of the most prestigious architectural galleries in the world. Unusually for an architectural gallery, the shows take the form of an installation, which generally extends onto an external terrace. All of this on the third and fourth floor of a toilet bowl manufacturer's showroom and office.

Living Design Gallery
Shinjuku Park Tower, 3-7-1 Nishi-Shinjuku, Shinjuku-ku ☎ 03-5322-6500. Open 10:30 am to 6:30 pm.
A prolific gallery with a new exhibition every seven days, fifty-two weeks a year! Architecture, furniture, product design are heavily featured. Amazingly good, amazingly consistent quality. Ozone Plaza, another exhibition space, and The Conran Shop are in the same building, as is the New York Bar and Grill, which offers the best place in Tokyo to sip beer and watch the city unfold fifty-two floors below.

sticks. This, combined with Tokyo's free visual planning laws, leads to some of the world's most unusual architecture, but these jewels lie hidden in the city.

Unlike other world capitals, Tokyo has no planned grand gestures, no sweeping boulevards, plazas, or piazzas. There is no space in which to stand back and admire a building. Even the new Tokyo International Forum belies its enormous size by the fact that you can never stand back far enough to see it in its entirety.

Tokyo's grand gestures are very much unplanned, the whole city having donned layer after layer of advertising and information. Buildings seem to wear glittering necklaces and tall hats. Signs whose fluorescent colors clash during the day drip with neon at night. Some buildings seem only to be an excuse for an enormous billboard.

An Architecture of Convenience

Tokyo's planned network of police boxes has become a world model, but the ever-growing network of convenience stores (konbini) is far more impressive. A recent study showed that the average walking time from any apartment in the city's twenty-three wards to a convenience store is four minutes. These twenty-four-hour fluorescent beacons have

••••••Hollywood for 120 million dollars, opened in Tokyo to long lines of nostalgic fams, some of whom had slept •

become the city's landmarks. Not only do they serve as your personal fridge and oven but also as a library, bank, color copy center, CD, video, and software shop. It's possible to stand and read the latest magazines for hours and hours, pay all your utility bills, pick up a pretty elaborate ready-cooked meal and a fresh salad, and check out the latest version of Final Fantasy before booking a ticket for the Giants game in the dome. When all the mobile phone numbers in the city got a few extra digits at the beginning of the year, a free docking port at all convenience stores updated your pre-programmed phone numbers there and then.

This thirst for ultraconvenience is changing the face of the city. The traditional Mom & Pop shops are dying away rapidly; the shoten-gai, or shopping street, is becoming a nostalgic weekend destination as the locations of the konbini pull people toward larger roads and intersections. Real shopping becomes more and more like entertainment. The use of the Internet for purchasing is only going to increase this trend.

Twenty million or so vending machines

Architecture Books and Bookstores

Most of Tokyo's architectural gems can be found with just two books in hand. Noriyuki Tajima's *Tokyo: A Guide to Recent Architecture*, which is part of the tiny, 10.5cm-square pocket book series by Ellipsis (ISBN 1-899858-01-6). All the outstanding buildings are covered: the good, the bad, and the ugly. Tajima's observation that the Tokyo Metropolitan Expressway is the most outstanding and important structure in the fabric of the city should be pondered as you zoom along.

Although *Tokyo: A Guide to Recent Architecture* is in English, it has no maps, so a good companion to it is *The Architectural Map of Tokyo*, published by TOTO Shuppan (ISBN 4-88706-098-X). It is published in Japanese, but the book is easy to navigate and has great maps.

When looking for books on Tokyo architecture, in particular check out the following:

GA Gallery
3-12-16 Sendagaya, Shibuya-ku. ☎ 03-3403-1581, fax 03-3497-0649. Open 10 am to 6:30 pm weekdays, 12 pm to 6 pm weekends and holidays.
The fabulously "brutal" home of Global Architecture publications. Great architectural bookstore and gallery.

Aoyama Book Centre, Roppongi
6-1-20 Roppongi, Minato-ku. ☎ 03-3479-0479. Open 10 am to 5:30 pm, Sunday 10 am to 10 pm.
Open almost twenty-four hours, probably one of the best places to spot architects waiting for the first train.

Aoyama Book Centre, Aoyama
Garden Floor, Cosmos Aoyama, 5-53-67 Jingumae, Shibuya-ku. ☎ 03-5485-5511. Open daily, 10 am to 10 pm.
One huge floor of books and magazines heavily weighted in the direction of the creative people who make up Aoyama. Faces onto the courtyard of the Women's Plaza at the back of the UN Building, with the added bonus of the supercool UN cafe next door.

overnight in front of the box office, but the feeling of most people after viewing the film was that although the

Tokyo has 1,237 neighborhood police boxes called koban, which come in all shapes and sizes. Tokyo police are very much a part of the community. They'll admonish kids for walking sloppily, and they know that Mr. Suzuki often comes home wobbly. If you need the train fare to get home, they'll lend it to you. Their main purpose, though, seems to be to give strangers directions, as the Japanese system of addresses is wonderfully arcane. The koban at the Hachiko Exit of Shibuya Station has been clocked giving out directions to a new inquirer every 20 seconds.

The Tokyo Metropolitan Police Department encourages architects of its koban to experiment, to try to reflect the feeling of the neighborhood (or something) in the koban. Our playful cops have also created a cuddly mascot called PEOPO ("people" plus "police"), which, when you think of it, sounds like the siren of an approaching patrol car. When you move into a new neighborhood, the police will drop about and ask questions that some might find obtrusive—"When do you usually get home from work?"—but they only want to be prepared if something should happen to you.

Where to Buy

POSTERS

The artistic quality and the paper and printing of the posters mounted in the train stations in Japan is very high. Because millions pass through the stations every day, posters are thought to be a highly effective means of advertising and are often coordinated with ads on TV and in print media. They stay up for an average of three days and make wonderful souvenirs. We leave it up to your imagination how to acquire one.

Another possibility is to visit the Ginza Graphic Gallery at 7-7-2 Ginza, Chuo-ku, where the best of Japanese graphic art is on display. They often have posters for sale.

populate Japan, of which Tokyo has its fair share. These machines dispense everything from canned coffee, cup noodles, disposable cameras, film, rice, flowers, ice, batteries, porn magazines, and videos, and are even more evidence that the city is constantly on the move, constantly on the spend. New drinks in newly designed cans come and go with the seasons. Over two thousand new drinks are launched this way each year, but only a handful make it to their first anniversary.

Puri-kura machines, too, continue their relentless invasion of the streetscape. Young girls no longer write in their diaries whom they meet—they use puri kura to document who they were with and when. The DJ scratch-and-dance machines add yet another dimension to the scene, with crowds watching the would-be dance star.

••••••• new monster was impressive, it wasn't Godzilla. (The original Godzilla was a midget in a rubber monster •

by Rick Kennedy, Mike Kleindl, and Robbie Swinnerton

HERE are short reviews of 116 of our favorite Tokyo-area restaurants. We have made no attempt to balance this coverage. The places listed are simply places we like and think you will, too. There are a fair number of French restaurants listed because we think they are one of the glories of the Tokyo restaurant scene. We think, actually, that it is easier to find a good French table in Tokyo than in Paris.

JAPANESE RESTAURANTS

CHICKEN AND YAKITORI

Birdland ** ¥ !

YUPPY YAKITORI

3-37-9 Asagaya, Suginami-ku. ☎ ***03-3392-8941**. Closed Sundays. No credit cards. Nearest station:* ASAGAYA.

Tokyo Q Symbology

*	very good
**	one of the best of its type in Tokyo
***	one of the best of its type anywhere
¥	less than ¥5,000
¥¥	between ¥5,000 and ¥10,000
¥¥¥	over ¥10,000
!	interesting decor
!!	startling decor
!!!	wow!

You sit around the charcoal grill at a counter seating twenty-one. It's a young, stylish crowd. There are flowers on the counter, and the serving dishes are pleasant to look at. Many people start with a platter of chicken-liver pate, which they spread on slices of toasted French bread. The set course of seven selections is ¥2,500. There is wine and some lovely sakes sold by the glass. Soft jazz murmurs in the background, and in the summer the floor-to-ceiling windows slide open to the street. (RK)

Botan * ¥¥ !

IN OLD TOKYO, CHICKEN SUKIYAKI

1-15 Kandasudacho,Chiyoda-ku. ☎ ***03-3251-0577****. Closed Sundays. No credit cards. Nearest station:* AWAJICHO.

"Button," in an old wooden building on an atmospheric block, offers a single dish they call torisuki-sukiyaki, made using tender free-range chickens from Saitama, cooked slowly over charcoal. The course is ¥6,300. Botan hasn't changed a bit since it opened more than a century ago. The maids still live in. To visit Botan is to slip gently back in time. (RK)

Monsen ** ¥¥¥ !!

YAKITORI AS HIGH ART

2-13-8 Azabu Juban, Minato-ku. ☎ ***03-3452-2327****. Closed Saturdays, Sundays, and holidays. No credit cards. Nearest station:* ROPPONGI.

At ¥12,000 for the set course, this is the most expensive yakitori you'll ever run across. But it's worth it—yakitori raised to haute cuisine. Monsen is far from the usual smoky, jocular yakitori emporium. Mr. Iwamoto insists that you reserve and not come alone. Monsen has the aspect of a country cottage: soft-lit lanterns on kyokabe walls, a rush ceiling, and a modest vase of flowers at the end of the counter. (RK)

Torie * ¥¥ !

CHICKEN STEW IN OLD TOKYO

1-2-1 Ikenohata, Taito-ku. ☎ ***03-3831-5009****. Closed Sundays and holidays. No credit cards. Nearest station:* YUSHIMA.

Gamecock from Saitama stewed over charcoal in an antique iron cauldron. Torie is a lovely old wooden building, and the Nakazawa family will pamper you as if you were their grandchildren. The course is ¥5,000. (RK)

Tori Fuku ("Happy Bird") * ¥

COUNTER EATING IN AN ATMOSPHERIC ALLEY

1-25-10 Shibuya, Shibuya-ku. ☎ ***03-3499-4978****. Closed Sundays and holidays. No credit cards. Nearest station:* SHIBUYA.

A classic little (seven stools) hole-in-the wall for yakitori, Tori Fuku is across the street from Shibuya Station in Nonbei Yokocho ("Drunkards' Alley"). A setting more evocative of cozy Japanese urban nightlife would be hard to imagine. Selections are laid out on a block of ice. Just point to what strikes your fancy. (RK)

•••••••When it was announced that a government panel of experts would be convened to discuss ways to raise the birth •

COUNTRY COOKING

Nanao ** ¥¥ !

STYLISH COUNTRY KITCHEN

1-5-10 Azabu Juban, Minato-ku. ☎ ***03-4301-7770.*** *Closed Sundays. Major credit cards. Nearest station:* ROPPONGI.

Early in the evening at Nanao, which opens at 5:30, conversation bubbles like a stew on the back burner, as everyone here seems to know each other, and all are enthusiasts of washoku ("Japanese food"). They are happily anticipating over the next hour and a half a succession of little jewel-like treats. Nanao is an entirely approachable entryway to the genuine delights, as opposed to the scholarly tasting rituals and virtuoso displays of technique, of Japanese cooking. (RK)

Negishi * ¥

BEEF STEW IN A BOISTEROUS SETTING

2-45-2 Kabukicho, Shinjuku-ku. ☎ ***03-3232-8020.*** *Open every day. No credit cards. Nearest station:* SHINJUKU.

Negishi, which specializes in an honest country beef stew laced with onions, carrots, and potatoes, is a very Shinjuku sort of place—a Tokyo version of New York's Carnegie Delicatessen. It serves food for people who take big bites, who like snappy service with mustard on the side, and who are not embarrassed to take advantage of value. Nobody goes much out of their way to come to Negishi, but as Kabukicho is Tokyo's Broadway, Negishi has about a million people who consider it their neighborhood joint. The stew set, with a bowl of mugimeshi and pickles on the side, goes for ¥1,260. (RK)

Robata * ¥¥ !

RUSTIC COUNTRY INN

1-3 Yurakucho,Chiyoda-ku. ☎ ***03-3591-1905.*** *Closed Sundays and holidays. No credit cards. Nearest station:* YURAKUCHO.

Robata is a survivor. Its gently decaying wooden building recalls the days of the Occupation, when the lights of the Ginza were dim and life was a struggle. To pull up a chair to Robata's ancient counter, which tilts a little, is to drift back to a less brittle, more homey, somehow more innocent Tokyo. Out on the counter will be several dozen platters with dishes like garlic mussels, sweet-and-sour pork ratatouille, salmon roe with cabbage, and jugged sardines. Mr. Inoue, Robata's soft-spoken proprietor, is a poet, a wearer of kimono, and a collector of pottery and paintings. (RK)

Yukun Sakagura * ¥ !

KYUSHU SPECIALITIES

1-16-14 Shinbashi, Minato-ku. ☎ ***03-3508-9296.*** *Closed Sundays, holidays, and first three Saturdays. No credit cards. Nearest station:* SHIMBASHI.

The atmosphere is something like a German beer hall—clamorous and guffaw-filled. Everything is laid out on the ten-meter-long counter for inspection: baskets of shellfish and bundles of delicate greens. Just take your waitress up to the counter and point to what you want. Tokyo people are unfamiliar with this food, such as the Mutsugoro, a fish served grilled, which comes from only one place in the world, Ariakekai Bay in Kyushu, where when the tide goes out fish-

Best "Old Tokyo" Restaurants

Botan
1-15 Kandasudacho, Chiyoda-ku. ☎ *03-3251-0577. Nearest station:* AWAJICHO.
The menu hasn't changed for over a hundred years, and the waitresses still live in. Free-range chickens cooked over charcoal. Course is ¥6,300.

Isegen
1-11-1 Kandasudacho , Chiyoda-ku. ☎ *03-3251-1229. Nearest station:* AWAJI-CHO.
From October through March, the dish is *anko-nabe,* anglerfish stew, for ¥3,300. Everybody eats in one huge tatami room in a marvelous old building.

Iseya
1-9-2 Nihonzutsumi, Taito-ku. ☎ *03-3872-4886. Nearest station:* MINOWA
Down-home tempura in perfectly preserved old building in old neighborhood bordering on the old courtesans' district. Kakiage donburi ¥1,500. Tenju ¥1,500. ¥300 for a dish of pickles.

Issa-an
2-14-3 Kami-Osaki, Shinagawa-ku. ☎ *03-3444-0875. Nearest station:* MEGURO.
Simple, unadorned buckwheat noodles beginning at ¥600.

Komagata Dojo
1-7-12 Komagata, Taito-ku.
☎ *03-3842-4001. Nearest station:* ASAKUSA.
About 190 years old and not changed at all. Loach is served two ways: Dojo nabe and Yanagawa, ¥1,300–¥1,400.

Torei
1-2-1 Ikenohata, Taito-ku. ☎ *03-3831-5009. Nearest station:* YUSHIMA.
Gamecock from Saitama cooked over charcoal in an iron pot, ¥5,000.

—Stella Regalia

ermen go after the fish on special sleds, plucking them from the mud with baitless hooks. (RK)

GENERAL

Hashimoto * ¥¥ !

HOME COOKING IN A COZY TATAMI SETTING
4-4-11 Roppongi, Minato-ku. ☎ ***03-3408-8388****. Closed Sundays. No credit cards. Nearest station:* ROPPONGI.
Barefoot, ponytailed Mr. Hashimoto cooks simple dishes like mushrooms, green peppers, and the tiny fish called shirasu in a piquant sauce. His ¥7,000 set menu of seven dishes is different every evening and would be a fine introduction to plain Japanese cooking for any foreigner inclined to be suspicious. It may also help that legs can be dangled under the table. The single sake, Tama no Hikari ("Light from a Crystal"), here poured from a handblown Swedish flask, would also be a fine introduction to the national tipple. (RK)

Kan Ran * ¥ !

TOKYO EQUIVALENT OF A SMART NY BAR
3-2-1 Higashi-Azabu, Minato-ku. ☎ ***03-5561-0615****. Closed Sundays and holidays. Major credit cards. Nearest station:* KAMIYA-CHO.
A masculine sort of place, bold and dark

with plenty of room to stretch out, a mix of modern design and good old things. Track lights play off backdrops of warm Japanese paper that is going to age beautifully, the place being just over a year old now. There is a table in the corner with a few comfortable chairs around it, as in a club. The thick, very wide counter is cut from one huge keyaki tree, one end resting on a rock hauled up from Shikoku. Especially recommended is the sashimi, served with exceptional wasabi and ginger in a paste. The sake is cooled in an ice bucket. Dishes average ¥1,000. (RK)

Nezu Club ** ¥¥ !!

¥4,000 KAISEKI IN OLD NEIGHBORHOOD

2-30-2 Nezu, Bunkyo-ku. ☎ ***03-3828-4004****. Closed Sundays, Mondays, and Tuesdays. No credit cards. Nearest station:* NEZU.

The entrance down a long, pebble-strewn corridor is theatrical. The massive table in the middle of the room, seating nine, is a lovingly waxed old English refectory table. An antique obi of subtle coloring is spread down the table's length, and in the middle is a shallow bowl of flowers of the field. The five-course set menu costs ¥4,000 and is pure and simple in the manner of inspired Japanese home cooking. Reservations (essential) are not easy to get. (RK)

Nobu * ¥¥¥ !!

RITZY SUSHI EMPORIUM

6-10-17 Minami-Aoyama, Minato-ku. ☎ ***03-5467-0022****. Open every day. Major credit cards. Nearest station:* OMOTESANDO.

Tokyo's glitterati and well-heeled camp followers have been appropriately wowed by the much-trumpeted homecoming of local-boy-made-good, Nobuhiso Matsuhisa, pal of Bob de Niro and chef to the stars in LA and NY. Those who know his other operations are underwhelmed by the glorified diner-style decor and noise levels. Nonetheless, the quality of the kitchen is undeniably superior. Nobu's trademark is his synthesis of Japanese technique, South American ingredients, and U.S. flamboyance—resulting in intriguing Chilean-influenced seafood and set-piece sushi arrangements given the full-out Californian treatment. Expect to pay top yen to rub shoulders with the fashionable set. (RS)

Parole ** ¥¥ !

HOME COOKING IN AN APARTMENT

4-4-12 Nishi-Azabu, Minato-ku. ☎ ***03-3409-5039****. Dinner only. Closed Saturdays and Sundays. No credit cards. Nearest station:* ROPPONGI.

Emiko Sakurai serves a set menu of eight or nine dishes for ¥5,000 in an ordinary apartment slightly revamped to accommodate a counter and a serious kitchen. She is an inspired manipulator of materials, an unfollower of recipes, and the rightness of her combinations can take the breath away. Oyster and celery soup. Sweet potatoes dusted with cinnamon. Mochi rice and marinated beef. She loves what she is doing, and it is a pleasure to be with her. (RK)

Showa Society * ¥¥ !

HEISEI-ERA CASUAL DINING

1-3-5 Naka-Meguro, Meguro-ku. ☎ ***03-3713-7431****. Open every day. Major credit cards. Nearest station:* DAIKANYAMA.

Not a retro-themed gentlemen's club but the epitome of contemporary crossover, Showa Society is Tokyo dining at its most stylishly casual. The menu revolves around prime seafood, chicken, and gamecock dishes, and while the underlying sensibility is Japanese, the seasonings are likely to be

voltage line. Police arrested the owners of a coffee shop called "Marijuana" for growing grass behind the shop.

Best Coffee Houses

Bon
3-23-1 Shinjuku. ☎ 03-3365-0358.
You get to choose your cup and saucer from the 450 museum-quality pieces on display, and you have your choice of two kinds of cream. The basic cup is ¥950, which means Bon is never crowded. Bon is seventy-five meters down the street from the big TV screen labeled "Studio Alta," its entrance marked by a discreet wooden sign.

Cafe Select de Sevres
2-30-10 Kitazawa, Setagaya-ku. ☎ 03-3466-1037.
With its walnut tables, stained-glass lamps, and ocher-colored walls, Cafe Sevres seems transported from the Left Bank of Paris. It offers perfectly made coffee, homemade cakes, and quiet solitude for reading Hemingway and writing your memoirs.

Chez Nous
3-15-2 Nishi-Waseda, Shinjuku-ku. ☎ 03-3208-4037.
On Waseda Dori in Takadanobaba. This is where to wait until the classic movie begins at ACT Cinema next door. A cup of cappuccino dusted with cinnamon costs ¥480.

Daibo
3-13-20 Minami-Aoyama, Minato-ku. ☎ 03-3403-7155.
A bowl of cafe au lait (here, "milk coffee") is ¥650. Dark and cozy.

Jazz A & F
Oriental Building, 2-2-3 Minamicho, Kichijoji. ☎ 0422-48-7323.
This is the ultimate jazz kissa (short for kissaten, Japanese for coffeehouse). With your cup of coffee (which you can nurse for hours) you get a slip of paper you can use to request your favorite vinyl jazz album and your favorite needle cartridge (from three) for the turntable and your favorite speaker (from three). A cool, solid wall of sounds, man, you dig?

PowWow
2-7 Kagurazaka, Shinjuku-ku. ☎ 03-3260-8973.
Spacious, with old chandeliers, antique chairs all different, and paneling throughout. Gallery on second floor, where there are sometimes concerts.

Rihaku
2-24 Kanda Jinbocho, Chiyoda-ku. ☎ 03-3264-6292.
Utterly charming retreat in the bookstore district. (Best bookstores for books in English, incidentally, are Subunso, Issei-do (second floor), and Kitazawa, all on Yasukuni Dori.)

Tsuta ("Ivy")
5-11-20 Minami-Aoyama, Minato-ku. ☎ 03-3498-6888.
In a private house next to Aoyama Gakuin, looking out on a beautifully tended garden. The music is mostly Mozart, sometimes Bach or Chopin, which the proprietor thinks best to drink coffee by.

Thai nam pla, Vietnamese coriander, or Chinese black bean sauce. The house specialty is homemade, unpressed tofu in three ineffable flavors. The waitresses dress in snappy brown homespun cotton tunics, and there is a terrace overlooking a quiet backstreet that's ideal for mellow summer evenings. (RS)

KAISEKI AND KO-RYORI

Aiya-tei *** ¥¥¥ !!!

OLD HOUSE AND GARDEN IN KAMAKURA

1-4-6 Sengaya, Kamakura. ☎ ***0467-24-6677****. Closed Mondays. No credit cards. Nearest station:* KAMAKURA.

In 1990, this classic Japanese house and garden belonged to a powerful politico, who lived here as though the world outside Japan didn't exist. That same year the house was remodeled as a traditional Japanese restaurant of the highest order, giving an impression of simple perfection. Yours is one of just nine spacious tatami rooms giving out on the garden. The zabuton are fine linen. The tatami and shoji are immaculate. The large table is mirror-like lacquer, even underneath. Your two waitresses, in handsome kimono, have the grace of ballet dancers, and when they kneel to slide open the door, there is no sound. The ¥5,000 lunch is a gift. In the evening, there are courses for ¥15,000, ¥20,000, and ¥30,000, and the illuminated garden is magical. (RK)

Daigo *** ¥¥¥ !!!

ON THE GROUNDS OF A TEMPLE

Seishoji, 2-3 Atago, Minato-ku. ☎ ***03-3431-0811****. Closed Saturdays. Credit: AmEx, DN, JCB. Nearest station:* ONARIMON.

Daigo is in the garden of a temple. You dine in a private tatami-mat room. In a corner there is a welcoming incense burner, timed to burn out at your arrival so as not to distract from the meal. Your maid greets you formally, forehead to tatami, then pours you a shallow lacquer dish of sake, just a mouthful, to titillate the taste mechanism. At this point you might want to push open the shoji to reveal the illuminated garden, mossy and cool in the evening. The basic course is ten or fifteen dishes of Buddhist temple food, which involves no meat or fish and costs ¥14,000. (RK)

Houmasa ** ¥¥¥ !!

KAISEKI AT THE COUNTER

3-2-1 Moto-Azabu, Minato-ku. ☎ ***03-3474-2880****. Closed Sundays. No credit cards. Nearest station:* ROPPONGI.

Mr. Hara composes the menu an hour before he opens, basing it on the results of his early morning forage through Tsukiji. He will ask you what style you would prefer the fish you have selected to be prepared in, then prepare it for you as you watch. The restaurant itself consists of a counter and a three-mat room in the back, and offers a vision of how perfect the world would be if only we could keep it simple. Say ¥15,000 per person. (RK)

Kakiden ** ¥¥ !!

KAISEKI WITH LEATHER COUCHES AND KOTO

3-37-11 Shinjuku, Shinjuku-ku. ☎ ***03-3352-5121****. Open every day. Major credit cards. Nearest station:* SHINJUKU.

Kakiden is a venerable school of the tea ceremony, which just happens to run a highly congenial restaurant open to the public. It's in its own architecturally striking building across the street from the busiest railway station in the world. The "mini kaiseki" course is a succession of eighteen or so small dishes, some no more elaborate than three black beans marinated in a provocative liqueur, for ¥8,000. The service is inspired by the tea ceremony: the young ladies in kimono who set your dishes so sweetly before you are all students of

afford to pay protection money, were arrested for jimmying open lockers in public baths and emptying wallets in

tea. The koto is played every evening from 6 to 8 pm. (RK)

Kogetsu ** ¥¥¥ !!

EXQUISITE SMALL DISHES AT THE COUNTER

5-50-10 Jingumae, Shibuya-ku. ☎ ***03-3407-3033****. Closed Sundays. Credit: JCB, UC. Nearest station:* OMOTESANDO.

With nine seats at the counter and a single six-mat room, Kogetsu is engaging in a Japanese way (attentive but never forward), absolutely immaculate (it looks as though it has just been unwrapped), and uncompromisingly dedicated to quality (many of the materials used are shipped directly to Kogetsu from Kyoto, because even Tsukiji dealers in rarities cannot provide everything Mr. Tsukiyama requires). Mrs. Tsukiyama in crisp kimono will place four little otoshi dishes, one by one, on the vermilion tray before you on the counter—perhaps a mouthful of shirako, or a cake of shiitake mushrooms en gelée, or inch-long baby endive in a light hollandaise sauce—dishes designed to set off your sake. Then perhaps a small plate of sashimi, consisting of two kinds of miniature scallops, backed up by several slices of hirame flounder, pink at the edges. The shoyu is diluted with broth to soften it. You'll be struck by the sheer workmanship of these dishes. A clear soup is enlivened by a corkscrew of citrus peel as thin as a thread. A pickle is encircled by a thin band of nori. You will find yourself looking at what is set before you the way a watchmaker regards a fine watch. Kogetsu is expensive, say ¥15,000 not counting sake. (RK)

Kyo wa Hana ** ¥¥ !!

KO-RYORIYA

7-6-9 Roppongi, Minato-ku. ☎ ***03-3405-8208****. Closed Sundays. Major credit cards. Nearest station:* ROPPONGI.

Kyo wa Hana ("Kyoto is a flower") is a fine example of a ko-ryoriya, a particular Japanese type of eating establishment where exquisite little dishes are assembled to order for a knowledgeable clientele, seated informally at a counter, and for whom a charmer in kimono will pour interesting sakes. This place is sparkling, and there is an immaculate three-mat room in the back for those not in the mood to enter into the general conversation at the counter. Courses for ¥6,000, ¥8,000, and ¥10,000, and most of the fifteen or so sakes go for ¥800 a crystal tumbler. (RK)

Sasaoka ** ¥¥ !!

SO JAPANESE, BUT WITH ITALIAN CHAIRS

2-17-18 Ebisu, Shibuya-ku. ☎ ***03-3444-1233****. Closed Sundays and second and forth Saturdays. Major credit cards. Nearest station:* EBISU.

There is no sign out front, no music, nothing on the walls. There is a counter for six and four tables. Everything seems a little smaller, a little more perfect, than in the real world outside. Young Mr. Sasaoka, who received his training at one of Tokyo's top traditional restaurants, has his fish shipped to him directly, thus saving a day, and he buys his seasonal vegetables directly from farmers in Kyushu and Shikoku. He is something

•••••••the back pockets of trousers while their owners were in the next room bathing naked in hot water up to their chin.

of a culinary genius. Lunch is ¥3,000 and ¥5,000, dinner ¥8,000 and ¥9,000. (RK)

Tamasaka * ¥¥ !!!**

UNFUSSY KAISEKI AT THE COUNTER

2-21-11 Nishi-Azabu, Minato-ku. ☎ ***03-5485-6690.*** *Closed Sundays. Major credit cards. Nearest station:* OMOTESANDO.

A young architect named Sato is responsible for the clean, open space on the ground floor. (Upstairs are several Japanese and Western-style rooms.) Incorporated into the design are details of classical Japanese houses that have been demolished. A counter seating ten looks out on a graceful garden, which, it is said, Mr. Sato had to persuade the landscape designer to keep simple. In the fall and spring the windows giving out on the garden are slid open. In the winter it is sometimes a snowscape. Sitting at the counter, you will have your own private chef working in front of you. He will, if he feels you are in the mood, explain what he is doing or perhaps give you a few hints on what to look for when you shop for particular materials. Lunch is ¥3,800, and the ten-course dinner menu is ¥8,000. I recently took to Tamasaka a jaded couple from San Francisco, where they say they eat Japanese food all the time. After our meal they told me, stunned, that they had never eaten Japanese food like this. (RK)

LOACH

Komagata Dojo * ¥

FISH OMELETTE IN A 200-YEAR-OLD BARN

1-7-12 Komagata, Taito-ku. ☎ ***03-3842-4001.*** *Open every day. Major credit cards. Nearest station:* ASAKUSA.

Only two things on the menu: Dojo nabe (loach stew) for ¥1,400 and Yanagawa (loach omelette) for ¥1,300. There are no tables: you sit next to a long board laid out on the tatami like everyone else in the neighborhood, the postman on a break and the two nattering grandmothers in kimono, who take this hallowed old place absolutely for granted. As at Yabu Soba in Kanda, another Old Tokyo tradition, the waitresses sing out their orders to the kitchen. (RK)

NABE POT

Ichinotani * ¥¥**

CHANKO NABE AS AN AESTHETIC EXPERIENCE

3-22-2 Uchi-Kanda, Chiyoda-ku. ☎ ***03-3254-0025.*** *Closed Sundays and holidays. No credit cards. Nearest station:* SUEHIROCHO.

From the rustic entrance to the wood-clad interior adorned with antiques and sumo memorabilia, Ichinotani exudes an old-world tranquility far removed from the electronic frazzle of nearby Akihabara. The master of the house is Mitsunari Kita, a former sumo wrestler who now prepares sashimi and charcoal-grilled fish of remarkable refinement. He also serves chanko nabe, not the Rabelaisian stewpot usually thought of, but a simple, gourmet version of the genre, containing no meat or chicken, just fish and vegetables of the highest quality. Expect to pay close to ¥10,000 each. (RS)

Isegen * ¥ !

ANGLERFISH STEW IN THE OLD DOWNTOWN

1-11-1 Kandasudacho, Chiyoda-ku. ☎ ***03-3251-1229.*** *Closed Sundays, weekends in July and August. No credit cards. Nearest station:* AWAJICHO.

The mood here is highly convivial, as everybody sits together in one great tatami room with tables inches apart, while cheery waitresses scurry about, bantering like barbers. The specialty is ankonabe, anglerfish stew, at ¥3,300 a serving. For an additional ¥500, you can end your meal with ojiya, an opportunity that should not be lightly passed up. This is a wonderful old place, where we would take friends from abroad if they had only one evening in Tokyo and we wanted to show them why we have chosen to live here ourselves. (RK)

NOODLES (SOBA, UDON, RAMEN)

Chotoku ** ¥ !!

TOKYO'S BEST UDON

1-10-5 Shibuya, Shibuya-ku. ☎ ***03-3407-8891****. Closed Mondays. Major credit cards. Nearest station:* SHIBUYA.

The waitresses wear crisp, blue cotton kimono and dazzling tabi, and are sweetly solicitous. The menu is a brocade-bound album of color photographs, and explanations are Japanese and literate English of the fifty or so variations available. The architecture of the place is notable, and huge speakers on either side of the room whisper Mozart or Vivaldi. This is no noodle joint. (RK)

Jikyu-an *** ¥ !

AMAZING SOBA, AMAZING GRACE

1-15-18 Minami-Asagaya, Suginami-ku. ☎ ***03-3314-6077****. Closed Mondays and third Tuesdays and Wednesdays. No credit cards. Nearest station:* MINAMI-ASAGAYA.

Many soba connoisseurs hold that this is the best soba in Tokyo, but Jikyu-an is more than just very fine buckwheat noodles. The lady of the house (the wife of the craftsman in the kitchen) places the dishes—many antique and all chosen with care—on your table with a grace inspired by the tea ceremony. Jikyu-an's attention to detail is suggested by their buying salt directly from the salt factory and grinding the crystals themselves. A meal here is a quintessential Japanese eating experience, and wonderful. (RK)

Koya * ¥

INVENTIVE RAMEN

8 San'eicho, Shinjuku-ku. ☎ ***03-3351-1756****. Closed Sundays and holidays. No credit cards. Nearest station:* YOTSUYA.

Koya specializes in ramen—noodles Chinese-style. The basic dish is a bowl of shina ("China") soba decorated with succulent slices of roast pork, which goes for ¥650. You can specify futoi (thick) or hosoi (thin) and choose from a list of broths and sauces. You add the final touch yourself with one or more of the Thai or Taiwanese condiments that Koya Karasawa, the proprietor, has tracked down and brought back from his exploratory expeditions abroad. The music at lunch has a baroque cast, but in the evening it's more likely to be unusual jazz, perhaps a cello sketching the outlines of "Sweet Georgia Brown." (RK)

Yabu Soba * ¥ !

TOKYO'S MOST FAMOUS SOBA SHOP

2-10 Awajicho, Chiyoda-ku. ☎ ***03-3251-0287****. Closed Mondays. No credit cards. Nearest station:* AWAJICHO.

Yabu has spawned almost fifty branches, which are all run by former apprentices. There is often a line, but you will find it no great inconvenience to wait on a bench in the narrow corridor at the edge of the little courtyard while the people who arrived before you finish their meal. The turnover is rapid. Yabu is a very Japanese place, with a sweeping expanse of immaculate shoji that can be slid open to reveal a garden. You'll probably want to curl up on the tata-

•••••••okuwagata beetles collapsed—a large okuwagata that formally went for ¥800,000 at the collector's corner of •

mi with most everyone else, at one of the low, comfortably worn lacquer tables. The service is a model of efficiency, with all orders sung out to the kitchen—an old Yabu tradition. This is where to come after braving that assault on the senses called Akihabara, just across the bridge. (RK)

ODEN

Otako Honten * ¥

EARLY EVENING WITH GINZA HOSTESSES

5-4-16 Ginza, Chuo-ku. ☎ ***03-3571-0057****. Closed Sundays. No credit cards. Nearest station:* GINZA.

People come to Otako, Ginza's old-line oden emporium, as to a sanctuary. The place is as plain and serviceable as a pair of disposable chopsticks, utterly frill-less. If you sit at the counter near the great bubbling tray of oden odds and ends, you'll be more easily drawn into the spirit of the place, and sitting next to you might well be a coterie of Ginza hostesses who have dropped in for some honest sustenance to carry them through a long night of flattery and sly charm. Sake goes with everything, the flasks piling up as you drink like saucers in a French cafe. (RK)

Nonki * ¥

DOWN-HOME VEGETABLE STEW

1-20-6 Mukogaoka, Bunkyo-ku. ☎ ***03-3811-4736****. Closed Sundays. No credit cards. Nearest station:* HONGO SANCHOME.

Nonki is Tokyo University's oden (vegetable stew) shop: its scruffy walls are covered with the calligraphic exercises of renowned scholars and renegade writers. It is frequented by students who read while they eat, by frazzled white-shirted wage earners who come in threes and fours and roll up their sleeves, and by ladies of the neighborhood who think of Nonki as a place for a quiet cup of tea and a dish of the lighter offerings. Nonki put up its noren in mid-Meiji. On the wall is a tin plate with Nonki's original phone number: 4736. (RK)

OKONOMIYAKI

Hiroki * ¥ !

UPSCALE OKONOMIYAKI HIROSHIMA-STYLE

2-14-14 Kitazawa, Setagaya-ku. ☎ ***03-3412-3908****. Major credit cards. Open every day. Nearest station:* SHIMOKITAZAWA.

Kadomae-san won't say what's in the white squeeze bottle that she squirts on her okonomiyaki, but when her secret hits the hot griddle the sizzle sounds like applause. Her creations resemble coarse Osaka-style okonomiyaki as closely as dandelions resemble roses. Hiroki is cozy, with most of its pleasant narrow space filled by the three-meter-long griddle counter and its twelve stools. Her family owns the largest oyster farm in Hiroshima, and every other day in season (from October to March) fresh oysters are flown in on ice—not in water. Water, she says, changes their taste. (MK)

Matsunami * ¥ !

GOURMET SAVORY FLAPJACKS

2-25-6 Nihonbash-Ningyocho, Chuo-ku. ☎ ***03-3666-7773****. Open every day. No credit*

••• department stores now goes for a mere ¥50,000. A high school in Kumamoto lined up 130 girls in their third year •••••

Best Brew Pubs

Puls Cecile
Akito Miyazaki (president), 2-1-1 Ohashi, Meguro-ku. ☎ 03-3481-6727.
If a restaurant's been open for ten years in Tokyo it's called an institution. And such is Puls Cecile. Located right on Yamate Dori, so it's easy to find. The atmosphere is laid-back and casual. Although the feeling is more restaurant than bar, they're happy to let you kick back and sip a few cold ones. They offer a variety of foods to complement the beers. With an emphasis on garlic, the dishes derive from a cross-section of world cuisine. Likewise, their beer selection has extensive representation from around the world. Check out Henninger, Brooklyn Lager, and the always fresh Tokyo Ale #3.

Cerveza
Masashi Hosomura (owner), Koko Roppongi Building B1F, 3-11-10 Roppongi, Minato-ku. ☎ 03-3478-0077.
The next time your co-workers drag you over to Roppongi, don't panic, steer them to Cerveza. Just a minute from Roppongi Station, this "not-as-well-known-as-it-should-be" bar offers one of the largest selections of beer in Tokyo. With a whole wall of refrigeration, you'll be guaranteed a well-maintained bottle every time. Looking through the glass doors, you can peruse their vast offerings: from Mickey's Big Mouths to Alexander Rodenbach, they have it all. Though don't worry if you can't decide; owner Hosomura-san is amazingly knowledgeable and always helpful with recommendations.

Rojak
Noboru Kobayashi (manager), 6-3-14 Minami-Aoyama, Minato-ku. ☎ 03-3409-6764.
Tucked away in the heart of Aoyama, Rojak offers us beer connoisseurs a very stylish setting for engaging our favorite activity: drinking good beer. Their menu, while not being very extensive, is perfectly selected. From Tokyo's underground favorite, Tokyo Ale #3, to the self-styled "world's strongest beer," Eku, there's bound to be the perfect choice for every taste. The Pan-Asian cuisine is

cards. Nearest station: NINGYOCHO.
You'll find a meal at Matsunami informal and jolly. Two strides will take you through the tiny garden and into the little entryway of the old wooden house, and two more into the single tatami room where everyone eats. The only furniture in the room is a half-dozen tables with grills set into their tops, the bottles of condiments and sauces off to the side. One wall is an expanse of windows, which rattle in their frames whenever a breeze comes up. The lights are dim, the atmosphere smoky, and everything seems to be quietly crumbling away. The course is ¥3,000. (RK)

SUSHI AND SASHIMI

Fukuzushi ** ¥¥¥ !!!
DIAMOND JIM BRADY SUSHI
5-7-8 Roppongi, Minato-ku. ☎ ***03-3402-4116.*** *Closed Sundays. Major credit cards. Nearest station:* ROPPONGI.
You enter on flagstones through a rock

•••••••and told them to take off their sailor blouses so teachers (some of them male) could check that their bras were •

all organic and should not be missed. If you're lucky (or famous) enough to be seated around the large tables in back, you can lounge in style with a fluffy pillow and a frothy beer.

Sugar Water

Sugawara-san (owner), 15-5 Sakuragaoka, Shibuya-ku. ☎ 03-3461-2188.
Need a good beer late night in Shibuya? Head over to Sugar Water. Just a few minutes from Shibuya Station and you'll be surrounded by a dazzling assortment of beer paraphernalia, as well as beer. Everyone sits around two tables, so the conversation starts flowing along with the drinks. Ask to see the attached gallery space, and don't forget to try the homemade tsukemono.

Tanne

Jo Umeda (owner), 1-32-15 Yoyogi, Shibuya-ku. ☎ 03-3373-6888.
After a warm day spent strolling through Yoyogi Koen, don't dream of that liter of Hoegaarden on draft, head over to Tanne and quaff one down. May as well have a big ole soft pretzel while you're at it. This great Yoyogi beer hall's menu of Teutonic fare perfectly complements the large selection of German and Belgian beers. Belly up to the bar and order that Hoegaarden, or allow owner Jo Umeda to decide by choosing one of his special selections of the day.

Popeye

Tatsuo Aoki (owner), 2-18-7 Ryoogoku, Sumida-ku. ☎ 03-3633-2120.
Next time you're in Ryoogoku to see the big boys dance Sumo, head to Popeye for a pint. With fourteen taps dispensing nama beer, this is as close to a multi-tap as you'll find in Tokyo. With a large selection of ji-beer, four to five of which are served on draft, you'll be able to sample a whole range of Japanese draft-brewed beer without having to leave Tokyo. The setting is a pleasant pub with a large-screen TV showing sporting events. The food is pub fare and quite tasty. The master, Aoki-san, is very well informed about the craft brewing scene in Japan. He is more than happy to talk beer as well as make recommendations as to his rotating selection of quality beer.

—Dave Yarrington

garden hedged by young bamboo so green they glow. Inside, you are greeted at a reception desk with a Brigit Riley print behind it, and ushered into the chic cocktail lounge to wait for seats at the sushi bar to become available. While waiting, sip a cup of green tea or something from the well-stocked bar, and leaf through the glossy Japanese fashion magazines in the magazine rack. When you are called to your place at the sushi bar, take your drinks. Your chair will be pulled out for you, and your place will be set with a linen napkin. Lunch starts at ¥2,500, dinner at ¥10,000. (RK)

Kizushi ** ¥

SUSHI FOR JADED CONNOISSEURS

6-17-2 Hongo, Bunkyo-ku. ☎ ***03-3811-5934****. Closed Sundays. No credit cards. Nearest station:* HONGO SANCHOME.
Kizushi is Tokyo University's very down-home sushi shop, a fine example of the breed. But it is more. If you call Yama-

••• regulation white and not the charcoal and salmon that is all the rage in Tokyo boutiques. The same high school •••••

guchi-san, Kizushi's master, a couple days before you plan to come, and tell him that you'd like something special, he will put his buying organization into gear so he can present you with a spread that may give you a whole new idea of what sushi can be. These would be things like a fish from Kyushu that is in season only a few weeks of the year, octopus eggs, a rare fish from Hokkaido that is known only by its Ainu name, a mollusk that Tsukiji can sometimes supply on special order but Yamaguchi gets direct from a personal contact. This is sushi for the explorer. (RK)

Miyako Zushi ** ¥¥ !

LUSH, TRADITIONAL SUSHI

1-10-12 Yanagibashi, Taito-ku. ☎ ***03-3851-7494.*** *Closed Sundays and holidays. No credit cards. Nearest station:* ASAKUSABASHI.

Miyako Zushi has no refrigerated cases of materials on display. There is no need, for customers get no choice. (How could they possibly know what's good? They are most unlikely to have been at Tsukiji before the sun came up.) Kato-san will put out on the plain wood counter a fistful of hand-cut slices of pickled ginger, then bring on the sashimi, the order of which will be carefully calculated. Then the sushi, on which Kato-san will brush his own soy sauce for you. The rice is hito hada, skin temperature, which makes it lush. (RK)

Saji *** ¥¥ !

REMARKABLE "HORS D'OEUVRES" BEFORE SUSHI

3-10-18 Jiyugaoka, Meguro-ku. ☎ ***03-3724-2424.*** *Closed Mondays. Major credit cards. Nearest stations:* JIYUGAOKA, KUHONBUTSU.

We are not the only ones who think Saji is a place apart. On the weekends, Saji's twenty-place counter is fully occupied minutes after it opens at 5 o'clock. For a treat, start off with "kobashi," Saji's seasonal hors d'oeuvres. It's not on the menu but will cost something like ¥3,000, depending. With this presentation of maybe five little dishes, you may never get to the sushi at all. Things like ikura with tonbori seeds, like shiroiebi with a dab of mustard, like okada (dried tofu) with shrimp slicked down with sake and shoyu in dashi stock, like kaibashira (miniature scallops in an ume plum sauce). Because presumably you will move on to nigiri sushi after this, the palate cleanser served with the kobashi is wakame seaweed, because the palate cleanser that will come with your sushi will be, of course, slices of pickled ginger. Saji offers fifty different kinds of sushi. Let them surprise you. (RK)

Takeno * ¥

WHERE TSUKIJI EATS LUNCH

6-21-2 Tsukiji, Chuo-ku. ☎ ***03-3541-8698.*** *Closed Sundays and holidays. They never heard of credit cards. Nearest station:* TSUKIJI.

Get there before noon, before Tsukiji shuts down and Takeno fills up with rubber-booted stall owners who have been running the daily fish auction since four in the morning. Over whiskey and water—as what may be lunch for you is dinner at the end of a furiously busy day for everyone else here—the talk is of food and the food business. These guys are, after all, pros. Prices are not displayed because they depend on the market price, but there is not a chance in the world that you will be overcharged. Sashimi moriawase ("assorted") goes for ¥700 a plate. The tempura moriawase at ¥600 a plate is a trencherman's delight. (RK)

••••••• has a rule that any student with hair not pitch black must dye it so. In high-school baseball, Gijuku High beat •

Yums Hoist's Five Favorites

Yums Hoist, importer of wine and exotic delicacies, possesses one of Tokyo's most finely tuned palates. We asked him for a short annotated list of his favorite places. He complied in his inimitable style as follows:

Kitajima-tei
7 San'eicho, Shinjuku-ku. ☎ 03-3355-6667.
The sign outside is far more like it than that of an ordinary ramen-noodle bar. OK, you found the restaurant after all, and that's invisible from the inside. This intimate restaurant feasts food lovers on perhaps the most candid French food in Tokyo.

Ne Quittez Pas
3-15-19 Higashi-Gotanda, Shinagawa-ku. ☎ 03-3442-2382.
The food here looks most unprecedented, even phony. Nevertheless, the trained palette can see all the dishes are composed subscribing to the real idea for restaurants: do it simply and do it brilliantly. You are to taste the best Beurre Blanc in your life.

Onma Kitchen
2-14-15 Shinjuku, Shinjuku-ku. ☎ 03-3341-8508.
A tiny, ramshackle Korean canteen in the heart of the planet's largest gay area. Eating here, especially the bibimpaf rice bowl and oxtail soup, is inescapably addictive. Don't bring the toilet roll on the counter to the loo. That is a napkin.

Sushi Izumi
6-6-9 Shimo-Meguro, Meguro-ku. ☎ 03-3793-9150.
Some might think the chef goes on too much about food and drink, but this is the place to go if you feel excited by twelve-month-old cod roe paste or a secret middle-of-the-tank bottle from a small but virtuous sake brewery. The sushi is decent, of course.

Rakutei
6-8-1 Akasaka, Minato-ku. ☎ 03-3585-3743.
The beautifully finished, pale brown wall sports solely a small flower in a bamboo vase. The flower looks most discreet in the restaurant, except for the owner/chef cooking sublime tempura. The perfect sophistication Tokyo should be proud of.

TEMPLE COOKING

Bon ** ¥¥ !!

VEGETARIAN FOOD IN AN OLD JAPANESE HOUSE
1-2-11 Ryusen, Taito-ku. ☎ ***03-3872-0375****. Closed Tuesdays. Major credit cards. Nearest station:* IRIYA.

Less a business than a benediction, there is a sweet gentleness about Bon that bespeaks its master's Buddhist inclinations. The house and garden are one of Tokyo's many hidden treasures. A finely detailed vegetarian course (from ¥8,000) is served, for which you are asked to come at 6:30 pm, so as not to be rushed. Quiet, fulfilling, civilized in a way that belies the concept "advanced civilization." (RK)

Gesshinkyo ** ¥¥ !!

ZEN VEGETARIAN SANCTUARY
4-24-12 Jingumae, Shibuya-ku. ☎ ***03-3796-6575****. Open every day. Major credit cards. Nearest station:* MEIJI-JINGUMAE.

Gesshinkyo is a paean to the manifold possibilities of fresh roots, greens, sea vegetables, and wild mountain herbs. It is serene but never austere, though it can feel that way after the hubbub of nearby Harajuku. The noren is made of coarse hemp; the tokonoma holds incense, a candle, and an ancient Buddha block print; the walls are of cracked mud, with wooden pillars and beams, lights diffused through washi. Owner-chef Toshio Tanahashi wears the simple indigo tunic of a novice monk. He learned his art at a Buddhist nunnery outside Kyoto, where the Zen vegetarian aesthetic is tempered by an earthy, rural understanding that the body must be nourished no less than the soul. There is no menu: the set dinner is a substantial ¥10,000 ten-course affair that will include as many as forty different seasonal vegetables, many of which you are likely never to have encountered before. (RS)

Sosai-bo ** ¥

VEGETARIAN PROVENDER AND SAKE

4-1-9 Meguro Honcho, Meguro-ku. ☎ ***03-3710-4336****. Major credit cards. Closed Mondays unless it's a holiday. Nearest station:* MUSASHI KOYAMA.

Most people knocking on the door of a Zen temple ask to be shown the way to enlightenment. When Sosai-bo's master knocked on the door of a temple in Kamakura, he asked to be taught how to cook. There is no hint here of that lofty otherworldliness that characterizes most places dedicated to the upper reaches of Japanese cuisine. Rather, there is a strong flavor of Zen here-and-nowness. There is an eight-mat tatami room in the back with tables a foot high. The walls, hung with brush-written homilies to sake, are cheap plasterboard showing an occasional dent. From the ceiling dangle four bare bulbs of a wattage so low the light doesn't reach into the corners, in which are stacked the usual detritus of a Japanese home: wicker baskets, shirts just back from the laundry, old magazines, and fishing equipment waiting to be repaired. The music is an unearthly mixture of the Beatles, Aretha Franklin, Madonna, and '50s bubblegum tunes about girls with names like Linda. Two huge sake refrigerators hold the fifty isshobin (magnums) on hand. There are seventeen varieties of Kikuhime ("Chrysanthemum Princess") alone. Your sommelier for the evening is a no-nonsense lady in jeans and white socks. She will whip off the top of a new isshobin and fill your glass to the rim in one motion (so that you have to take your first sip with the glass on the table), while talking half to you and half to herself. She is very knowledgeable. The two people in the little kitchen—the master and his dedicated assistant—usually bring to your table the dishes they have just prepared and can answer any questions. Although temple food ostensibly aims for simplicity—Sosai-bo's stocks are so simple that the quality of the water is critical—some of these dishes can have a dozen ingredients, being simplified versions of dishes with thirty. In general, though, the clarity of vegetarian dishes plays off well against the soft subtleties of

••••••• president, thus effectively Japan's next prime minister. Among the three contenders for the party presidency ••

sake. The Yasai nana-shi mori plate of seven vegetable hors d'oeuvres is ¥2,000. The Zen course is ¥3,500. Sake goes for ¥600 to ¥5,000 a glass. (RK)

TEMPURA

Hayashi *** ¥¥¥ !!

TOKYO'S BEST (AND MOST EXPENSIVE) TEMPURA

1-12 Nihonbashi Muromachi, Chuo-ku.
☎ ***03-3241-5367****. Closed Sundays. No credit cards. Nearest station:* MITSUKOSHIMAE.

The most exquisite tempura in Tokyo, served with gentle dispatch in a very traditional little place of utter refinement. Everyone who comes here knows exactly what's going on. Reservations are essential for a place at the ten-seat counter for the ¥14,000 course, and you are asked to arrive as close to 6 o'clock as you can, for in tempura timing is everything. Conversation here is subdued, the mood tranquil. (RK)

Iseya * ¥ !

OLD-LINE TEMPURA SHOP IN OLD PART OF TOWN

1-9-2 Nihonsutsumi, Taito-ku. ☎ ***03-3872-4886****. No credit cards. Closed Wednesdays. Nearest station:* MINOWA.

Everyone knows where Iseya is. It's the neighborhood tempura joint. People come on bicycles, and the youngest of the family is wheeled in, in a stroller. Because Iseya takes no reservations, there's usually a line of half-a-dozen or so, but nobody minds waiting for a few minutes, as everyone knows everyone else, and it is an occasion to catch up on the gossip. Inside, the floor is stone. There are four low wooden tables with benches, and in the back, two small tables on tatami. The lightbulbs are in old-fashioned fixtures. (When one of the fixtures breaks, the master orders a replacement from a factory in Hokkaido

Where to Buy

DRIED SEASLUG ROE

Available from Maruki, a famous dealer in chimi (high-class exotic foods for kaiseki restaurants), in Tsukiji. At ¥100,000 a kilo, it is the most expensive food available in Tsukiji.

that has been making them since Meiji: his instinct is to preserve.) The shoyu containers on the tables are antiques. Iseya's tempura is rough-and-ready, Edo-style, heavy on the soy sauce. It is not served to you piece by piece as in the lofty establishments in the Ginza, but all scraped together in a savory mess, like a Mexican omelette. When Kyoto people complain about the koi (darkly pungent) taste of Tokyo food, Iseya's tempura is what they are talking about. Iseya's customers, on the other hand, would find delicate, Kyoto-style tempura—the kind served in the Ginza—effete. (RK)

Mikawa ** ¥¥ !

SUPERIOR TEMPURA WITH A HOMELY TOUCH

3-4-7 Nihonbashi-Kayabacho, Chuo-ku.
☎ ***03-3664-9843****. Open every day. No credit cards. Nearest station:* KAYABACHO.

Hidden away down a narrow, unmarked alley, Mikawa is as homely and unprepossessing as a neighborhood izakaya. Two modest, scuffed tatami rooms hold ten people at a pinch, with seats for eight more at the wooden counter. Modest it may look, but the food is of the highest order: this is where Tokyo's chefs come to eat tempura. The cooking style is Edo-mae (Tokyo traditional), using only the same fish and vegetables that were available here in the shogun's capital 150 years ago (the

Obuchi had the least popular support, but evidentally in the LDP scheme of things it was simply Obuchi's turn. An

Restaurants with Stylish Decor

Carmine Edochiano
9-13 Arakicho, Shinjuku-ku. ☎ 03-3225-6767. Nearest station: YOTSUYA SAN-CHOME.
The understated elegance of this old house, once a ryotei, with its tatami, tokonoma, scrolls, and flowers, blends seamlessly with the modern Italian artwork Carmine admires. Such a tasteful setting is the best showcase for the uncomplicated Tuscan food that Carmine excels at. (MK)

New York Grill
Park Hyatt Hotel, Top Floor, 3-7-1-2 Nishi-Shinjuku, Shinjuku-ku. ☎ 03-5322-1234. Nearest station: SHINJUKU.
Bold and brash, this place is swank, with thirty-foot ceilings, ebony floors, huge paintings bright as flame against charcoal granite and slate-blue walls, and the dazzle of Tokyo far below. Top floor service, too, with prices to match. The food from the open kitchen is usually quite fine but can be uneven at times. Those who miss Gotham will feel at home. Cool live jazz in the bar. (MK)

Stellato
4-19-17 Shiroganedai, Minato-ku. ☎ 03-3442-5588. Nearest station: HIROO.
With its imposing chandeliers, walls decorated in gold and silver, and a blazing log fire, Stellato is a magnificent post-modern baronial dining room for the twenty-first century. (RS)

Tableaux
11-6 Sarugakucho, Shibuya-ku. ☎ 03-5489-2201. Nearest station: DAIKAN-YAMA.
Tableaux has more gilt than a merry-go-round and the same dizzying excitement. The overall effect is Italian baroque meets Rodeo Drive: lustrous, opulent, and slightly decadent. Most people love the ride. (MK)

Yuu-an
Shinjuku Park Tower B1, 3-7-1Nishi-Shinjuku, Shinjuku-ku. ☎ 03-5322-6427. Nearest station: SHINJUKU.
Burnished metal screens, lanterns of paper and bamboo, walls of packed mud, and zabuton cushions of indigo cotton: Yuu-an's interior (like its food) is a brilliant blending of traditional refinement, rural simplicity, and sleek urban sophistication. (RS)

exception being asparagus spears). The anago is sublime. The top course is just ¥6,800, though the top ingredients are reserved for the à la carte menu. (RS)

TOFU

Goemon * ¥¥ !!!

TOFU DISHES IN A MAGIC GARDEN
1-1-26 Hon-Komagome, Bunkyo-ku. ☎ ***03-3811-2015****. Closed Sundays. No credit cards. Nearest station:* HAKUSAN.
Of the eight or so Tokyo restaurants whose menu is built around tofu, Goemon is the most charming. Enter the lantern-lit alley, and by the time you have walked the thirty meters of cool, moss-covered paving stones leading back to the restaurant itself, you will have experienced a mood change. In summer, the shoji screens of the main

building are open to a garden and to the much-sought-after mountain huts with room for five or six. Goemon's basic course is ¥5,500. (RK)

TONKATSU

Katsuyoshi ** ¥ !!

TONKATSU IN A FARMHOUSE KITCHEN

Ebisu Garden Place, 4-20-3 Ebisu, Shibuya-ku. ☎ ***03-5421-0080****. Open every day. Major credit cards. Nearest station:* EBISU.

Tonki's tonkatsu is fun—to Tokyo what the pastrami at the Carnegie Delicatessen is to New York. Maisen's tonkatsu, served in what used to be a public bath, is majestic and very good. I have to say, though, that the tonkatsu served up by Katsuyoshi, whose main business is in Shizuoka, is on another level entirely. The sesame oil is from a famous producer and is made to house specifications. The koromo crust adheres perfectly, and as each cutlet is served on a handmade wire net, any residual oil drains away. You have your choice of pig. On the more expensive left-hand side of the menu, where you should order from, the pigs are from Kagoshima, with the rosu (chop) going for ¥2,000 and the more tender hire (fillet) for ¥2,500. Tonkatsu connoisseurs can call ahead to arrange to be served an even more special cut for ¥4,000 to ¥5,000. On the cheaper right-hand side of the menu, the pigs come from Katsuyoshi's own spread in Iwata. The ¥1,200 set lunch packs 'em in, but in off-hours the pace is leisurely. (RK)

Maisen * ¥ !

TONKATSU IN AN OLD PUBLIC BATH

4-8-5 Jingumae, Shibuya-ku. ☎ ***03-3470-0071****. Open every day. No credit cards. Nearest station:* HARAJUKU.

Pretty good tonkatsu at Maisen, which has done a roaring business for as long as anyone can remember. The tip-off is the care they take with the sauce, which at most tonkatsu parlors is that barely viscous "Bulldog" sauce from a bottle. Maisen brews its own, which comes in three versions: regular, astringent, and a version with apples and onions especially concocted for the kurobuta ("black pig") tonkatsu. Service is informed and precise by crisply uniformed waitresses. The atmosphere is that of a modish cafeteria. The comfortable back room, which was formerly a public bath, is preferred. Hirekatsu teishoku (regular fillet course) is ¥1,500. Jo hirekatsu teishoku (a more tender fillet) is ¥2,200. Jo hirekatsu kurobuta teishoku (fillet of the more toothsome Chinese "black pig") is ¥2,800. (RK)

Tonki * ¥

TONKATSU AS A TOKYO INSTITUTION

1-1-2 Shimo-Meguro, Meguro-ku. ☎ ***03-3491-9928****. Closed Tuesdays. Credit: DC, JBC, Visa. Nearest station:* MEGURO.

One of the great sights of Tokyo. Crisply uniformed minions prepare with surgical precision the classic (as in Model T Ford) Japanese dish called tonkatsu, which is deep-fried breaded pork cutlet garnished with a mound of shredded cabbage, over which is dribbled the sauce called Bulldog. Tonki is always crowded, so first order hirekatsu (trust me), then drift to the rear near the little garden, order a mug of beer, and observe the proceedings. When your order is ready, you will be called to the surgically scrubbed long counter and served with sweet but startlingly efficient grace. Seconds of shredded cabbage are for the asking. (RK)

phrase that richocheted through the media for a week and caused Obuchi, in a wry gesture, to serve cold pizza to

Best Sidewalk Cafes

Aux Bacchanales
1-6 Jingumae, Shibuya-ku. ☎ 03-5474-0076. Nearest stations: HARAJUKU, MEIJI-JINGUMAE.
This is a Left Bank student hangout, an always crowded refuge for French ex-pats who miss cabbage soup and the reek of Gauloises, a place for deliciously cheap omelettes and salad Nicoise. Fashion models play foosball. Overworked waiters yell out orders in bad French. This is Paris in Tokyo. (MK)

Brasserie Les Halles
AXIS Building, 5-17-1 Roppongi, Minato-ku. ☎ 03-3505-8221. Nearest station: ROPPONGI.
Roppongi has long needed a place to sit and watch the street life. Too new to have acquired a regular crowd, and with its faux Art Deco decor, Les Halles seems unsure of itself. But with its seventy wines and serious food, it will soon find its niche. The ¥1,500 weekend brunch is a steal. (MK)

Cafe des Pres
5-1-27 Minami-Azabu, Minato-ku. ☎ 03-3448-0039. Nearest station: HIROO, *Exit 3.*
The tables are chipped and the parquet floor is scuffed, but the women in their Chanel suits don't seem to mind. This cafe wears its civilized, Right Bank sophistication lightly. Sit at a tree-shaded table and write your memoirs, as the young waitress in a smart black skirt, heels, and white blouse brings another glass of champagne on a silver tray. (MK)

Cafe Madu
iNi Building, 1-8-9 Jinnan, Shibuya-ku. ☎ 03-5456-7533. Nearest station: SHIBUYA.
Fashionable hangout on a fashionable street. There's a rack full of the latest French fashion magazines to leaf through, while you nibble your pannini and sip your Campari soda and watch the girls go by. (RK)

Cafe Michelangelo
29-3 Sarugakucho, Shibuya-ku. ☎ 03-3770-9517. Nearest station: DAIKANYAMA.
Fashionable Daikanyama offers some of the best people-watching in Tokyo, and this is the place in Daikanyama to do it. The espresso is fine, and they have commendable focaccia sandwiches and plenty of dolces—plus a strong array of grappas. (RS)

UNAGI (EEL)

Yama no Chaya ** ¥¥¥ !!

EEL IN AN OLD TEAHOUSE IN A GARDEN
3-10-6 Nagatocho, Chiyoda-ku. ☎ ***03-3580-3055****. Closed Sundays. Major credit cards. Nearest station:* AKASAKA MITSUKE.
Yama no Chaya is at its most appealing just after the siege of winter has lifted, and you can slide back the old-style shoji to let the evening breeze into your private tatami room and look out on a garden coming alive with greenery. Somehow, the polished patina of this rambling old place, the genuinely simpatico staff, and the fineness of the meal, which is organized around eel, a dish as exquisite as foie gras, all come together to illuminate the evening. Yama no Chaya ("Mountain Teahouse") began

•••••••reporters waiting to interview him. Two million in ¥10,000 notes was found floating lazily down a river in

ninety years ago as a kashiseki, where you could rent rooms in which to drink tea and compose haiku (well, yes, and to engage in dalliance, too, I suppose). It is situated in its own woodland glen, next to a famous temple. Dinner costs ¥18,000. (RK)

Nodaiwa ** ¥¥ !!

TOKYO'S MOST FAMOUS PLACE FOR EEL

1-5-4 Higashi-Azabu, Minato-ku. ☎ ***03-3583-7852.*** *Closed Sundays. No credit cards. Nearest station:* KAMIYACHO.

You can drop in off the street for a quick eel meal at one of the tables on the first floor. Unaju (eel and its juices laid out on a bed of rice) costs ¥1,400. Up the baronial staircase of this Edo-era stone building is where to go to tuck into an eel banquet in a private room. The rooms are small, as if to emphasize the intimacy of the experience. The old-style shoji are crisp, the ceiling is beamed, and it is as quiet as a park at sunrise. Nodaiwa serves its unagi in a lacquer box set in a metal pan holding an inch of hot water, to keep your eel from cooling too fast. Eat slowly as unagi is exceedingly rich. The ¥6,700 basic course brings so much food you may not be able to finish. Nodaiwa has a branch on the rue Saint-Honore, Paris. (RK)

YOSHOKU

Grill F * ¥ !

JAPANESE VISION OF WESTERN FOOD

Gotanda Ekimae, Shinagawa-ku. ☎ ***03-3441-2902.*** *Closed Sundays and holidays. No credit cards. Nearest station:* GOTANDA.

In the time of the Emperor Meiji, when the cooks of Japan got their first good look at Western food, they saw meat, potatoes, heavy sauces, and lots of deep frying. When they tried to replicate what they saw, they inevitably gave the resulting dishes a Japanese twist. Over time, they developed a whole repertoire of Japanese versions of Western dishes. That repertoire still exists, frozen in time. It is called yoshoku (literally, "Western food"), and what it brings to mind, more than anything else, is the sort of food that might be served to officers of the Portuguese army on field maneuvers. Yoshoku is worth our attention because it's hearty, filling, and cheap, and because the places that serve it recall a funkier, more relaxed Japan. Yoshoku restaurants are only found in the older sections of the city, in the back alleys. Grill F is an excellent example of the genre. Its brick building is strangled by ivy, and its battered sign says "Grill F, Fransu ryori" ("French cooking"), but if this is French cooking, I'm Charles de Gaulle. The menu, scrawled in a hand not used to writing cursively, looks like a mistake with its Bifteck a la Hambourg for ¥1,200 and its Stewed Boeuf for ¥1,800. It's not a mistake, though. It's yoshoku. (RK)

FOREIGN RESTAURANTS

AMERICAN

7025 Franklin Avenue * ¥ !

TOKYO'S BEST HAMBURGER

3-15-18 Higashi-Gotanda, Shinagawa-ku. ☎

Kawagawa prefecture. In spite of the appointment of Seiko Noda, known for her miniskirts and at 37 the youngest

***03-3441-5028**. Open every day. No credit cards. Nearest station:* GOTANDA.

Named after the address of the hamburger palace in LA where Mr. Matsumoto studied the art of grilling ground beef for five years. He turns out Tokyo's best burgers, with variations like avocado-burgers, chili-burgers, and mushroom-burgers. Open and airy, with a little courtyard for balmy weather, a working fireplace for brisker weather, and built-in bookcases with books for browsing. Red wines and a champagne for those in a decadent mood. (RK)

New York Grill ** ¥¥ !!!

VIEW FROM THE SUMMIT

Park Hyatt Hotel, top floor, 3-7-1-2 Nishi-Shinjuku, Shinjuku-ku. Open every day. ☎ ***03-5322-1234**. All credit cards, except Masters. Nearest station:* SHINJUKU.

The place is aptly named: you might as well be in New York. The kitchen is open to view, with a rack of chickens rotating on spits and decorative jars of steeping condiments. Two-story-high ceilings, Italian leather chairs, bravado graphics, and sparkling napery. The menu is designed to titillate jaded expense-account eaters used to putting away a lot of food. You get your own individual warm loaf of bread, and olive oil is poured into a side dish for dipping. Take friends here to transport them away from Tokyo, away from it all. Dinner is a la carte. Lunch is ¥4,200, which lets you roam a wonderful appetizer buffet before settling into a main dish like grilled lamb chops served with spiced pear, cranberry chutney, green beans, and mashed potatoes. While you are in the area, consider visiting the Ozone Design Center next door, with its two floors of Conran Shop furniture and implements for living. (RK)

Stellato ** ¥¥¥ !!!

BRASH POWER DINING IN SLAM-GLAM STYLE

4-19-17 Shiroganedai, Minato-ku. ☎ ***03-3442-5588**. Open every day. Major credit cards. Nearest station:* HIROO.

You'll either love or hate the ersatz Moroccan architecture, the chandeliers, log fire, and fin-de-siècle baronial dining room decor. The glam flirts perilously close to kitsch at Stellato, but the food is excellent and entirely serious. Chef Masahito Ueki's creative synthesis of influences epitomizes the best of modern American cuisine while never forgetting its Japanese roots. Thus foie gras with sato-imo yam, or Colorado lamb chops spiked with garam masala. Do not fail to try his superb Dungeness crab croquettes. A predominantly expat crowd gathers here for power dinners, retiring when replete to the bar for brandies or to the rooftop lounge for expensive Havanas. (RS)

The Tokyo Restaurant * ¥¥ !

TOKYO MEETS SOHO IN A REFITTED BANK

2-4-1 Minami-Azabu, Minato-ku. Open every day. ☎ ***03-5418-7555**. Major credit cards. Nearest stations:* TAMACHI, MITA.

Housed in the shell of a now-defunct bank (spot the safe embedded in one wall), TTR has the cool ambience of a downtown New York loft: vertiginous ceilings, wall-sized monochrome photographs, exposed heating ducts, and a jazzy soundtrack. The menu mirrors the look. It's new-wave Pacific Rim cooking with an urban edge—eclectic, vertical, sometimes overindulgent, but always priced for a casual night out. The Tuna Tower is highly recommended, so is the killer mashed potato. You can also drop by to cradle a drink in the ground-floor bar, or for a light snack on the intimate mezzanine level. (RS)

•••••••cabinet minister since the end of the war, the general public appeared unimpressed with Prime Minister Obuchi's

Yonchome Cafe ¥ !

RICK'S CAFE AMERICAINE

4-28-10 Koenji-Minami, Suginami-ku. ☎ ***03-5377-1726.*** *Open every day. No credit cards. Nearest station:* KOENJI.

This is a wonderful place, very Tokyo, but you have to be in the mood. The food is an exact replica of that offered by a not-very-conscientious roadside diner in, say, Chillacothe, Ohio, which is why it gets no stars. Typical dish: fried fish with tartar sauce, served with coleslaw, French fries, carrots, and corn for ¥850. You come to Yonchome Cafe because it's fun and because Koenji has four jazz houses and a kilometer-long covered shopping mall, and because the Inokashira Line from Shibuya (change at Kichijoji) has cars with two headlights close together and looks straight out of Buck Rogers. We prefer the back room, with its tin ceiling, wooden park-bench banquette, Grand Picture Palace stained glass window, and corkboard wall, where local photographers thumbtack up their latest black-and-white prints. (RK)

CHINESE

Bodaiju * ¥ !

CHINESE VEGETARIAN

4-3-14 Shiba, Minato-ku. ☎ ***03-3456-3257.*** *Closed Sundays. Credit: AmEx, DC, Diners. Nearest station:* TAMACHI.

If you are suspicious of vegetarian food because of its reputation for righteousness, Bodaiju will be an awakening. At Bodaiju the exclusion of meat (and milk, eggs, and butter as well as onions and garlic) bears no intimation of deprivation. Quite the reverse: the cooks, who are all from Hong Kong—which by all accounts, still harbors the finest Chinese chefs in the world—and who have never cooked any other way but strict vegetarian, respond to the challenge of not being able to draw on easy flavors by virtuosities of invention. The basic course is ¥4,000, and a la carte dishes run ¥1,000 to ¥1,800. (RK)

Chikuro Sanbo * ¥

OVER-REACHING CHEAP CHINESE

2-21-8 Kichijoji Honcho, Musashino. ☎ ***0422-23-3363.*** *Closed Wednesdays and third Thursdays. Credit: Diners, Visa, AmEx. Nearest station:* KICHIJOJI.

Although Chikuro Sanbo does all it can within the bounds of politeness to keep the crowds down, by covering the tables with clear sheets of plastic, pumping in elevator music, and illuminating the place as though it were an emergency room, you'll still probably have to make a reservation by the middle of the week if you want a table on the weekend. The reason is that in Tokyo we have plenty of cheap Chinese places where everything comes in a bowl, and plenty of expensive ones with filigreed furniture and chopsticks of genuine ivory, but only a handful of relatively cheap Chinese places that are cooking their hearts out. I mean, what sort of cheap Chinese place is it that sets five different hors d'oeuvres on the table as an overture? (RK)

Den-en-kyo ** ¥¥ !!

CHINESE WITH ANTIQUES

4-17-8 Yoga, Setagaya-ku. ☎ ***03-3709-3910****. Open every day. No credit cards. Nearest station:* YOGA.

Den-en-kyo is run by the Son family, and everyone involved is Chinese. Waitresses wear jeans and either T-shirts or high-collared Chinese silk blouses. The à la carte menu first lists a dozen "Grandma's Favorite Dishes," then runs through a couple hundred offerings, with no chuka clichés, before ending with variations on Dim Sum for ¥580 to ¥900. The restaurant is on the first floor of a modern apartment building, but there is an attempt to blunt the modernism of it all by tricking the entrance out with lily pads and bold calligraphy on an old door. Inside, there are antique tansu, shelves of pottery, and wooden chairs dark with use and age. Den-en-kyo's Beijing-style cuisine is based on Chinese medicinal herbs, which impart a nutmeg-like ground bass to these light, flavor-intense dishes. (RK)

Fu Min * ¥ !

AOYAMA'S FAVORITE CHEAP CHINESE PLACE

5-7-17 Minami-Aoyama, Shibuya-ku. ☎ ***03-3498-4466****. Closed Sundays. No credit cards. Nearest station:* OMOTESANDO.

Great negi wonton (¥1,300) and kisetsu yasai to umi no sachi itame (¥3,000), a kind of Chinese Salade Nicoise. Fu Min, spacious and run with dispatch, is Aoyama's neighborhood Chinese joint and, as such, is an order of magnitude better than the best Chinese places on the Upper West Side of Manhattan, which would be its cultural equivalent. There are courses for ¥6,000 and ¥8,000. (RK)

Hokkaien ** ¥¥

BACK ROOMS IN BEIJING

2-12-1 Nishi-Azabu, Minato-ku. ☎ ***03-3407-8507****. Open every day. Major credit cards. Nearest station:* NOGIZAKA.

Unless a gourmet friend has briefed you beforehand, you would have little reason to suspect that Hokkaien is any different from the standard Chinese restaurant anywhere in the world—a thoroughly nondescript entryway (albeit here with a sulky parrot on a perch just inside the door), a rambling arrangement of rooms, lights a little too bright, lime-green tablecloths that harmonize with nothing, and a Chinese staff inclined to lean up against the nearest wall. I list it here because Hokkaien's kitchen works to a standard as high as any Chinese place in town. The basic strategy is to pick one dish—the crispy Peking Duck, for example—and ask for advice on what would go with it. Odds are the forthcoming suggestions won't be on the menu. A meal should run ¥6,000, more or less. (RK)

Hu Tong Si He Fang * ¥ !

DUCK AS LUSH AS PIG

3-12-34 Hiroo, Shibuya-ku. ☎ ***03-5485-6682****. Open every day. No credit cards. Nearest station:* HIROO.

A cheery Chinese factotum oblivious of the local lingo will come to the table to slice the whole bird (¥4,900, easily enough for two) into domino-sized chunks with a

•••••••polled by the *Asahi Shimbun* thought the new government had any chance of getting the economy back on track.

crude but terrible cleaver, which could slice a piece of paper as it falls. Skin Only or Skin With Meat costs the same, the difference being that Skin Only is Peking and Skin With Meat is Canton. Either way, you roll up what has been laid out for you with slivers of leek and cucumber into a crepe and lather on a spoonful of black-bean sauce. The result is as right and as simple as a charcoal-grilled chopped-sirloin hamburger. (RK)

Tonpo * ¥

CHINESE STIR-FRY

3-24-9 Jingumae, Shibuya-ku. ☎ ***03-3405-9944****. Closed first and third Sundays. No credit cards. Nearest station:* HARAJUKU.

Stir-fried variations made from scratch of natural ingredients by Miss Ryo Kan Mei from Beijing and her mountainous brother. All dishes either ¥1,000 or ¥1,300, with Miss Ryo's exquisite gyoza dumplings, deftly rolled out by hand to your order, going for ¥1,000. No atmosphere at all—just good eating. (RK)

(Maison de) Yu Long *** ¥¥¥ !!

CHINESE WITH SILVER CHOPSTICKS, WINE

4-13-18 Akasaka, Minato-ku. ☎ ***03-3589-955****. Closed Sundays. Major credit cards. Nearest station:* AKASAKA MITSUKE.

Think of this food as Chinese kaiseki, the sort of meal you would be served if you were the guest of honor at a banquet in Beijing organized by the Chinese Foreign Ministry, which is trying to soften you up. Mr. Suzuki, the amiable maitre d', will bring you an elaborate menu detailing set courses running from ¥7,000 to ¥20,000. The menu, he will tell you conspiratorially, is for people who feel safer with a plan sketched out for them. After spending a polite amount of time with it, wave it away. Instead, tell Suzuki you have in mind spending, say, ¥8,000, and that you'd prefer him to oversee the proceedings. By all means consider wine, too. Yu Long is one of the few Chinese establishments outside the big hotels where it is possible to match wine with food. Dinner will take two hours, toward the end of which you will be able to make out the faint whisperings of some sophisticated jazz. (RK)

Zuien Bekkan * ¥

CHEAP CHINESE FOR BIG EATERS

2-7-4 Shinjuku, Shinjuku-ku. ☎ ***03-3351-3511****. Open every day. Credit cards: Visa. Nearest station:* SHINJUKU SANCHOME.

Zuien Bekkan has no ambience, but it does have some of the best Chinese food in Tokyo. They specialize in Beijing-style cuisine, uncomplicated and hearty, prepared as it would be at home—sauteed, stir-fried, or steamed—served quickly and with no pretensions. The staff seems to take no special notice of the miracles they bring to the table. Two of Zuien's most popular dishes are #82, mixed vegetables and egg wrapped in a pancake, and #163, boiled dumplings. If you plan to eat before 8:30 pm, make a reservation. The jasmine tea is served in unbreakable plastic cups. (MK)

ECLECTIC

Aviland * ¥

TOKYO FROM A MEDITERRANEAN ANGLE

2-8-4 Mita, Meguro-ku. ☎ ***03-3715-2970****. Closed Sundays. No credit cards. Nearest station:* MEGURO.

Although this tiny place is always too crowded and has been forced by its popularity to schedule two seatings each evening to accommodate people willing to wait thirty minutes or more for seats, its

Cheap French Places

Cou-cou
1-16-2 Kami-Meguro, Meguro-ku. ☎ 03-3792-2975. Nearest station: NAKA-MEGURO.
Gingham tablecloths, empty bottles of cheap vin rouge, Pernod posters, and a tasty menu that's reliable (if never too ambitious)—all in a wonderful setting by the cherry-lined banks of the Meguro-gawa, the Meguro River. (RS)

L'Habitude
3-5 Minami-Yamabushicho, Shinjuku-ku. ☎ 03-3260-8784. Nearest station: KAGURAZAKA.
The off-off Kagurazaka location may be obscure, but the French-trained cooking crew know their origins. You can expect top-value prix-fixe meals that satisfy at this no-frills bistro. (RS)

Le Mange-Tout
22 Nandomachi, Shinjuku-ku. ☎ 03-3268-5911. Nearest station: KAGURAZAKA.
Dinner courses for ¥3,800 and ¥4,800, which is not fantastically cheap, but this is serious food, lovingly prepared. A sophisticated, fun-loving clientele that is happy to be in Tokyo. (RK)

Mannebiches
1-16-8 Nezu, Bunkyo-ku. ☎ 03-3824-0484. Nearest station: NEZU.
Owner-chef Yamamoto grows his herbs outside the front door, bakes his own baguettes and pain de campagne, and serves up bourgeois cuisine that's well above average. In short, he's created a neighborhood super-bistro in one of the city's most traditional areas. (RS)

Pas Mal
2-13-3 Mejiro-dai, Bunkyo-ku. ☎ 03-3945-9908. Nearest station: MEJIRO.
For ¥2,300, choose from seven hors d'oeuvres and seven main courses. A delightful little place with the feel of a country cottage. An atmospheric, tree-lined walk from Mejiro Station past Gakshuin, the Peers' University. (RK)

Premier
5-19-9 Hakusan, Bunkyo-ku. ☎ 03-3944-5257. Nearest station: HAKUSAN.
Premier is intimate, friendly, and refreshingly free of all pseudo-Gallic ostentations. At ¥2,800, Chef Wakamura's hearty three-course dinners represent one of the best bargains in town. (RS)

imaginative offerings remain a remarkable value. Dishes from the very full menu chalked up over the counter are Japanese variations on dishes you would find on the French, Italian, and Spanish Rivieras, and run ¥500 to ¥600—with which you'll probably want to drink the Beaujolais. (RK)

Ken's Chanto Dining * ¥¥ !!

TRENDY NISHI-AZABU—ASIAN FUSION

1-15-4 Nishi-Azabu, Minato-ku. ☎ ***03-5771-5788.*** *Open every day. Major credit cards. Nearest station:* HIROO.
The eponymous Ken'ichiro Okada, a Kansai-based celebrity chef, has developed a style you could term "Pan-Asian fusion food." His primary sources are Japanese, Korean, and Chinese, with extra flourishes from Indochina and even Italy—as if Wolfgang Puck had been born in Kobe, or Ter-

ence Conran in Hong Kong. Some offerings are inventive and inspired, others less so. At heart this is grazing food, born of the izakaya tradition, aimed at the sleek, fashionable crowd for whom the chic-cool interiors form an ideal backdrop against which to chat, pose, flirt, or just to see and be seen. (RS)

Kri Kri * ¥ !

ETHNIC STEW

3-38-12 Yoyogi, Shibuya-ku. ☎ ***03-5388-9376****. Closed Tuesdays. Major cards, except AmEx. Nearest station:* SANGUBASHI.

Nobody knows what "Kri Kri" means or is able to say what kind of a restaurant this is, but nobody cares. Sturdy wooden tables, bric-a-brac picked up on their travels by the Honmas (she serves; he, in a beaded African skullcap, cooks). There's an eclectic collection of CDs (Arab coloraturas, Peruvian tin flutes, jazz from Preservation Hall) and a great ragbag of dishes from all over: moussaka (¥1,100), shish kebab (¥1,100), cheese fondue for two (¥2,500), steak tartar (¥1,800). A little rummaging around in the wine bin can produce a good bottle at a fair price. (RK)

Tableaux ** ¥¥ !!!

GRAND THEATER OF EAST-WEST CUISINE

11-6 Sarugakucho, Shibuya-ku. ☎ ***03-5489-2201****. Open every day. Major credit cards. Nearest station:* DAIKANYAMA.

Tableaux has an attitude—they think all the world's a stage and why not eat well during the show? Tableaux's spacious set is stunning: gold wallpaper, vermilion-and-black parquet floor, moss-green velvet drapes, and gold-framed mirrors ever so artfully cracked. Akira Watanabe, the Milano-trained chef, juxtaposes Italian, French, Southeast Asian, Japanese, and Californian influences not for melodrama but to create an original cuisine, which is consistently appealing and stylishly presented. Tickets for two, including wine, will average around ¥15,000. (MK)

FRENCH

Apicius *** ¥¥¥ !!!

BACKROOM AT THE GARRICK

1-9-4 Yurakucho, Chiyoda-ku. ☎ ***03-3214-1361****. Closed Sundays. Major credit cards. Nearest station:* YURAKUCHO.

Those who are weary of Tokyo French menus that twinkle daintily can find respite here. This old-line establishment has something of the feel of a mahogany-paneled men's club, with a sporting rifle hung behind the bar, a bear rug on the floor, brass door handles shaped like antelopes, and the odd Cezanne and Chagall scattered about for color. Apicius is known for its confident way with venison, teal, partridge, and pheasant, which come from its own spread in Hokkaido. Apicius has its own built-in wine cellar, where slumber rack upon rack of classic Burgundies. Coming here for a meal will cause you to ease the waistcoat buttons and enjoy one or two glasses of vintage port and a Habana cigar at the denouement. Harrumph. (RK)

Argent ** ¥¥ !

CLASSIC BISTRO IN WORKING-CLASS BANLIEU

1-25-12 Nakacho, Meguro-ku. ☎ ***03-3792-4445****. Closed Sundays. Major credit cards. Nearest station:* MEGURO.

Argent is a quiet neighborhood bistro offering superb French food at reasonable prices. You get a hint of the pleasures in store as you enter. Hanging under the

••• next day, as the yen slipped disasterously, said such intervention is inevitable. The Post Office said the weak •••••

eaves are several hams, cured and dressed by the chef himself. Once inside, you will find in the alcove the evening's desserts cooling on a rack—perhaps fresh custards or a strawberry almond tart. Argent is small, with a simple decor of dark wood, floral tablecloths, and fresh flowers. Dinner for two, including wine, will be less than ¥15,000. (MK)

Au Petit Paris ** ¥¥ !!

LITTLE FRENCH JEWEL

6-23-2 Shirogane, Minato-ku. ☎ ***03-3449-7301****. Closed Mondays. Major credit cards, except Masters. Nearest stations:* HIROO, MEGURO.

Au Petit Paris is a tiny temple of gastronomy, so perfect in its details that an unsympathetic observer might call it precious. There are lace curtains at the single little window; there are antique engravings in gilt frames on the walls; the chandeliers have delicate cut-glass globes; the majestic plates are by Villeroy & Boch. People tend to talk in whispers here, as if fearful of breaking a spell. The dinner course of classic dishes, perfectly turned out, is ¥6,000. (RK)

Au Temps Jadis * ¥ !!

CREPES AND CIDER

1-5-4 Jinnan, Shibuya-ku. ☎ ***03-3770-2457****. Closed Wednesdays. No credit cards. Nearest stations:* SHIBUYA, HARAJUKU.

Au Temps Jadis ("Times Past") is a fine place to sit at a wooden table and wash down a lovingly made thin crepe with a bowl of cider. It is in an airy, atmospheric basement with a high ceiling and large French doors, which can be thrown open when the weather is soft so you can sit in a shaded, leafy courtyard if you are in the mood. The basement is an antique space that evokes a quieter, gentler Tokyo, with its tile floor and great wooden library shelves holding bottles of French cider, Belgian beer, mineral water, and jars of homemade fruit compote. There is a fireplace. The ¥2,200 set lunch brings a bowl of cider, a finely constructed little salad, the crepe of the day, a seriously lush dessert, and coffee or herbal tea. (RK)

Aux Bacchanales * ¥ !

SIDEWALK CAFE

1-6 Jingumae, Shibuya-ku. ☎ ***03-5474-0076****. Major credit cards except in cafe. Open every day. Nearest station:* HARAJUKU.

Aux Bacchanales, Tokyo's first real sidewalk cafe, gives out on Meiji Dori and is a premier spot for scouting local talent. It opens at 10 am for cafe au lait, morning croissants, and light omelettes. As the day progresses, the regulars settle in to scan the papers, catch up on their correspondence, and monger a little gossip, while toying with a cup of espresso or tinkering with an aperitif. Aux Bacchanales's restaurant next to the cafe is nothing fancy, but it has just the right touch of French insouciance. You might be greeted at the door with, "But monsieur, if you 'ave no reservation, I regret. . . . But ah, wait a moment. Permit me to give you a reservation right now! In ziz way we 'ave zolve ze problaim." (RK)

Bistro de Bizen * ¥ !

NOSTALGIC FRENCH

4-3 Kanda Surugadai, Chiyoda-ku. ☎ ***03-3295-8538****. Closed only on holidays. Major credit cards. Nearest station:* SHIN-OCHANOMIZU.

Although only fifteen years old, Bistro de Bizen brings to mind those heady days just after the war, when Tokyo was in the process of defining itself, when Shinjuku sported a little jazz place every fifty meters, when coffee houses played the complete symphonies of Beethoven through huge speakers to music lovers who had brought the score, and when the baths enlisted squads of comely ladies in shorts and halter to scrub backs. We have come a long way, but still. . . . Bistro de Bizen's setting would have been deemed forward-looking back then, but now it seems too open to public scrutiny—diners look out on a store selling female apparel, a coffee shop, and commuters scurrying home. It's a little like dining in a dirigible. In spite of these reservations, Bistro de Bizen is a fine little restaurant, a good place to dine after hammering out a synopsis with your publisher or after an afternoon's browsing for books in Jinbocho. (Think of a rendezvous at the little bar of the Yama no Ue Hotel, five minutes away.) The ¥5,500 basic course offers foie gras as one of its two hors d'oeuvres, a gift at that price, of course. (RK)

Bistro de la Cite * ¥¥ !

WELL-WORN BISTRO, A TOKYO LANDMARK

4-2-10 Nishi-Azabu, Minato-ku. ☎ ***03-3406-5475****. Closed Mondays. Credit: AmEx, Diners, Visa. Nearest station:* ROPPONGI.

This is the most ancient of Tokyo's cozy little French holes-in-the-wall, having been established in 1973. The entranceway is three feet wide, so customers entering have to defer to customers leaving by flattening themselves against the wall. The wooden floor is gently warped and creaks. The walls are hung with a profusion of testimonials, engravings, prints, caricatures, menus, and broadsides, which have accumulated, like moss, over the years. There is an antique coatrack for macintoshes and opera capes, and built into the wall is an ancient icebox—the best way to keep fish, of course. Courses from ¥7,500. (RK)

Bistro Sanno ** ¥¥ !

BISTRO OBLIVIOUS OF FASHION

3-5-8 Akasaka, Minato-ku. ☎ ***03-3582-7740****. Closed Sundays. Major credit cards. Nearest station:* AKASAKA MITSUKE.

Named after a nearby shrine, Bistro Sanno is as dependable, as unerring, as spare of non-essentials as a quartz movement. It has been on Tokyo gourmets' little list for years. Akasaka seems too gaudy for such a well-mannered restaurant, which keeps its prices in line by eschewing expensive silverware and crystal, whose plates are utterly plain, and whose wine card lists nothing for anyone seeking notoriety by springing for a famous bottle. While the polished service here proceeds from genuine concern and the standard of preparation is high—several cuts above the grandmotherly fare dished out by the typical Paris bistro—there has been no attempt to gussy the place up to justify a tariff that gives pause. The typical check for two will run ¥25,000, good value for a meal that will stick in the mind for as long as you like. (RK)

Brasserie Bernard * ¥¥ !

WHERE THE HUNGRY FRENCH GO

7-14-3 Roppongi, Minato-ku. ☎ ***03-3405-7877****. Closed Sundays. Major credit cards. Nearest station:* ROPPONGI.

In Tokyo, when you itch for plain, honest

Japan has 20 million or so vending machines, one for every six people. On many Tokyo intersections, there's a bank of vending machines on all four corners, offering things to eat, things to drink, and life's daily necessities. Here you see machines vending hamburgers, popcorn, a pep drink improbably called Pocari Sweat, and condoms for the man on the go, to match his blood type.

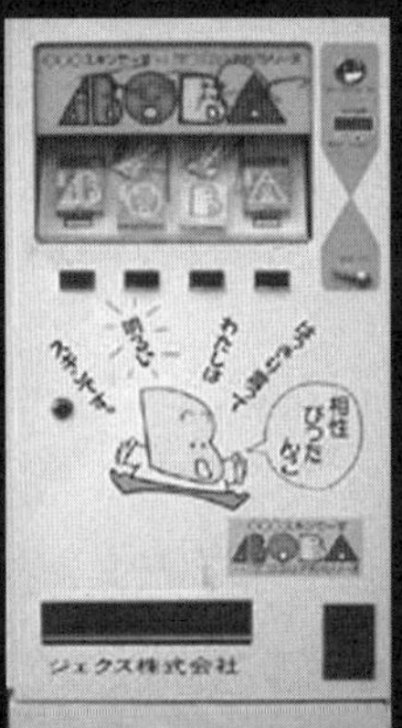

Here is a machine offering canned coffee (iced in summer, hot in winter), a machine dispensing bowls of noodles, and next to it a machine selling hot water for your noodles, and a machine selling just about any battery you could ever want.

bourgeois cooking, Brasserie Bernard is your man. BB's soupe de poisson (always a touchstone) is thick, shot through with essence of lobster, and very satisfying. There's confit de canard, roast pigeon, rabbit stew, and a bull's-eye boudin noir (black-pudding sausage) served with slices of baked apple. BB is where to go for that infusion of filet de boeuf sauce Bordelaise and bottle of Burgundy, which some foreign palates require periodically in order to maintain equilibrium. (RK)

C'est La Vie ** ¥¥ !

CLASSY SUBURB'S LITTLE FRENCH PLACE

2-55-10 Den-en-chofu, Ota-ku. ☎ ***03-3722-4508****. Closed Tuesdays. Major credit cards. Nearest station:* DEN-EN-CHOFU.

Den-en-chofu is Tokyo's poshest suburb. Its residents—well-traveled, experienced eaters—drop in here not only because it's handy but because Monsieur 'Ashimoto is hard working, inventive, and offers remarkable value for money spent. The basic ¥5,500 course brings two hors d'oeuvres, then some finely tuned pasta on a chilled plate, then a fish like amadai cooked al dente with a sauce of white miso and sesame or maybe a free-range chicken smoked on the premises, followed finally by an intricate dessert. The ¥6,500 course includes meat. Afterward, perhaps a walk in the park on the other side of the station. (RK)

Cote d'Or *** ¥¥¥ !!!

TOKYO'S BEST FRENCH RESTAURANT

5-2-18 Mita, Minato-ku. ☎ ***03-3455-5145****. Closed Mondays. Credit: AmEx, Diners, UC, Visa. Nearest station:* TAMACHI.

Chef Saisu and Bernard Pacaud won two Michelin stars for their L'Ambroise in Paris, in a meteoric eighteen months—faster than it had ever been done before. Then Saisu, perhaps a little homesick, returned to Tokyo to open up his Cote d'Or and shoot for the stars here. It's as simple as perfection: the closer you look the finer it seems. Basic dinner course in the summer is ¥15,000, and in winter ¥18,000. People come here to eat alone, not wanting to be distracted by the need to converse with a tablemate. I imagine Cote d'Or would easily be two Michelin stars if it were in France. To me, in Tokyo it's an easy three. (RK)

Crescent ** ¥¥¥ !!

ESCOFFIER WOULD BE AT HOME HERE

1-8-20 Shiba Koen, Minato-ku. ☎ ***03-3436-3211****. Major credit cards. Open every day except Sundays in August. Nearest stations:* DAIMON, ONARIMON.

Crescent, founded in 1947, purveyor of banquets to the Imperial Palace, is a grand old pile. In the main dining room on the second floor, the curtains are heavy brocade, the brass fixtures are polished daily, and the tablecloths are woven with the house emblem. Over an antique Sheraton sideboard is a 1772 engraving of strollers on Pall Mall. Upper class Tokyo dines at Crescent in a mood of well-bred celebration: to welcome Aunt Yoshiko back from her safari or to bid the youngest daughter Godspeed on the eve of her departure for Wellesley. The feeling is of an empire in gentle decline, a useful corrective, you may find, to the feeling of being consumed by the atomic-powered city left behind Crescent's great oak door. I prefer to dine upstairs in one of Crescent's private rooms. The Viscount Room looks out on the massive gate of Zojojo Temple across the street, and an illuminated Tokyo Tower is in the middle distance. (RK)

••••••• begin selling lottery tickets. Prime Minister Obuchi delivered his first speech to the Diet, outlining what the •

La Belle-de-Jour ** ¥¥ !!
FIN DE (PREVIOUS) SIÈCLE
4-37-22 Hakusan, Bunkyo-ku. ☎ ***03-5395-4841****. Closed Sundays. Major credit cards. Nearest station:* SENGOKU.
A perfect belle époque restaurant (mahogany paneling, brass fixtures, Tiffany lamps) in a down-to-earth part of town where one would never expect to find such a careful reconstruction. There are dishes like Roti d'agneau au pistou et les légumes provençals for ¥2,400, and classic Burgundies are drunk from outsized glasses. Afterward, perhaps a stroll through the nearby Rikugien Garden, one of Tokyo's most flamboyant. (RK)

Le Lys dans la Valée* ¥¥¥ !!!**
ESCOFFIER-INSPIRED MENU IN PRIVATE HOUSE
2-7-15 Nishikata, Bunkyo-ku. ☎ ***03-5684-0770****. Closed Sundays and Mondays for lunch. Major credit cards. Nearest stations:* TODAI-MAE, KASUGA.
In a beautiful Meiji-era Japanese house filled with Western antiques, classical French cuisine is presented as though it were a fairy tale. It would be unthinkable that you would ever hear recorded music here. The dining room looks out on a garden with backlit trees. Dishes like medallions of venison in a blueberry and cinnamon sauce are brought to the table under silver bells. The wine cellar is a separate building. Expect to pay ¥50,000 for two. (RK)

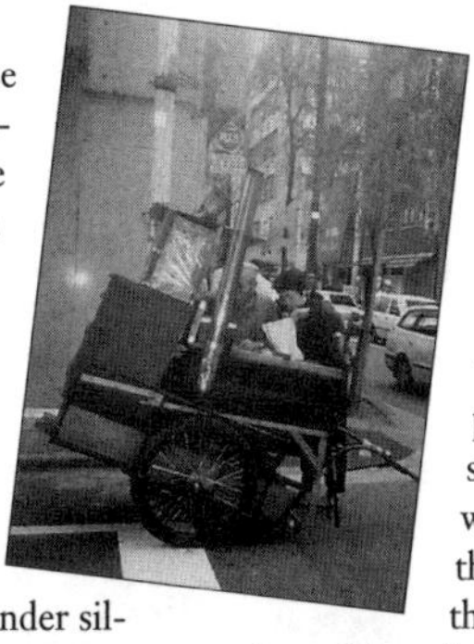

Le Mange-Tout * ¥ !
ATMOSPHERIC STUDENT CAFE
22 Nandomachi, Shinjuku-ku. ☎ ***03-3268-5911****. Closed Sundays. No credit cards. Nearest stations:* KAGURAZAKA, ICHIGAYA.
Gallery posters thumbtacked up on the walls. French soul music from a set of bookcase speakers, overlaid by the grumble of the dumbwaiter bringing dishes down from the tiny kitchen upstairs. The conversation is in Japanese, English, and French about the city, about the great photographers, about living arrangements. There is laughter. The ¥5,800 dinner menu includes an hors d'oeuvre, fish, meat, and dessert. Wine from ¥2,800. One of Tokyo's best cheap French places. (RK)

Le Manoir d'Hastings * ¥¥¥ !**
BEST FRENCH IN GINZA
8-12-15 Ginza, Chuo-ku. ☎ ***03-3248-6776****. Open every day. Major credit cards. Nearest station:* SHINBASHI.
This place is in one of the dimmer Ginza arrondissements, a block from the Dai-Ichi hotel. The facade is worryingly pretentious, and there's that awful name. But apprehension evaporates on being met at the door by the orotund maître d', who is most accommodating and who is backed by an attentive staff. (When my companion expressed a desire to smoke, everyone in the room was asked, discreetly, whether this would be acceptable; on this occasion, it was not.) Chef Igarashi cooks with the flair of Chef Saisu of Cote d'Or, my maximum accolade. Comes first a mere spoonful of Igarashi's blood pudding. Of course this has to be exquisite if it is to work at all. It is. The matter-of-fact menu gives few hints of the Igarashi touch. It is unusual to be offered cassoulet, normally a plodding Norman

•• intended to do to get the economy back on track. (Sample pronouncement: "The most important element in ••••••

pudding of beans and sausages, as a starter, but here it appears in a ramekin of miraculously married materials, including beef marrow and tiny flickers of truffle. The fish soup, served under a porcelain bell, is silky unto decadence. Lunch courses are ¥4,000 and ¥6,000; dinner courses ¥7,500 and ¥12,000. (RK)

Ne Quittez Pas ** ¥¥¥ !!

MOST ORIGINAL FRENCH IN TOKYO

3-15-19 Higashi-Gotanda, Shinagawa-ku. ☎ ***03-3442-2382****. Closed Mondays. Major credit cards. Nearest station:* GOTANDA.

Chef Tanabe is an original. Former member of Japan's Olympic boxing team, he taught himself how to cook. He is always experimenting with dishes like watermelon soup and sardines stuffed with foie gras. Most of his experiments are successful and therefore mind-expanding, but a number are interesting disasters. Still, this is an acceptable price to pay for sitting at what one visiting French chef called "the most creative table in Tokyo." Tanabe's menu, every day newly inscribed in Tanabe's bold hand, details a ¥10,000 three-course dinner, always built around fish. This is an open, airy, immaculate first floor of a town house, surrounded by a garden. The floor is wood, the furniture from the century before. There is a different set of chairs at each table. The competent, unservile staff dress all in white—pleated shirts, sneakers. (RK)

Omiya * ¥¥

MEAT AND POTATOES—AND WINE

2-1-3 Asakusa, Taito-ku. ☎ ***03-3844-0038****. Closed Mondays. No credit cards. Nearest station:* ASAKUSA.

In Asakusa, Tokyo's raucous old downtown with its cobblestones and willow trees, its nostalgia-tinged striptease theaters, and its annual samba festival, you expect the unexpected. But even in Asakusa, Omiya is a wonder. Omiya is a perfect replica—as if caught in amber—of the best French restaurant in, say, Cincinnati, Ohio, vintage 1953. Think of it as a high-class French truckstop and you'll have it. The focus is on beef, dependable no-nonsense classics like boeuf Bourguignonne with Madiera sauce, boeuf Stroganoff, and queue de boeuf, as well as serious sirloins. Omiya's wine list is exceptional, with classic Burgundies running back to 1964. Omiya is noted for its homemade sherberts. (RK)

Passe Simple ** ¥¥ !!!

FRENCH FOR IMPOSSIBLE ROMANTICS

2-12-1 Shirogane, Minato-ku. ☎ ***03-3444-5711****. Closed Sundays and Mondays. No credit cards. Nearest station:* TAKAWADAI.

Passe Simple, in an elegant old Japanese house on a quiet back street, is the restaurant of former French cultural attaché Patrice Julien and his beautiful Japanese wife. He cooks, she greets. The ivy-smothered house is open and airy, with a built-in grove of bamboo, fine old sliding doors, and a welcoming veranda set with cafe tables and chairs. Great attention has been paid to decorative details. There are old Tokyo shop signs on the wall, and placed just so are a venerable medicine cabinet, a windup phonograph with its huge horn, and a baby carriage holding an antique sake-warming apparatus. In the evening, the tables are lit with oil lamps and old paper lanterns. Flowers and greenery abound. The set menu in the evening is ¥6,500. At the end of the meal you are presented with your bill, written by brush. (RK)

Restaurant Beaux Arts ** ¥¥ !!

CHARMING FRENCH OVER A FRAME SHOP

3-17-30 Shimo-Ochiai, Shinjuku-ku. ☎ ***03-3950-1889****. Closed Sundays. Major credit cards. Nearest station:* MEJIRO.

Lettered across the facade of this handsome stucco building: "Sakaiya Art Materials Since 1934." Over this frame shop, up a narrow flight of stairs, in what was formerly an atelier with a lofty ceiling and good light, is the restaurant. The tables are set with immaculate nappery, with long candles in silver holders. This is a French restaurant with something of the quiet perfection of a teahouse. The ¥7,500 course menu, which changes daily, is written by hand on handmade paper and brought to you by a waiter in black tie, wing collar, and long black apron. There's a rambling old public bath across the street, in case you are in the mood for a preprandial dip. (RK)

Shiratori ** ¥¥ !

STEAK AND BURGUNDY

3-2-18 Sakura, Setagaya-ku. ☎ ***03-3706-7158****. Closed Tuesdays and second Mondays. Major credit cards. Nearest station:* KAMI-MACHI.

Shiratori does things its own way, from baking its own crusty loaves to sporting a wine list that's 90 percent Burgundy. It's not concerned to be thought of as "refined"—the pictures on the walls look as though they were brought down from the attic, and the unfinished ceiling, though sprayed peach to match the tablecloths, wouldn't be out of place in an auto body shop. The rugged rug looks made for the floor of a factory, and in a corner by the entrance, decanters and corkscrews clutter the top of a stack of unopened crates of wine from famous domains. It's clear people don't come to Shiratori to congratulate each other on their good taste, but to drink brave wines at good prices while eating heartily. If you are alone, unshaved, and would like to read a magazine during dinner, you can eat at the counter at the bar in the other room. (RK)

Vincent *** ¥¥¥ !!

FRENCH FOR SELF-INDULGING

5-18-23 Roppongi, Minato-ku. ☎ *03-3589-0035. Closed first and third Sundays. Major credit cards. Nearest station:* ROPPONGI.

The feeling here is of unembarrassed good living. The room is as large as a tennis court, with a high ceiling. There are tapestries and original oils and prints on the walls. A huge Art-Deco mirror, a bronze statue of Mercury, silver candelabra, Venetian glass chandeliers and sconces. On the sideboard is a brace of classic cookbooks in French by Chef Etsuo Jo's mentors. Almost everything is served under well-worn silver bells. The lace doilies under the soup plates are real lace. The cheese tray is lush and the dessert cart towering. There seems to be a waiter for every table. (RK).

ITALIAN

Aroma Fresca ** ¥¥ !!

CHIC MILANO TRATTORIA

2-22-10 Ebisu, Shibuya-ku. ☎ ***03-5449-***

••• people.") The speech was generally perceived as blah blah blah, with the *Asahi Shimbun* saying it "lacked vision, •••••

Cheap Italian Places

Carmine
21 Nakamachi, Shinjuku-ku. ☎ 03-3260-5066. Nearest station: KAGURAZAKA.
One of the first efforts to put serious Italian food on a Tokyo table at reasonable cost. To get started, Carmine Cozzolino had to ask neighborhood carpenters and plumbers to lend a hand for all the pasta they could eat. The place was a success from Day One, and now Carmine owns the upscale (and very fine) Carmine Edochiano in Yotsuya and drives around town in a Ferrari. (RK)

De Niro
1-8 Nihonbashi Hakozakicho, Chuo-ku. ☎ 03-3639-1475. Nearest station: SUITENGU-MAE.
De Niro has built its reputation on good seasonal fare and modest tariffs. That's why it's an established favorite with folks from the nearby financial district. (RS)

La Bettola
1-21-2 Ginza, Chuo-ku. ☎ 03-3567-5656. Nearest station: GINZA.
It would be remarkable to find such sophisticated Tuscan cucina at such budget prices anywhere: in Ginza it's unheard-of. Unfortunately you've got to be persistent as well as lucky to book a table. (RS)

Savoy
2-7-10 Kami-Meguro, Meguro-ku. ☎ 03-3714-5160. Nearest station: NAKA-MEGURO.
They do things with poise and style here: intensely aromatic wood-fired pizzas, simple antipasti, and a good range of pastas—all to the accompaniment of '40s swing over the sound system. (RS)

Taverna
2-15-10 Takadanobaba, Shinjuku-ku. ☎ 03-3232-1997. Nearest station: TAKADANOBABA.
Ide-san, the owner-chef of this cozy basement eatery, serves up three-course meals for less than the cost of the antipasti at most Tokyo trattorias. He acquired his skills (and value-for-money ethic) in Rome, where he returns every year for further inspiration. (RS)

4797. *Major credit cards. Closed Sundays. Nearest station:* HIROO.
With only eight tables, Aroma Fresca is not large but feels spacious, with its subtle colors of white and beige and its transparent textures. A glass-walled walk-in wine cellar separates the open kitchen from the dining room. Mr. Tazawa, the manager and self-taught designer, and his friend Mr. Harada, the chef, formerly of Gino's (another of Tokyo's best Italian restaurants), started their restaurant less than a year ago, but Aroma Fresca already has a seasoned confidence and draws a stylish crowd, from fashion models and businessmen to young couples on a first date. The menu is printed up daily and features dishes from throughout Italy, given a sophisticated twist by Mr. Harada. (MK)

Carmine Edochiano ** ¥¥ !!

TUSCAN COOKING IN A LOVELY OLD HOUSE
9-13 Arakicho, Shinjuku-ku. ☎ **03-3225-6767.** *Closed Sundays. No credit cards. Near-*

est station: YOTSUYA SANCHOME.

The house was formerly a ryotei: until a few years ago, the gentry came here to be served delicacies and be entertained by geisha. Now the tatami mats are covered by carpets, except in one stunning Japanese-style room looking out on a floodlit garden, where eight guests can relax on overstuffed cushions at a low table set with sparkling glasses and crisply folded napkins. On the walls, classical and modern Italian prints and drawings are hung just far enough away from Japanese scrolls depicting pine trees in the mist. On a tansu, there is a silver tray with a silver tea service. Several of the old doors, evidence of the genius of Japanese carpentry, have been fitted with fixtures made in Milan, and the little lights set in the ceiling were manufactured in Bologna. In some magical way, it all works beautifully, and it's a treat to an eye seeking refuge from the city's lugubrious stretches of leaden concrete and screeching chromium. The menu is good honest Tuscan dishes lovingly prepared. (RK)

Cucina Hirata *** ¥¥ !!

SOPHISTICATED MODERN ITALIAN

2-13-10 Azabu Juban, Minato-ku. ☎ ***03-3457-0094****. Closed Sundays. Credit: AmEx, Visa, Diners. Nearest station:* ROPPONGI.

This finely tuned place would be a hit in any city in the world—Masaru Hirata is a master of the Italian style, with twists of his own. His faithful clientele, though, tend to be well-heeled, and he caters to them, so it can be very expensive if you get carried away. Just stick to the marvelous platter of antipasti misti for ¥3,000 and one of Hirata's silky pasta for around ¥2,000 and you'll be safe. Or slip into Hirata's wine bar on the floor below for a light snack. (RK)

Elio ** ¥¥ !!

URBANE ITALIAN INN

2-5-2 Kojimachi, Chiyoda-ku. ☎ ***03-3239-6771****. Major credit cards. Closed Sundays. Nearest station:* HANZOMON.

Elio is my favorite Italian restaurant, but Umberto, my favorite Italian waiter there, disagrees with me. "No, no," he says, "Elio is not ristorante. Is like a locanda—how you say—an inn. More comfortable, more relaxed." Elio specializes in food from Calabria and Sicily. Their grilled sea bass is delicately crisped, with the flesh as silky and moist as fish only hours from the sea can be. Served with Tokyo's best roasted potatoes, a few slices of roasted red pepper, and a squeeze of lemon, this dish exemplifies Elio's uncomplicated approach. The mood here is infectiously gregarious. Waiters rush back and forth across the terrazzo floor tending to their guests' needs, as you look longingly at each passing dish wishing you could order it, too. (MK)

Gino ** ¥¥ !

TINY, COZY ITALIAN

3-10-9 Roppongi, Minato-ku. ☎ ***03-3402-2227****. Closed Sundays. Major credit cards. Nearest station:* ROPPONGI.

The kitchen at Gino has the dimensions of a pool table, but because the menu is focused down hard on just five dishes on any particular evening it is not noticeably overextended. The seven small but well-appointed tables are only inches apart, but there is no spareness of decorative bric-a-brac, some of which verges on the high baroque. The wall just inside the entrance is hung with elaborately framed comments and photos, including one of a happy Jimmy and Rosalynn Carter (he had just lost the presidency), who managed on two separate evenings to shake their security

•• was cancelled because of objections by Kyoto residents. This was taken to be a sign that democracy can work in ••••••

escort and flee to Gino, where they knew there would be no room for supernumeraries. (RK)

Il Cantuccio * ¥ !

SIMPLE, FRESH TUSCAN COOKING

2-10-13 Kitazawa, Shibuya-ku. ☎ ***03-3414-0456.*** *Major credit cards. Open every day. Nearest station:* SHIMOKITAZAWA.

Il Cantuccio is a laid-back refuge from the crowds of Shimokitazawa. The floors are oak, the bentwood chairs comfortable, and the tables draped with dark green linen, the color of fresh basil. Warm red brick and cool white stucco walls arch gently into the ceiling. Angelo Cozzolino, brother of the famous Carmine, describes his own Tuscan food as simple and fresh. His gnocchetti, the smaller, more sophisticated sibling of gnocchi, are hard to beat, especially the humble but heavenly potato gnocchetti with a sauce of three cheeses. Highly recommended also are the grilled isaki and the Tacconi freschi: large, square, freshly-made noodles with duck meat sauce. Every Monday Angelo offers a discounted course menu for only ¥3,000. And on Thursdays he prepares a special pizza menu. (MK)

Il Pinolo ** ¥¥ !

RELAXED ITALIAN THAT KNOWS ITS PLACE

1-8-7 Higashi-Azabu, Minato-ku. ☎ ***03-3535-6860.*** *Closed Sundays. Major credit cards. Nearest station:* KAMIYACHO.

Il Pinolo is not at the top rank of Tokyo's Italian restaurants—not on a par with the exquisite and expensive Yamazaki or the highly polished hotel restaurants Attore and Bice—but this is simply because Il Pinolo prefers to be less formal. Unlike more rarefied Italian places, Il Pinolo's kitchen is open to view, the whole place can be opened up to the world outside, its little wine cellar off the back room is not much more elaborate than a dedicated wine drinker would have at home, and there seem to be several patterns of silverware in circulation. But the imaginative menu—not a single pasta, pomodoro, parmesan cliché is in evidence—is lovingly prepared. Truth to tell, we never ate so well in Tuscany. Next time I go, I plan to sit at the counter and have a bowl of Tuscan bean soup lubricated by a swirl of olive oil on top, a plate of the cold tagliolini with caviar sauce, and a glass of wine, which will come to less than ¥4,000. (RK)

La Pineta ** ¥¥ !

FIRST-CLASS NEIGHBORHOOD ITALIAN

3-4-2 Yagumo, Meguro-ku. ☎ ***03-372-7098.*** *Closed Sundays. Credit: AmEx, Masters, Visa, JCB. Nearest station:* TORITSU DAIGAKU.

You sit down to a table (one of just four) whose napkins must have been folded by someone trained in the art of flower arranging. There will be set before you an amusement of toasted thin bread smeared with pate, with two kinds of olives and a couple of caperberries on the side. On the

•••••••Japan. After Mita Industrial Company, a major manufacturer of office equipment, went belly up it was found that

table are homemade breadsticks and a dish of unsalted butter. Everything has been carefully bought: erotic tomatoes, sweet lemons, sparkling fresh fish, baby lamb for the lamb-lovers. The sauces are constructed with balsamic vinegar from Modena; the garnishes of peas and beans are first parboiled, then sauteed in butter. The espresso is pungent, and there is cheese. Fingerbowls come with a sprig of mint. (RK)

Oseille * ¥ !

NEIGHBORHOOD TRATTORIA

5-50-1 Jingumae, Shibuya-ku. ☎ ***03-3409-9454****. Closed Sundays. No credit cards. Nearest station:* OMOTESANDO.

Just around the corner from Kinokuniya, one of the world's classiest supermarkets, this little place, recently spruced up with a new upstairs dining room, still maintains a high level of presentation because the residents of Aoyama insist on it. The two chefs prepare everything from scratch, turning out textbook examples of trattoria classics. Tripe ¥1,800. Penne al gorgonzola ¥1,400. A trustworthy collection of wines. (RK)

Riva degli Etruschi ** ¥¥ !!!

IN A TUSCAN VILLA

3-15-13 Minami-Aoyama, Minato-ku. ☎ ***03-3470-7473****. Closed Mondays. Major credit cards. Nearest station:* OMOTESANDO.

Riva is for people who are at home in Italy and with the Italian table. Seconds after you sit down, your glass is filled with prosecco, unbidden. The Italian owner's wife brought back with her the fixtures, the furniture, the linen, the custom Ginori plates big enough to hold a boar's head, and the red terra-cotta tiles. There are 130 wines on the wine list, broken down by region, and 30 grappe. The two young Italian chefs make their own bread and rolls and their own fantasy desserts, and may cause to be put on the table at the end of the meal unlabeled frosted bottles of their own wildly complex liqueurs. The menu embraces pheasant, pigeon, rabbit, and venison. Upstairs, under the old roof of the house demolished to make way for this smart new building, is a tavern where meat is roasted on a spit and wine is by the glass. (RK)

Yamazaki ** ¥¥¥ !!

CLASSY MODERN ITALIAN

1-22-8 Minami-Aoyama, Minato-ku. ☎ ***03-3479-4657****. Closed Sundays. Major credit cards. Nearest station:* NOGIZAKA.

Because their homemade breadsticks are beautiful and their antipasti intricate (baby frogs' legs in an herbal tempura, for instance) you know right away that the details are going to be right. The long, off-white wall is hung with just two engravings, both interesting, and the restroom is a restrained lark. Madame Yamazaki is a woman of uncommon taste. She has trained a number of chefs who have gone on to make their mark at places more in the public eye. Yamazaki itself is listed in none of the local restaurant guides—I suspect because Madame Yamazaki forbids it.

She founded her place fifteen years ago, well before Italian became the rage, and she had the confidence to tag it with a name that doesn't even hint at what she is doing. That's class. (RK)

KOREAN

Matsuya ** ¥

FIERY KOREAN STEWS

1-1-17 Okubo, Shinjuku-ku. ☎ ***03-3200-5733****. Open every day. No credit cards. Nearest station:* SHINJUKU.

Matsuya serves simple, hearty country cooking for Tokyo's sizable Korean population. You leave your shoes outside the door and sit on colorful square cushions on a hard linoleum floor, as if at a rural hostelry in Cholla province. The walls are cluttered with jars of medicinal liquor and signs in hangul. Some people come to drink, others to snack; almost everyone finishes with kamjatang, a rugged hotpot of pork backbones cooked at your table in a fiery, stick-to-your-ribs chili sauce. Stomach-warming and sinus-opening, this is Korea's secret weapon against the chill gales of winter. (RS)

MEXICAN

Fonda de la Madrugada ** ¥¥ !!!

A MEXICAN HACIENDA DEEP IN SHIBUYA

2-33-12 Jingumae, Shibuya-ku. ☎ ***03-5410-6288****. Open every day. Major credit cards. Nearest station:* MEIJIJINGUMAE.

Descend the winding stairway, and you'll find yourself in the courtyard of a hacienda. No expense has been spared on this subterfuge: everything from the wrought ironwork and mounted toro's head to the strolling, serenading mariachis has been imported from Mexico. This is not a glorified tacos-and-refried-beans joint nor is the provender Tex-Mex. The restaurant prides itself on serving authentic Mexican cuisine. Try the jalapenos rellenos, deep-fried chiles stuffed with cream cheese; or the marinated cactus, with its pleasant okra-like sliminess; or the arroz con mariscos, a risotto with garlic, scallops, crab, squid, and two kinds of shrimp; or the enchiladas, three chicken enchiladas each with its own sauce: green tomato, red tomato, and mole—and you'll know they are serious about their food. Somehow all the decor gimcrackery here works. Maybe it's a trick of the lighting or the cool courtyard atmosphere, but if you lean back and look up at the five-meter-high ceiling, you expect to see stars. (MK)

NATURAL FOOD

Natural Harmony * ¥ !

CREATIVE ORGANIC DISHES IN A RUSTIC SETTING

Jingumae 3-38-12, Shibuya-ku. ☎ ***03-3405-8393****. Open every day. No credit cards. Nearest stations:* HARAJUKU, GAIENMAE.

Natural Harmony hand-lettered up its name on the window four years ago, moved in the endearingly rough tables and chairs made for a country cottage, painted

•••••••percent over the year before—a sure sign of a depressed economy. The Japan High School Baseball Federation

Best Wine Bars

Aux Amis des Vins
2-5-6 Ginza, Chuo-ku. ☎ *03-3567-4120. Nearest station:* GINZA.
The ground-floor restaurant puts on airs, but the "brasserie" upstairs is as relaxed and convivial as an izakaya. Both draw from the same formidable cellar, assembled by oenophile owner Hiruto Maruyama. (RS)

The Rocks
1-26-22 Shoto, Shibuya-ku. ☎ *03-3469-0125. Nearest station:* SHIBUYA.
If you've been to Sydney, you'll recognize the name. And you won't be disappointed by the extensive array of wines from Down Under at this small, spare, but very welcoming wine bar. (RS)

Requiem
Hirano Building 1F, 6-24-6 Jingumae, Shibuya-ku. ☎ *03-5485-1426. Nearest station:* HARAJUKU.
This intimate little place offers over 300 wines, with a daily choice of twelve by the glass. The chef turns out Italian food with imagination, and the dinner course for ¥3,600 is a bargain. Hope you like Mozart, though—it's the only music played. (MK)

Scala Dei
1-3-9 Azabu Juban, Minato-ku. ☎ *03-5575-6667. Nearest station:* AZABU JUBAN.
Forget the pompous interior and the strange Euro-Asian cuisine; nowhere in town has a better selection of wines by the glass. (RS)

Vino Hirata
Endo Building 2F, 2-13-10 Azabu Juban, Minato-ku. Nearest station: ROPPONGI.
A leisurely space with minimalist decor, Vino Hirata is a gem, with everything from the sparkle of the glasses to the polished service just right. The wine list proffers a select, but extensive, collection of mostly Italian reds and whites, with twenty-four wines by the glass. The food is impeccable. Reservations essential. (MK)

"Living in Harmony with Nature is a Blessing for Us and Mother Earth" across the white-washed back wall, and chalked up the day's menu on the blackboard. Since then it has established itself as one of Tokyo's best natural-food establishments and a favorite of advocates of pure living. David Bowie drops by when he's in town. The best dishes are the flaky onion pizza, risotto, huge piled-up salads, and soups, which, however, may need a pinch of salt. You'll find, I think, that a glass of sake works well with this food, particularly in the colder months. (RK)

SPANISH

La Playa ** ¥¥ !

TAPAS, PAELLA, AND HEROIC WINES FROM RIOJA
2-14-4 Shibuya, Shibuya-ku. ☎ ***03-5469-9505****. Closed Sundays. Major credit cards. Nearest station:* SHIBUYA.
For ¥8,500 (not including wine, of course), after a welcoming glass of Osborne fino and a dish of the lusty olives that Toru Kodama (better known as Carlos), smuggles in, come the tapas, which make up the first half of the meal. Things like tortilla pie, beautiful jamon serrado, which Carlos makes himself and ages for six or

Where to Buy

FINNISH BREAD

The Finns make some of the most characterful bread in the world—Tumma Setuuri, Peruna Lingu, Hapan Lingu, Happan Ruis Vuoka, and Happamaton Miniputti, for example. You can find them all at Kinokuniya in Aoyama.

seven years, Iberian blue-veined goat cheese served with Carlos's own marmelade, his silky gazpacho, his exceedingly tender calamares en su tinta, white asparagus from Shikoku with anchovy sauce, sardines served with orange slices, shrimp in an avocado, stewed tripe, and his subtle albondigas meatballs. After the tapas, you can go a number of ways: roasts or grills or perhaps a saffron-drenched paella. Throughout, you can drink magnificently from a constantly evolving wine list chock-full of Rioja Reservas, Gran Reservas, and Reservas Especiales, ten to twenty years old. Our last meal at La Playa ended with a glass of 1834 Madiera. (RK)

Maika ** ¥ !

CHARMING NEIGHBORHOOD SPANISH

5-28-15 Okusawa, Setagaya-ku. ☎ ***03-3722-2037****. Closed Tuesdays and third Wednesdays. Major cards, except AmEx. Nearest station:* JIYUGAOKA.

This is a giving little place. Everywhere there is evidence of loving attention to detail. Large Spanish pots are arranged just so on a shelf over the door, there is a profusion of dried flowers in an earthenware crock, and in a nook there's an antique engraving in an old frame. A miniature crystal chandelier hangs over one of the four tables. The excellent Sangria (¥3,500 the decanter) is a concoction of red wine, apples, oranges, lemons, gin, sherry, brandy, and a tinge of sugar—no shortcuts. The garlic toast is moistened with olive oil and sprinkled with paprika for color. Big iwashi sardines are first fried in olive oil, then marinated for four days to intensify the flavor and soften the bones. In the salmon canapés, the salmon is deep-chilled to provide a contrast to the melted cheese. Every dish is arranged with flair and presented on Spanish pottery plates and platters that reflect the same honest rural genius as Japanese pottery. (RK)

Poco a Poco * ¥ !

TAPAS BAR

3-1-24 Jingumae, Shibuya-ku. ☎ ***03-3404-5888****. Closed Saturdays and Sundays. No credit cards. Nearest station:* OMOTESANDO.

Señor Nishino, who carries himself like a hidalgo, loves to talk about Spanish food, wine, and history to people who drop in to Poco a Poco for tapas and a glass of amontillado. He also has tucked away a remarkable collection of fine Spanish vintages, which he might be persuaded to uncork for significantly less than you would pay elsewhere. It is pleasant to wind down an evening here with a banana flambéed in an antique rum, followed by a cup of espresso, then perhaps a snifter of fine Spanish brandy and a Habana cigar. (RK).

SWEDISH

Lilla Dalarna * ¥ !

SWEDISH HOLE-IN-THE-WALL

5-9-19 Roppongi, Minato-ku. ☎ ***03-3478-4690****. Closed Sundays. Major credit cards. Nearest station:* ROPPONGI.

Lila Dalarna is the smallest restaurant in Roppongi. A few decorative Scandinavian

•••••••game. Sony took off the market a best-selling video camera with a "night shot" function which, if used during the •

objects are self-consciously scattered about, and the little tables are set with simple white plates and plain tableware, less Scandinavian modern than Scandinavian farmhouse. The hearty, bearded gourmets from the Sweden Center just up the street usually start with thick Kosta Boda beakers of icy aquavit. There's a small and charmingly idiosyncratic selection of wine, but for the most part this is beer food. Homemade rye rolls. (RK)

Stockholm * ¥¥ !!

VIKING

6-11-9 Roppongi, Minato-ku. ☎ ***03-3403-9046****. Open every day. Major credit cards. Nearest station:* ROPPONGI.

You descend into a brick-walled, candle-lit bomb shelter in the basement of the Swedish Center, to be waved to black leather Barcelona chairs in the bar. You are not encouraged to go straight in, possibly because the restaurant has learned that customers ushered immediately into the presence of the smorgasbord table are susceptible to heart spasms. Use the time to settle in with a barely viscous aquavit (¥800), poured reverently from a bottle encased in a block of ice. In time, you will be led to your table and seated in chairs that look borrowed from a Viking parliament. Your fellow diners are likely to be a convivial cluster of Japanese businessmen at one of the tables for eight, and couples who have known each other long enough to visit the smorgasbord table separately. (Stockholm is no prelude to seduction. It is, first of all, unremittingly square, with all the cutaway flash of a middle-American men's club, corny arrangements of Broadway tunes tinkling in the background. Besides, you will be too full.) Lunch is ¥3,500; dinner ¥5,800. (RK)

THAI

Keawjai * ¥ !

WHERE THE THAI EMBASSY GOES FOR LUNCH

2-14-9 Kami-Osaki, Shinagawa-ku. ☎ ***03-5420-7727****. Open every day. Credit: JCB, UC, Masters, Visa. Nearest station:* MEGURO.

Marble floors and tabletops. Paper napkins folded architecturally. A little brass vase of real carnations. Filigree fingerbowls. You can choose to sit in one of the wrap-around banquettes, all carved wood and shimmering fabric, for an illusion of intimacy. Young Japanese bloods in double-breasted suits bring their young ladies here for an elaborate feast (set menus at ¥2,000, ¥4,500, or ¥7,500—the last being enough for two) washed down with a ¥3,000 bottle of sparkling wine called Cafe de Paris, brought to the table with great dignity in a tin ice bucket by a waiter in white tunic with brass buttons. If they dimmed the lights, they could charge half again as much. (RK)

Rice Terrace ** ¥¥ !

BANGKOK FLAVORS, BISTRO AMBIANCE

2-7-9 Nishi-Azabu, Minato-ku. ☎ ***03-3498-6271****. Closed Sundays and holidays. Major credit cards. Nearest station:* HIROO.

The ultimate Thai bistro, both intimate and sophisticated, with wonderful food to support the relaxed surroundings. The menu ranges from intricately carved veg-

•• day, revealed people's underwear under their clothes. Five people fell ill after eating Italian olives, prompting jars ••••••

etable hors d'oeuvres served with spicy, tangy shrimp sauce through the authentically piquant yam salads to the delectable rice dishes of its name. Chili levels are generally kept in check, in deference to local sensitivities, but all the ingredients and seasonings are full-on authentic. The second-floor dining room feels rather cramped, so aim to reserve one of the downstairs tables. (RS)

TURKISH

Bosphorus Hasan * ¥ !

TURKISH COMFORT FOOD

3-6-11 Shinjuku, Shinjuku-ku. ☎ ***03-3354-7947****. Open every day. Major credit cards. Nearest station:* SHINJUKU SANCHOME.

Hasan Ulan cooks the most satisfying Turkish food east of Lake Van. Service is unhurried, so just order a plate of his meze appetizers with a bottle of Efes beer (or a half of raki) and settle in for the evening. The dolmades are succulent, as is the spicy lamb-meat, Sis Kofte. There is no belly dancing. To reach the dining room, tastefully decorated with arabesque tiles, you must pass the open kitchen: this allows Hasan to greet his customers as they arrive and depart, and also gives you a chance to inspect the day's specials—exactly as at any self-respecting eatery in Anatolia. (RS)

VIETNAMESE

Dusit Thien Duong ** ¥¥ !!!

TOKYO'S BEST VIETNAMESE, NO QUESTION

Century Tower Building, 2-2-9 Hongo, Bunkyo-ku. ☎ ***03-5800-0099****. Closed Sundays. Major credit cards. Nearest station:* OCHANOMIZU.

Dusit Thien Duong, with branches in Bangkok and Bern, inhabits a dramatic space designed by a British architect, with a high, clear-glass ceiling curving like a breaking tidal wave. The oshibori are scented. The chopsticks are silver. The wine list comes in a Hermes leather binder. The wicker chairs are very comfortable, and there is enough space for a Vietnamese lady in flowing black aodai to wheel a large serving cart up so she can arrange your dishes at table. There is a splendid nine-course set dinner menu for ¥7,000. (RK)

Huong Viet * ¥

BARGAIN-BASEMENT SAIGON STREET FOOD

5-3-3 Higashi-Nakano, Nakano-ku. ☎ ***03-3364-6304****. Closed Mondays. No credit cards. Nearest station:* HIGASHI-NAKANO.

When Tokyo's cognoscenti crave Vietnamese food without the authentic edges smoothed off, Huong Viet is where they always end up. The decor is sparse but cheerful: bottles of rice liquor, the obligatory map, a full-scale mural of Vung Tau beach. The young chefs (all recently arrived in Japan) serve up all the standards: spring rolls (both fresh goi cuon or crispy cha gio), multifarious dumplings, and noodles (notably the fiery Hue-style bun bo). Don't miss the cha chung, best described as an Indochinese version of a Spanish omelette. Wash it all down with Saigon 333 beer. (RS)

••••••of Italian olives to be taken off supermarket shelves all over the country. A man and a woman, both confined to

IZAKAYA: SAKE BARS

compiled by Robbie Swinnerton and Tony Trollope

LIKE the pubs of Ireland and the brown cafes of Amsterdam, the izakaya (little, very Japanese places to drink sake and nibble little things from a menu that has been refined over decades) are national treasures. Sometimes you hear them called "nomiya." In the service of cultural research, Robbie Swinnerton and Tony Trollope have spent a considerable amount of time zeroing in on Tokyo's most characterful izakaya, such as the following.

Akaoni *** ¥¥ !

TOP OF EVERYBODY'S LIST

2-15-3 Sangenjaya, Setagaya-ku. Closed Sundays and holidays. No credit cards. ☎ ***03-3410-9918****. Nearest station:* SANGENJAYA.

People who make lists invariably put Akaoni right at the top of the list of their favorite izakaya in Tokyo. Akaoni ("Red Devil") looks nondescript, both inside and out, but they take their sake very seriously. There are over

Tokyo Q Symbology

*	very good
**	one of the best of its type in Tokyo
***	one of the best of its type anywhere
¥	less than ¥5,000
¥¥	between ¥5,000 and ¥10,000
¥¥¥	over ¥10,000
!	interesting decor
!!	startling decor
!!!	wow!

100 listed, none of them inferior. So, too, with the food: the master is considered a doyen among izakaya chefs. Call ahead to reserve, and they will ask if you want the mixed sashimi plate: the correct answer is "yes." The water, served in recycled sake bottles, is brought into town from a noted spa. All pungent brands of tobacco are banned. (RS)

Aki *** ¥ !!!

LITERARY PUB

2-24-7 Kichijoji Honcho, Musashino-shi. ☎ ***0422-21-1353****. Closed Sundays and holidays. No credit cards. Nearest station:* KICHIJOJI.

Aki is for adults. People feel comfortable dropping in alone after work and reading a novel while they wind down. The food is inventive and the sakes are first class, as the owner, a gentle soul who dresses in the comfortable homewear of 100 years ago, is a former sake maker. New arrivals are introduced to everyone, and when someone leaves, everyone says goodbye. (TT)

Aun * ¥¥ !

FULL-BLOODED SAKE IN ANEMIC SETTING

3-10-6 Akasaka, Minato-ku. Closed Sundays and holidays. Major credit cards. ☎ ***03-3584-3331****. Nearest station:* AKASAKA-MITSUKE.

Aun is squeaky-clean, almost feminine in its fastidiousness. But it houses arguably the most impressive range of hard-to-find premium sake in all of Akasaka, an area not unknown for its love of the fruit of the grain. After the nation's top sake brewers hold their annual tasting at the nearby Prince Hotel, this is where they like to adjourn. They can relax among kindred spirits here, and they know Aun's kitchen crew prepares excellent creative side dishes. (RS)

Banshu ** ¥ !!

ANTIQUES AND REPARTEE

4-31-12 Ogikubo, Suginami-ku. ☎ ***03-3393-0856****. Closed Sundays, sometimes second Saturdays. No credit cards. Nearest station:* OGIKUBO.

Matsui-san and his wife built this little shack forty years ago with their bare hands. Over the years they filled it with antique bowls and dishes and other curiosities, all of which are for sale. No need to order: Matsui-san will improvise your meal right in front of you while keeping up a constant stream of banter. As such, he provides an excellent introduction to the delights of Japanese home cooking. Amateur cooks take the place over once a month to show each other the dishes they've been working on. The house sake is Tesshu, a delicious junmaishu. (TT)

Daizen * ¥ !!

HALF SMART NEW YORK BAR, HALF IZAKAYA

1-10-7 Gotanda, Shinagawa-ku. Open every day. Major credit cards. ☎ ***03-3473-8739***.

Izakaya Etiquette

The culture of the izakaya has its own prescribed etiquette, no matter how rough-and-ready (or how expensive and exclusive) the premises. On entering, make clear how many people you are (an upraised finger or three does the trick). When seated at either counter or table, you will be served a miniature otoshi (taster dish) and asked what you want to drink: most people start with a small beer to slake the thirst. When you're ready for sake, the primary question is always: hot (say "atsukan") or cold (ask for "rei-shu")? You will also want to order a side dish or two. This is not only to balance the alcohol intake: food actually enhances appreciation of the drink. Sashimi fish and sake are a marriage made in heaven. Sometimes only snacks are available; in other places you can construct a full meal. But as a rule of thumb, izakaya with premium sake usually serve food of similar quality. (RS)

Nearest station: GOTANDA.
A big place, five times the size of a typical izakaya, with wide wooden floorboards, brick walls, old beams with joinery notch cuts, and house plates and platters handcrafted to designs that have been around for a couple hundred years. Dishes run ¥400 to ¥900, and there are a couple dozen sakes for ¥700 to ¥1,100 a glass, poured so generously the lacquer masu in which the glass nestles is half-filled, too. (TT)

Enoki ** ¥ !

TINY, LIVELY, FULL OF FUN
Nonbei Yokocho, Shibuya-ku. Closed Sundays and holidays. No credit cards. ☎ ***03-3407-5320***. *Nearest station:* SHIBUYA.

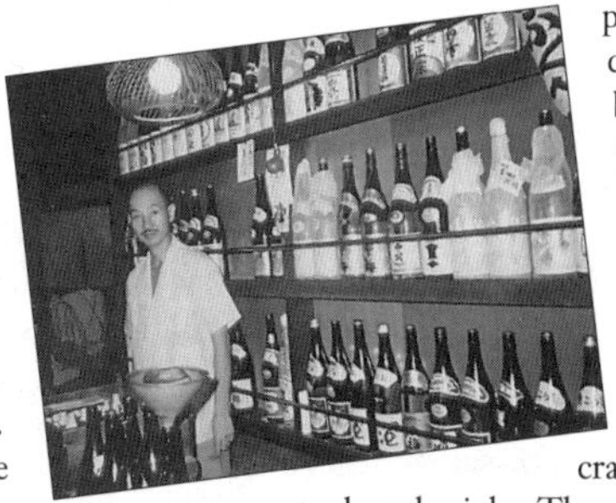

Chizuru Doi, a natural hostess, presides over Enoki, which is six stools, a counter, and a hotplate. Doi-san is an innovative cook and likes to play around with Spanish and Italian recipes. Wine is on hand, and she keeps two grades of sake, the better of which you won't get if you don't ask for it. Nonbei Yokocho ("Drunkards' Alley"), a quintessential Tokyo experience, is just across the street from the Hachiko Exit of Shibuya Station. Ask at the police box. (TT)

Fukube * ¥¥

AS IF THE WAR HAD NEVER HAPPENED
1-4-5 Yaesu, Chuo-ku. ☎ ***03-3271-6065***. *Closed Sundays and holidays. No credit cards. Nearest station:* TOKYO.
A drinking hole of the old school—indeed one of a fast-disappearing breed. You can tell it's been in business for sixty years: a patina this thick does not come overnight. Fukube is shabby and as well-worn as the coats of the salarymen who cram in here after work each night. The air can be blue with cigarette smoke. But they keep excellent sake on tap, especially their winter taruzake, drawn straight from the cedar barrel.

••• pushed their wheelchairs off a cliff into Lake Biwa. The Japan Communist Party, in a major policy reversal, •••••

They also do a remarkable job of replicating the kind of simple, no-frills snacks that people in 1939 used to nibble on while they drank. (RS)

Hachimaki Okada ** ¥¥¥ !!

POWER IZAKAYA

3-7-21 Ginza, Chuo-ku. ☎ ***03-3561-0357****. Closed Sundays and holidays. Major credit cards. Nearest station:* GINZA.

Tucked into an alley behind Matsuya, this little jewel of an izakaya caters to company presidents and like establishment figures who, just because they have been promoted to elevated positions in the hierarchy, have never gotten out of the habit of downing a few flasks of sake after work. Last time we were there, the Minister of Transportation was in attendance, his big black limousine idling outside. More expensive than most izakaya, you'll get out for around ¥12,000. But very fine, with waitresses in kimono. (TT)

Hananko * ¥¥ !

COMFORTABLE, DISCREET, HIGH QUALITY

1-16-9 Toranomon, Minato-ku. Closed weekends and holidays. Major credit cards. ☎ ***03-3502-8705****. Nearest station:* TORANOMON.

Hananko is the yin to next-door Hanataro's yang. It draws a mature crowd, which is surprising since the two brothers who run it are both still the right side of their mid-forties. Igarashi the younger acts as floor manager, dispensing drinks and advice on the menu. His elder brother stands behind the cedarwood counter, assembling side dishes of remarkable quality and fielding the banter from the middle-management types, who take over the low upholstered counter chairs. The food is all free of chemical additives. The best sake is served in crystal glasses with flecks of gold leaf. (RS)

Hanataro ** ¥¥ !!

FRIENDLY, CLASSY, MID-BUDGET

1-16-9 Toranomon, Minato-ku. Closed weekends and holidays. Major credit cards. ☎ ***03-3591-8970****. Nearest station:* TORANOMON.

Hanataro is intimate but never overly informal. It's quiet and relaxed—much like the people who frequent it. The serving staff are welcoming to strangers (whether local or foreign) and helpful with suggestions (they have several set-price sake-tasting courses). There are seats for twenty along three sides of the counter: invariably they are full. Since Hanataro is one of Tokyo's essential izakaya experiences, reservations are advised. (RS)

Ichimon * ¥¥ !!

YE OLDE WORLDE SAKE SHOPPE

3-12-6 Asakusa, Taito-ku. Closed Sundays and holidays. Major credit cards. ☎ ***03-3875-6800****. Nearest station:* IRIYA.

A massive sake barrel sits on the roof; the interior is an antique-lover's dream; the staff wear traditional indigo tunics; the mama-san dispenses homilies with her sake from behind a rustic counter. In short, it's virtually a pastiche of what a traditional izakaya ought to look like. But since the food and drink are excellent and the mood is timeless, Ichimon remains the best spot in Asakusa to take your rest after a day among temples and bazaars. (RS)

Iseto * ¥¥ !!!**

TRADITION REIGNS

4-2 Kagurazaka, Shinjuku-ku. Closed Sundays and holidays. No credit cards. ☎ ***03-3260-6763****. Nearest station:* IIDABASHI.

Mr. Kaname Kamayama oversees the proceedings at Iseto (which looks like the set of an NHK period drama) with enormous dignity. He never stirs from his position

••••••announced it would recognize the legitimacy of the Emperor. It was revealed that the Seikan tunnel between •

behind the long wooden counter, where he warms the only sake, Hakutsuru, over charcoal until it is skin temperature. He will not serve it to you cold. If someone is talking too loudly he will admonish them, so everyone talks in whispers. Last order at 8:40 pm precisely. Will you believe me if I tell you Iseto is a delightful place? (TT)

Kagiya *** ¥ !!!

CLASSIC PROLETARIAN TAISHO NOMIYA

1-24-5 Negishi, Taito-ku. Closed weekends and holidays. No credit cards. ☎ ***03-3872-2227****. Nearest station:* UGUISUDANI.

Kagiya is twenty-five years old, going on a century. It's situated in a perfectly preserved old wooden house that's like a time warp back to a far less complicated era. Shimizu-san, the silent, austere master, smokes short Hope cigarettes and tucks a fan down the back of his apron. He discourages female customers who arrive solo or in groups, though he tolerates couples who observe appropriate decorum. The literary ghosts of Tanizaki and Kafu surely look down from above with total approbation. (RS)

Kanda Komachi ** ¥¥ !

A CUT ABOVE THE REST IN KANDA

3-22-2 Uchi-Kanda, Chiyoda-ku. Closed Sundays and holidays. No credit cards. ☎ ***03-3254-0025****. Nearest station:* KANDA.

Though it looks little different from the thousand other drinking holes in the warren of alleys around Kanda Station, Kanda Komachi is special. The proprietress, Matsumori-san, is a true connoisseur of good sake. She lists six dozen varieties on her menu (not counting new arrivals and seasonal specials), three of which she selects each day as an introductory "set menu." Matsumori-san, who always wears kimono, is equally particular about the food she serves. Be sure to try the crispy deep-fried conger eel spines: you will never want to eat potato chips again. (RS)

A Brief Sake Glossary

We are living in a veritable golden age for sake. Overall demand for Japan's traditional tipple may be dropping, but never before have so many brewers produced such a rich variety of high-grade sake. And the good news is they're increasingly available at specialist Tokyo izakaya. A little knowledge of the terminology and lore can illuminate the entire izakaya experience.

Atsukan: the term for sake that is served hot.

Choko: small, thimble-sized sake cups.

Daiginjo-shu: sake brewed with only the inner 40 percent of the rice grain; tends to exhibit rich, fruity, flowery flavors; can be very pricey.

Ginjo-shu: sake brewed from rice polished to 50 percent of its original size; the purer carbohydrate results in more subtle flavors.

Jizake: "locally brewed sake." This is no guarantee of quality, but small companies often make more individualistic brews.

Junmai-shu: "pure rice sake" containing no extra brewing alcohol or other additives.

Koji: the cultivated rice at the core of the fermentation process.

Ko-shu: "aged sake." Most sake should be drunk young, but some are aged for years, concentrating the flavors and developing a rich, yellow color.

Masu: square cedarwood boxes often used for drinking cold sake.

Nigori-zake: thick, unfiltered sake the color of milk.

Nihonshu: "Japanese sake," a general term often heard instead of just plain "sake"

Rei-shu: "cold sake." Most high quality sake is only drunk chilled or at room temperature, since heating destroys the subtleties.

Tokkuri: flasks (usually 180 ml or 360 ml) for serving hot sake.

Komahachi * ¥

PLEBEIAN AND PROUD OF IT

5-12-4 Shiba, Minato-ku. Closed Sundays and holidays. Major credit cards. ☎ ***03-3456-1271***. *Nearest station:* TAMACHI.

Komachi is bright, inexpensive, and hugely popular. What elevates it above the lowest common denominator are the creative variations on standard pub grub, the handful of quality sake bottles in the fridge, and the friendly ministrations of its ever-cheerful master. And since half the staff are mainland Chinese, no one has any hang-ups over language/culture/behavior differences. (RS)

Kuriya ** ¥¥ !

CLASSY HOLE-IN-THE-WALL

1-14-15 Gotanda, Shinagawa-ku. Closed Sundays and holidays. No credit cards. ☎ ***03-3441-4944***. *Nearest station:* GOTANDA.

Kagiya is barely bigger than the proverbial broom closet, yet it sparkles like a miniature gem among the dingy back streets of Gotanda. The master, Kotake-san, used to run a bookstore; judging from his taste in nihonshu, he must have sold only modern classics. His constantly rotating cellar is always first-rate, and so are the snacks. Kuriya seats eight people in comfort, ten in elbow-nudging proximity. The regulars are accepting of new faces, as long as they know their place. (RS)

Little Okinawa ** ¥¥ !

THE SPIRIT OF THE SOUTHERN ISLES

8-7-10 Ginza, Chuo-ku. Open every day. Major credit cards. ☎ ***03-3572-2930****. Nearest station:* SHINBASHI.

Little Okinawa is the most cheerful, welcoming place in Tokyo to explore the drink and the food of the Ryukyu Islands. The ingredients and cooking techniques may be closer to Chinese than Japanese, but the way they're knocked back is 100 percent homegrown. The beverage of choice is the Okinawan firewater known as awamori, premium aged varieties of which are dispensed from ceramic pots arrayed on the counter next to the plates of fermented tofu, bitter melon, and simmered pork belly. (RS)

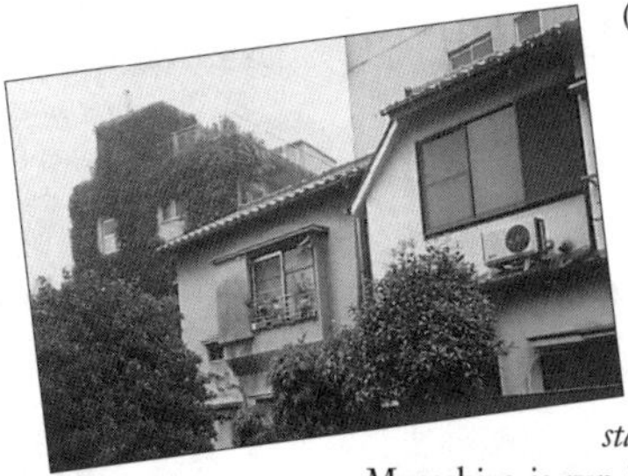

Mokichi ** ¥¥ !

RURAL FARE, BOISTEROUS COMPANY

Kagurazaka, Shinjuku-ku. ☎ ***03-3267-5307****. Closed Sundays and holidays. No credit cards. Nearest station:* KAGURAZAKA.

Mokichi is a celebration of mountainous Yamagata Prefecture. To give Tokyoites a taste of backwoods informality, they cram everyone in around large communal wooden tables, which can trigger the kind of neighborly bonhomie and sharing of drinks now all too rare at sophisticated urban izakaya. Yamagata produces some of the best sake in Japan: start your exploration with the eponymous Mokichi or premium Dewazakura. (RS)

Musashiya ** ¥ !

GENTLE OLD ROOM IN YOKOHAMA

3-133 Nogemachi, Yokohama. Closed weekends. No credit cards. ☎ ***045-231-0646****. Nearest station:* SAKURAGICHO.

Musashiya is run by the two white-haired sisters Kimura, daughters of the founder. Most people sit around two antique wooden tables, but there is a pleasant little tatami area out back that gives out on a little grove of bamboo. The rafters are hung with the calligraphy and sketches of cus-

Where to Buy

KALEIDOSCOPES

Mukashi-kan, 2-13-8 Azabu Juban, Minato-ku.

The kaleidoscopes come from around the world. The most expensive is Captain Nemo's Kaleidowave from the U.S. at ¥3 million. It operates like a submarine periscope and gives the dazzled viewer control over most parameters, so it is like making your own stained glass window. We prefer the more delicate Fenix and Palor, also from the U.S., for a piffling ¥60,000. There must be a couple hundred different kaleidoscopes available here, and stopping in after having indulged yourself at Monsen, Tokyo's best yakitoriya, next door, is something of a visual dessert.

••• able to agree on a late-night, last-ditch plan to put Japan's banking system back in order is that the plan is •••••

tomers. House rules: nobody can enter after 8:00 pm and you are limited to three beers or three glasses of sake. No need to order: ¥1,900 brings a set of eight little dishes, which you will find set off your sake perfectly. (TT)

Nezu no Jinpachi ** ¥ !!

PICTURESQUE OLD HOUSE IN OLD DOWNTOWN

2-26-4 Nezu, Bunkyo-ku. ☎ ***03-5685-1389****. Closed Sundays, open holidays. No credit cards. Nearest station:* NEZU.

This is most everyone's dream of what an Old Tokyo drinking place must have been like, and Nezu is a wonderful Old Tokyo neighborhood. There's a low wooden counter with seven stools and three lacquer tables on tatami in the back, and it couldn't be more cozy. The owner, a lovely, modest lady, had to promise not to change anything before she was allowed to take the place over from the former proprietor. Try to get there as close to 6:00 pm as you can. (TT)

Sakanatei * ¥ !

CASUAL PUB WITH RULES

2-23-15 Dogenzaka, Shibuya-ku. ☎ ***03-3780-1313****. Closed Sundays and holidays. Major credit cards. Nearest station:* SHIBUYA.

Takatsuka-san and his wife like things simple: home-cooked food, early-period Beatles music, and quality sake (but not necessarily in that order). Their pub is a relaxed operation, but the sign on the door makes their philosophy clear: if you don't want to drink sake then don't come in. Cell phones are banned, and the seats closest to the open kitchen are no-smoking. The vegetables are organically grown whenever possible. (RS)

Uo-san * ¥

THE ROUGH-AND-READY SOUL OF SHITAMACHI

1-5-4 Tomioka, Koto-ku. ☎ ***03-3641-8071****. Closed Sundays and holidays. No credit cards. Nearest station:* MONZEN-NAKACHO.

Uo-san is coarse, cramped, noisy, and always crowded with salt of the shitamachi earth. Generic sake, as dispensed by the ever-cheerful mama-san from giant ceramic flagons, costs a mere ¥150. Few of the numerous fish dishes are over ¥500. This is the rough-hewn, blue collar, low-city Tokyo experience: not the place to bring a first date, or perhaps for women drinking on their own. (RS)

Sakebayashi Hanna ** ¥¥ !!

SAKE, STRAIGHT NO CHASER

1-25-2 Minami-Aoyama, Minato-ku. ☎ ***03-3405-9888****. Closed weekends and holidays. No credit cards. Nearest station:* NOGIZAKA.

This is a purist's pub: a counter and four small tables; wooden walls adorned with vintage sake labels; cool jazz on the stereo; and, apart from one microbrewed beer, nothing to drink except nihonshu. It is run single-handedly by a friendly woman of a certain age, who dispenses tasty side dishes from platters set out along the bar. The sake costs either ¥1,000 or ¥1,500, depending on the grade; the food is all ¥500 per dish. Why can't other places keep things so relaxed and straightforward? (RS)

Where to Buy

PAPER LANTERNS

Washikobo, near Nishi-Azabu crossing on Roppongi Dori. ☎ *03-3405-1841.* The shop will sell you a paper lantern for ¥1,500. They also carry kites and fans and all manner of things made of Japanese paper (washi).

Sake-no-ana *** ¥¥ !!

A MECCA FOR PREMIUM SAKE

Ginza Rangetsu, 3-5-8 Ginza, Chuo-ku. ☎ ***03-3567-1133****. Open every day. Major credit cards. Nearest station:* GINZA.

The magnums arrayed on the shelves behind the stylish curving counter represent just a fraction of what Sake-no-ana has to offer. There are over 100 different nihonshu varieties listed, from standard high-street brands to special brews rarely available to the public. Despite the care and quality (and the ritzy address), it's not undemocratic or unreasonably pricey—making it an ideal place to embark on a voyage of discovery around the extensive geography of Japan's liquid national treasures. (RS)

Sasashu ** ¥ !

SAKE AND CHARCOAL-GRILLED SALMON

2-2-6 Ikebukuro, Suginami-ku. ☎ ***03-3393-0856****. Closed Sundays and holidays. No credit cards. Nearest station:* IKEBUKURO.

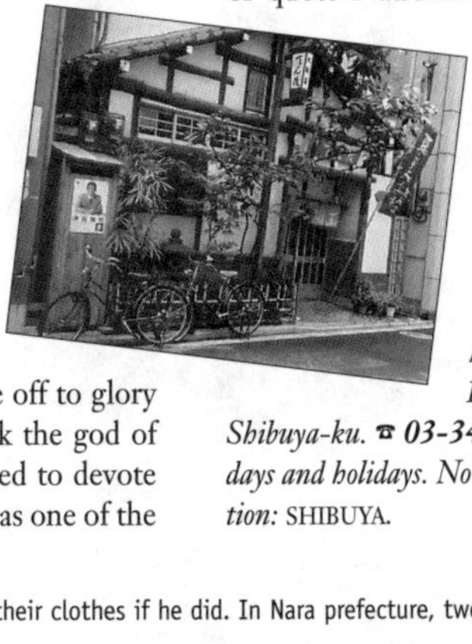

Mr. Sasagawa was in the Kamikaze Corps about to take off to glory when the war ended. To thank the god of war for sparing him, he decided to devote his life to good sake. Sasashu has one of the best selections in the city, as he sends his own truck out to pick up small-production sake that otherwise would never make it to Tokyo. *The New York Times* has called Sasashu "the Carnegie Hall of Nihonshu." The Japan Nihonshu Association meets here. Call ahead and ask to sit in the back with Sasagawa-san as he grills salmon steaks and wild duck sent to him by his ex-Kamikaze buddies up north. Every once in a while, at the end of a particularly congenial evening, he'll stage a contest to see who can brush the most vivid kanji on the shoji screens. (TT)

Suzuden ** ¥

BLUE-COLLAR VALUES, WHITE-COLLAR CROWD

1-2-15 Toranomon, Minato-ku. Closed weekends and holidays. ☎ ***03-3580-1944****. No credit cards. Nearest station:* TORANOMON.

For such a scruffy, crowded joint, Suzuden inspires fierce loyalty from its legion of fans. That's because nowhere else in Tokyo purveys top-grade sake with such utter lack of pretension—or at such charitable prices. The men (and the occasional woman) who cram the long, low tables are an aware bunch, mostly middle-class business types and bureaucrats, who talk trade statistics or quote Natsume Soseki. Isono-san, the gentle, white-haired master, is a sake buff who leads study tours to noted breweries around the country. (RS)

Tamakyu *¥¥

A DEFIANT SURVIVOR

1-30-4 Shibuya, Shibuya-ku. ☎ ***03-3461-4803****. Closed Sundays and holidays. No credit cards. Nearest station:* SHIBUYA.

••• female students if they would take off their clothes if he did. In Nara prefecture, two pigs, a weasel, a badger, a •••••

Ken Straiton likes to wander Tokyo's back alleys. He's got an eye for the city—its signs and storefronts and delivery bicycles and tiny one-bench parks. People with an eye for Tokyo like Ken's find wonders in the patina of an old ivy-covered mailbox and the fanciful design of a manhole cover.

アトリエ
わよう
NYU

FANTASIA
CHARITY SHOW

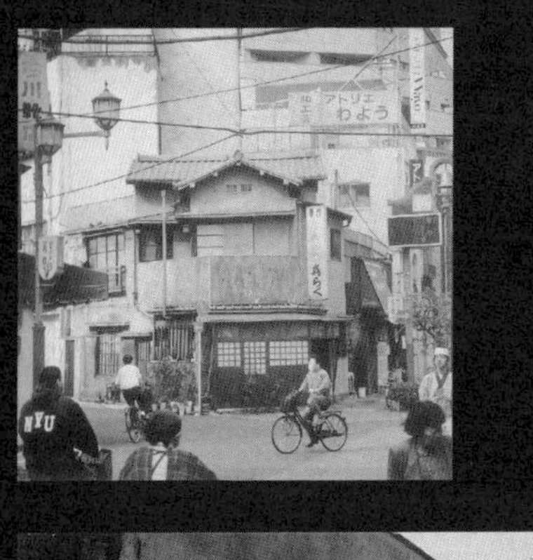

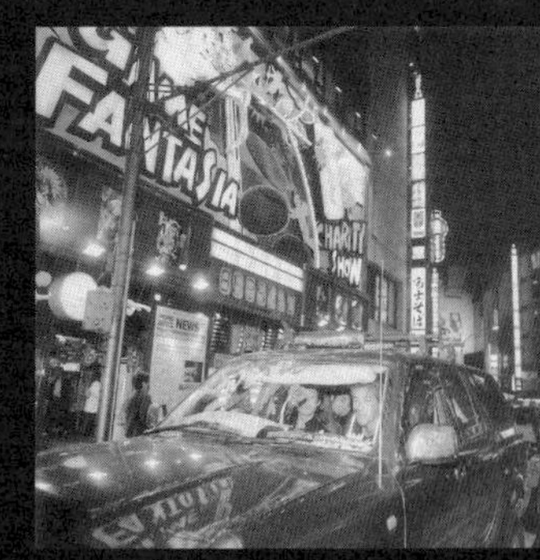

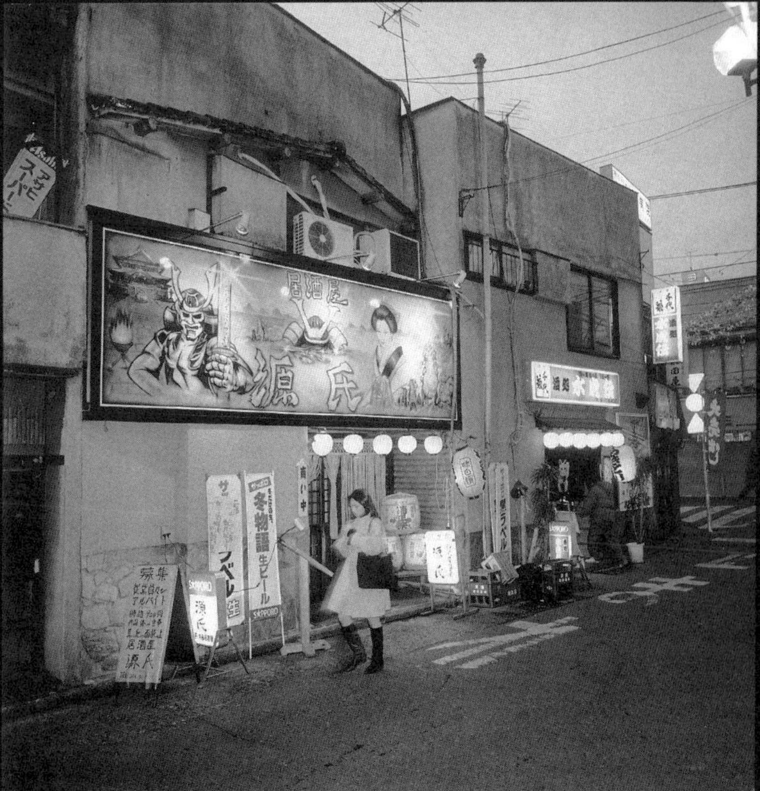
居酒屋
源氏
冬物語
生ビール
SAPPORO
商い中
黒ラベル
募集
居酒屋
源氏

Tamakyu's place in the izakaya Hall of Fame rests solely on its bloody-mindedness. Having defied the developers, this drafty wooden shack (with its one tree) is surrounded on three sides by a trendy multi-story mall. Although the sake is generic, the welcome less than overwhelming, and the prices (all unlisted) rather high, Tamakyu is always busy. This is what all of Shibuya used to look like. To hoist a drink here is to thumb your nose at the trashy modern consumerism that has now taken over the area. (RS)

Tarafuku Manma ** ¥ !!

A COUNTRY INN WITH JAZZ

1-14-3 Nishi-Azabu, Minato-ku. ☎ ***03-3479-0532****. Closed first to the fifth of every month. No credit cards. Nearest station:* ROPPONGI.

Run by a happy Buddha, this is a place for hearty eaters. Sixty items on the menu, with many displayed on outsized platters on the counter, so just point to what strikes your fancy. Most everything goes for ¥500 to ¥1,000, and you can ask for a half portion ("han-nin mae"). Try a bowl of the nikujaga beef stew with potatoes and onions for ¥800, and finish with the excellent ochazuke. The plates and platters are by some of Japan's best country potters. (TT)

Yorozuya Matsukaze ** ¥¥ !

RUSTIC TAVERN

1-24-5 Nishi-Ikebukuro, Toshima-ku. ☎ ***03-3986-1047****. Closed Sundays and holidays. Major credit cards. Nearest station:* IKEBUKURO.

Amid the sleazy attractions of Ikebukuro's gaudy nightlife district, Yorozuya Matsukaze is a haven of rustic calm. The weatherbeaten wooden frontage bespeaks a venerable roadside tavern in some rural backwater. The walls are of darkened timber and beaten mud. People drop in to quaff sake out of simple glass tumblers. They come to chat, perhaps to flirt, maybe even to lubricate their libidos, but never to get falling-down drunk. It's not that kind of place. (RS)

Yuuan * ¥¥¥ !!!**

POST-MILLENNIAL IZAKAYA

Shinjuku Park Tower B1, 3-7-1 Nishi-Shinjuku, Shinjuku-ku. ☎ ***03-5322-6427****. Open every day. Major credit cards. Nearest station:* SHINJUKU.

Yuuan redefines the izakaya for the twenty-first century. It's a hushed space of elemental textures: burnished metal screens, gleaming stone, rural mud, and lanterns of paper and bamboo. You sit at a counter formed from a single massive cedar trunk, slit in half laterally. The sake is served chilled in crystal glasses. The seasonal tidbits are homely but inventive like the surroundings—a perfect blend of kaiseki, farmhouse, and contemporary urban sensibilities. (RS)

•••••••lemur and a tiger cub caused havoc when someone let them out of their cages on an expressway. The head of •

SENTO: PUBLIC BATHS

by Alex Urbansky

THERE are about 1,500 sento (public baths) in Tokyo. Their modest ¥385 entrance fee is made possible because the city government chips in.

To many people, a visit to the local sento at least once a week is as necessary to their well being as an occasional memorable meal or a periodic sexual release. And like those life-fulfilling experiences, the feeling after a good soak is that this one always seems to have been the best yet.

To live in Tokyo and never partake of a sento shows a pitiful unawareness of life's essential sweetness.

Daikoku-yu

32-6 Senju Kotobukicho, Adachi-ku. ☎ ***03-3881-3001.*** *Closed Tuesdays. Nearest station: fifteen-minute walk from* KITA SENJU *on the Hibiya Line.*

Daikoku-yu, way out in the northern suburbs, is a classic bathhouse well known to bath connoisseurs. It is, as they say, worth the trip. Daikoku-yu is built in miyazukuri style—in the elaborate style of a royal residence, with a facade like an Indian temple. There is as much space inside as a Roman bath. The lobby looks like a suburban living room, with a big TV, a doll collection, and comics scattered about. There is a tatami area with low tables for après-bath beer and snacks, while looking out on a deep, mossy pool filled with carp. Daikoku-yu's roomy sauna costs ¥400, which is a little expensive for this working-class neighborhood, so it is never crowded. The sauna is well lit and harbors no TV or loudspeakers, which is fine, as sweating in a sauna is essentially a solitary activity. The excellent roofed rotenburo (outdoor bath) is in a garden. Bathers sit in the garden or lounge half-in and half-out of the bath while contemplating the trees and the stone lantern. The pace here is roughly that of a drowsy turtle. For those in need of stimulus, there is a serious jet bath. There is a wonderful old ceiling in the changing area, and there are three serious massage chairs in the lobby. *For beer, exit the bath and turn right. There's a little sake shop seventy-five meters down the street on the right.*

Ginza-yu

1-12-2 Ginza, Chuo-ku. ☎ ***03-3561-2550.*** *Closed Sundays. Nearest station:* GINZA.

Ginza-yu is far removed from any romantic vision you might have of a traditional Japanese bath. It is simply a cleaning machine. This is where Ginza hostesses come in the early evening before work to steel themselves for a long night of forced smiles or after work to heave a sigh of relief. On the men's side, Ginza characters settle in, mumbling to themselves and studiously not acknowledging the presence of fellow bathers. They sink into the glorious hot water, emerging three long minutes later the color of boiled lobsters. There are no separate showers, no sauna, no cold pool, no rotenburo, no massage chair, no TV, no drink dispenser. There is just a pool of very hot water, with a jacuzzi section for the thrill seekers, and a wonderful mosaic of Ginza Yonchome on the back wall of the men's section and a mosaic of a summertime fireworks display in the women's. In the immaculate changing room there is only a weighing machine, a fire extinguisher, and a rack of fans and copies of the latest issue of the Chuo Ward newsletter. The bath is just a few blocks down the street from the Seiyo hotel, one of Tokyo's three most elegant small hotels, whose bar makes a fine martini. Ginza-yu is in a bleak location, next to an overhead expressway. Very noir, don't you know.

Konparu-yu

8-7-5 Ginza, Chuo-ku. ☎ ***03-3571-5469.*** *Open every day. Nearest station:* GINZA.

The bath called Konparu-yu is just three doors down from Kyubei, probably Tokyo's most famous sushi place, where the

Where to Buy

TENUGUI

Kunoya, at 6-9-8 Ginza, Chuo-ku. ☎ 03-3571-2546.

Tenugui are cotton towels used at the bath or to wipe the sweat from your brow. Kunoya has shelves full of beautifully printed tenugui beginning at ¥800 each. They make fine gifts.

top course, served by ladies in kimono on dishes by Rosanjin, a famous potter and restaurateur of the 1930s, goes for ¥30,000. A particular delight, then, is first to indulge in this sushi (let's say ¥70,000 in all for two), followed by a leisurely bath next door (¥770 for two). Konparu-yu is pre-Meiji and is still run by the same family, the matriarch of which sits on tatami at her old-fashioned wooden bandai, which lets her keep an eye on both the men's and women's bath. There is a magnificent kamidana, Shinto altar, up in the rafters. Like all old sento, it's very simple. There's no sauna, no stand-up showers, and no rotenburo. There are only two baths for each sex, one labeled "atatakai" (hot) and one labeled "nurui" (tepid). Believe me, nurui is hot enough. Submersion in very hot water is wonderfully relaxing, of course, because your muscles cannot resist the heat and after about ten seconds just collapse. You can buy everything you need to take a bath here: soap, towel, your choice of a razor for ¥30, ¥60, or ¥90, and tiny vials of shampoo and rinse, as well as a change of underwear and a new pair of socks. You'll be given a plastic bag to take your wet towel home with you after the bath. I'm thinking that only in Tokyo would you find a public bathhouse on one of the city's most expensive and glamorous streets.

Oh Edo Higashiyama Onsen

3-1-6 Higashiyama, Meguro-ku. ☎ ***03-3712-0356****. Closed third Tuesdays. Nearest station:* IKEJIRI-OHASHI *on the Shin-Tamagawa Line.*

The Grand Edo onsen is a spanking new four-story building in the Higashiyama district of Ikejiri-ohashi in Meguro Ward. Its traditional whitewash and blue-tile roofing over the entrance give an old-fashioned flavor to the brand-new look. But Oh Edo's variety of baths plus whirlpool, steam, sauna, and massage are definitely for the modern-day bather. A big draw is the medicinal benefit of soaking in real onsen waters. The owners say it was pure luck that they found a hot spring on their building site, and that old, familiar sulphuric smell of onsen water permeates Oh Edo. You can float in the "longevity" waters in the outdoor rotenburo or indoors in the "peace" bath, lounge in the "resting" and "walking" pools, or fight back in the "let the water hit you" jet bath. Or you can try all of them and leave with your skin looking like a prune. The rotenburo is tepid but warm enough to make the crisp outside air pleasurable. A forty-five-minute massage is available for ¥4,000; a fifty-minute acupuncture session is ¥5,000; and

Where to Buy

PIPES AND SMOKING GEAR

Ginza Kikusui, 6-9-6 Ginza, Chuo-ku. This shop stocks mostly Danish, French, and English pipes, including blustering Meerschaums and General Douglas MacArthur corncobs (¥500). Classical Japanese pipes (kiseru) made of silver and gold cost a mere ¥250,000 but are not, for some reason, big sellers.

you can rent a private room with an elaborate airline-type reclining chair for an hour-long after-bath snooze for ¥400. There is a restaurant that is more like a cafeteria, and a rather smoky lounge with TV blaring. The drawback to modernization here is the ubiquitous fluorescent lighting, tasteless modular furniture, synthetic carpeting over cement floors, and the overall feeling that you're in a school gym. Gone is the feel and smell of warm, wet cedar. Smoking is permitted anywhere except in the bath itself, so don't be surprised to see a few bodies drying off for a quick smoke and then heading back for another dip. All reasons why the place is loved by its regulars. Weekends are crowded. A visit mid-day, mid-week might be a little more peaceful.

Monozono Yokujo

3-4-8 Nakano, Nakano-ku. ☎ ***03-3382-4446****. Closed Wednesdays. Nearest station:* NAKANO *on the Chuo Line.*

Monozono-yu devotees are hooked on that delicious frisson that comes when you go directly from a sauna into a cold bath. The sauna here (for ¥300 extra) is a blistering 105 degrees, and the cold bath, positioned right in the middle of the proceedings, is big enough for six and—most unusual—is roiled by jacuzzi, which of course makes it seem even colder. After four or five cold-bath/sauna cycles, you won't be able to tell the difference between hot and cold, and your nerves will have the tensile strength of bubblegum. Bathers recover in a teahouse overlooking a garden with a carp pool. Some bring novels. There is a gentle electric bath and a bath that directs an underwater blast of water at each side, while you rest your head on a pipe chilled by cold water running through it—most refreshing. There's also a mist sauna with unobtrusive jungle sounds and, really as an afterthought, a small rotenburo. The water is from a deep well. *The beer is just around the corner. Nakano is a lively neighborhood with lots going on.*

Kamata Onsen

2-23-2 Kamata Honcho, Ota-ku. ☎ ***03-3732-1126****. Closed Wednesdays. Nearest station:* KAMATA *on the Keihin Tohoku Line.*

In Kamata, there are a number of onsen (baths which get their hot water straight from the bowels of the earth), but too many of them are finding custom slipping away as the city develops around them, cutting them off by driving highways through the old neighborhoods. Kamata Onsen is in the middle of a changing community, too, but it prospers because it gives everyone what they want. It opens at ten o'clock in the morning (most baths open

••••••percent, the lowest in 40 years. The Ministry of International Trade and Industry showed off its new robot that •

around three o'clock in the afternoon), its sauna is free, and there's after-bath karaoke in the public room on the second floor. In addition, you can bring in a video to watch with friends in a little six-seat theater, and the massage chair is state-of-the-art. There is a cold bath just large enough for one person, and two non-onsen baths, one a denkiburo (an "electric bath" with a weak current running through it, for mild titillation). There are two onsen baths, both with digital gauges showing the temperature of the water to a tenth of a degree centigrade. The onsen water, here as black as gunpowder tea, leaves the skin soft. Kamata Onsen is a no-nonsense bath, and there is no rotenburo for the local sybarites. *There's beer out the door to the left and around the corner, and just up the road there's a fine little sushi shop that does a roaring business delivering right to the bath.*

Fuji no Yu

2-1-16 Tamagawadai, Setagaya-ku. ☎ ***03-3700-3920****. Closed any day with "2" as the last digit—2, 12, 22—except when this day falls on Sunday, in which case the bath will be closed on the following Monday. Nearest station: eight-minute walk from* YOGA *on the Shin-Tamagawa Line.*

Most Tokyo public baths are scrambling to appeal to a new generation which takes it for granted that even people living in a one-room apartment have their own private, knees-up bath. Thus the recent proliferation of electric baths, jacuzzi, hi-tech massage chairs, and high-definition TV sets in the lobby. Fuji no Yu is on a different wavelength. The family who run Fuji no Yu think bathing should be an aesthetic experience. The lobby is dark and cool, with an arrangement of flowers in a pottery vase and perhaps some lingering incense.

Just Yu

The "yu" in the name of many baths is the Japanese character for "hot water." In Japanese, "mizu" (drinking water) and "yu" (hot water) are written with different kanji, suggesting the special place of divine hot water in the Japanese scheme of things.

The only furniture is a well-worn wooden bench. No TV. The tiles on the floor are handcrafted. The lobby could be a place for drinking tea. In the changing room, there is no plastic, no chromium, no showers, even. A couple of pastoral oil paintings and an old *Asahi Shimbun* tin sign that must have been there for fifty years hang on the white plaster walls. The clock, fan, and scale are antiques, as is the hair dryer, which costs ¥20 to use. Paper lanterns dilute the fluorescent lighting. The sauna (for men only: it used to be for women only, but female customers were few so sides were switched) is of Scandinavian dimensions. It and the cold bath and a tiled expanse where odalisques could lounge occupy a separate room. There's no electric bath and only a halfhearted massage bath. The centerpiece is a classic bath of hinoki (Japanese cypress), which miraculously softens the water; it is like bathing in silk. From high over the bath, water drips, plunk–plunk–plunk, into the bath—Fuji no Yu's only music. There are old-fashioned wooden washing stools and buckets. Fuji no Yu is not particularly easy to find. You will probably have to ask someone the way. They will point you with some pride to their neighborhood bath. "Naka naka ii," they will probably tell you. "A pretty nice place."

•• can walk up and down stairs. As U.S. unemployment hit 4.3 percent, the lowest in 28 years, unemployment in •••••

Where to Buy

FISHING GEAR

Sansui, 3-16-2 Shibuya, Shibuya-ku.
☎ 03-3400-3698.

The razor-cut precision of a fine fly, the pristine perfection of a bamboo rod, and the intricate gearing of a fly-fishing reel appeal to something deep down in the Japanese soul. (In fact, Shimano, Japan's foremost manufacturer of reels, also makes beautiful bicycle gearing systems.) Everything the fly-fisherman could imagine wanting, including bumper stickers making public his passion, are available at Sansui, a two-minute stroll from Shibuya Station. They've been in business since 1902.

Nozawalando

4-4-11 Nozawa, Setagaya-ku. ☎ ***03-3421-7171****. Closed Mondays. Nearest station: twelve-minute walk from* KOMAZAWA-DAIGAKU *on the Shin-Tamagawa Line.*

In 1977 the city changed its mind about rotenburo (outside baths). Rural rotenburo where the sexes bathed together always had a delicious whiff of licentiousness, but in Tokyo the sexes bathed separately, so the city assembly thought: Why not? Nozawalando embraced the opportunity and installed Tokyo's first legal rotenburo. It is the work of a skilled stonemason: shallow and large enough for you to lie prone as the breeze fans your face and the water, heated to not much more than skin temperature, laps your weary frame. In this world of temptations, it is the closest you will ever get to returning to the womb, and when you drag yourself out of the bath there is room to relax stretched out on the duckboards next to the bath with your towel under your head as a pillow. There is a vigorous electric bath and a herbal bath of unsubtle scent. Inside bathers can slide open glass doors to the outside, turning the whole bathhouse into a rotenburo. There are fluffy rugs in the sauna, which cost an additional ¥350, and there is considerably more room at the hot-and-cold faucets than is usual, for vigorous scrubbing sessions. In the carpeted and chandeliered lobby, ramune, old-fashioned lemonade, goes for ¥100 the classic bottle, and there are two first-class massage chairs (five minutes for ¥100), for which there may be people waiting. *There is beer just across the street.*

Soshigaya Onsen

3-36-21 Soshigaya, Setagaya-ku. ☎ ***03-3483-2611****. Open every day. Nearest station: five-minute walk from* SOSHIGAYA OKURA *on the Odakyu Line.*

Soshigaya Onsen is a natural hot spring, its soft water heated naturally by Mother Earth. Located in one of Tokyo's posher wards, it is several cuts above your standard public bath. Actually, Soshigaya Onsen has more in common with the lush marble-and-chromium private baths for weary executives, which cost ten times as much. Soshigaya Onsen's basic fee—thanks to an indulgent city government that looks on public baths the way the Roman senate looked on bread and circuses—is just ¥385. For ¥1,000, though, you get access to a whole range of bathing experiences, beginning with a roomy sauna with a five-minute sand glass at each place. There's also a twenty-five-meter swimming pool lined with palm trees; a waterfall to stand under to let water pound down on your head and shoulders; a steam-mist sauna that is like being in a tropical rain forest; a place where you can have needle sprays tickle you from 360 degrees; a herbal pool with silky pitch-black water; and a wonderful invention called the "Acqua Massage," which directs water under the pressure of a fire hose at you underwater—it's like sitting in a water wind tunnel. Your ¥1,000 will also get you a bag containing a large fluffy towel and a small tenugui towel, a small bar of soap, and vials of shampoo and rinse. Also for sale are clean underwear and a range of toiletries. In the carpeted lobby, racks hold the latest newspapers and magazines for all tastes, from comics to literary commentary. The walls are hung with modern prints and paintings, and there is a daily arrangement of seasonal flowers. For ¥4,000 you can have a forty-minute massage. *Beer is available on the corner. For some well-crafted sushi, turn right at the corner onto the main street, and a short stroll will bring you to Kinzushi (☎ 03-3483-1413).*

Yu Paaku Nobilando ("Hot-water Park Stretching Land")

1-24-1 Soshigaya, Setagaya-ku. ***☎ 03-3484-6768.*** *Closed Mondays. Nearest station:* SOSHIGAYA OKURA *on the Odakyu Line.*

This being Tokyo, where square meters on the ground are the fundamental measurement of wealth, the owners of this new bath decided to cut back on space devoted to the lobby (which as a result has all the charm of a bus-terminal waiting room, with the bath's mechanically refined, if a shade brutal, massage chair consigned to a dim corner like a scolded child). The lockers in the changing room are so close together there is a constant stream of apologies from bathers trying to keep out of each other's way. The idea was to give priority to the baths themselves, which as a result are wondrously spacious. The main bath is the size of a quarter of a tennis court, and in it is an electric-bath corner and several variations on the jacuzzi, where water under considerable pressure buffets you from the front or the side, or tickles the bottoms of your feet while you lean back, your neck resting on a chromium pipe chilled by the cold water coursing through it. Without leaving the main bath, you can enter a glass-walled room the size of a closet, punch a button on the wall, and have a stream of warm water from above pound your shoulders and the top of your head. The main bath is large enough for you to find a quiet, un-jacuzzied corner to sink into—a rare luxury. The cold bath (at 16.6 degrees centigrade, according to a digital gauge) is large enough for a half-dozen cold-water disciplinarians at a time, and the outdoor rotenburo, the finishing touch, is the largest of any Tokyo sento so far inspected. The rotenburo is suffused with fragrant herbs, which color the water. There are eighteen herbal variations, which change every other day. Some bathers call ahead to find out the herb of the day. This is a new Swedish-modern bath, with clean architectural lines, expansive tiling, and the lighting of an emergency room—a somewhat startling contrast to the somber lighting and mossy dark-wood world of the traditional bath. *Beer is available on the premises for ¥250 a can.*

Gokuraku-yu

2-40-14 Kamiogi, Suginami-ku. ☎ ***03-5382-4569****. Closed Tuesdays. Nearest station:* OGIKUBO *on the Chuo Line.*

Gokuraku-yu must be Tokyo's smallest sento. The men's and women's baths are each only the size of an ordinary Tokyo 2 LDK apartment (that is to say, two rooms: a living room and a dining area with kitchen). There are just fourteen scrubbing stations. But there's a tiny sauna, two small and shallow tiled jacuzzi, and a denkiburo (electric bath) that can jolt. Fluorescent lights throughout and an immaculate varnished floor give the place a clinical air. There's no room for a lobby, so bathers tend to linger après-bath in the changing room, where the TV is gabbling away, and there are cold drinks from a vending machine. Grim. Management is aware that things are not ideal at Gokuraku-yu, so they provide an hour's free time at the karaoke bar on the second floor. It's like a Ginza hostess bar, with velvet couches, a piano, a bar, and a tiny stage. It's a fine thing to see people from the neighborhood enjoying themselves here after the bath: barefoot, drinking beer from the vending machine in the corner (¥200 cheap), and warbling away about lost love in a Kyushu fishing village. A bath at Gokuraku-yu is a perfect preliminary for a dinner of soba at famous Homura-an nearby.

Hakusan-yu

2-28-11 Narita-Higashi, Suginami-ku. ☎ ***03-3311-2396****. Closed Mondays. Nearest station: fifteen-minute walk from either* MINAMI-ASAGAYA *or* SHIN-KOENJI *on the Marunouchi Line.*

Hakusan-yu is a real neighborhood bath: the dignified old gentleman on his way in asks you if it's crowded; the girl at the desk clips the toenails of an old lady who finds it difficult to do it herself; and tots of both sexes scamper naked and giggling back and forth between mother's bath and father's. It's a huge old rambling summer-camp of a bath, which has recently been indifferently renovated with varnished pine and cheap tiles, but it remains unselfconsciously the genuine article. It doesn't really matter that the sauna (¥300 on top of the ¥385 basic price) is laid out awkwardly or that the cool pool is only big enough for a single panting refugee from the sauna at a time. The taki (waterfall) is heated (decadent, some think); there is a serious electric bath (where you sit innocently soaking between two electrodes while an electric current courses through your body); and the large, landscaped, still-water rotenburo (outside bath) is open to the sky. After the bath, armed with a beer from the shop just around the corner, you can gaze out on the floodlit moss garden large enough to walk in, waiting for your companion to emerge, late as usual.

Yuamilando

4-2-10 Eifuku, Suginami-ku. ☎ ***03-3328-4639****. Closed Mondays. Nearest station: three-minute walk from* EIFUKUCHO *on the Inokashira Line.*

Most baths are laid out on a square grid.

••••••that have stayed out of trouble for 10 years. Researchers at Tokyo and Meiji Universities showed off a software •

Everything is at right angles, as though to accommodate troops being drawn up for review. Yuamilando's layout is a good deal more relaxed. The roomy cold bath is triangular, and the electric bath and the massage bath are kidney-shaped. The washing stations are scattered about in nooks so you can scrub down away from the crowd if you like. There is a baroque sensibility at work here. In the sauna, which is arranged like a mini–Greek amphitheater and costs a reasonable ¥300, with two towels thrown in—the music might be Scarlatti. There are Greek columns at the entrance and Egyptian columns in the carpeted, movie-palace lobby. In one washing area, there is a faux eighteenth-century mosaic of a Christlike figure ascending to heaven, accompanied by winged cherubs fresh from the bath. It should be noted that the water in the cramped roofed rotenburo is lit from below by blue lights, an annoying distraction, but there is a little garden (curiously uninspired, though, after all these flights of fancy) with a little bench to recover on. There is a pleasant pine-scented mist bath. *Beer is available on the premises for ¥300 a can.*

Imado Onsen

2-8-3 Imado, Taito-ku.
☎ 03-3873-3609.
Closed Fridays. Nearest station: ASAKUSA.

The walk to Imado Onsen from Asakusa Station is a twenty-minute stroll along the landscaped south bank of the Sumida River, through one of Tokyo's oldest and funkiest neighborhoods. The neighborhood defines the bath. Some of Imado Onsen's customers have been coming here since before the war. Tacked up on the walls are tattered posters asking for volunteers to help at the local summer festival and placards flamboyantly autographed by a baseball star, a stand-up comedian, and the master of ceremonies of a late-night soft-porn TV program—all of whom are regulars. You can stash your dirty laundry in one of the coin-operated washing machines, and it will be ready for you when you are ready to reenter the real world. Everybody knows everybody, of course. The little sauna, clearly installed well after such things became fashionable, is free. Rent a sauna towel for ¥100, or not, as you like. The baths are shallow, encouraging supine soaking. Every bath opens out into the large garden, with its carp pool and palm trees and a bath of its own in a rocky grotto. It is said that this outside bath offers a splendid view of the summer fireworks display on the Sumida. *Beer comes easily to hand at the sake shop two minutes away.*

Where to Buy

WETSUITS/DRYSUITS

Marine Plaza Genova, Toshimazu, 2-45-10 Higashi-Ikebukuro, Toshima-ku. ☎ 03-3985-7719.

Despite the grandiose name, this is an honest-to-goodness Mom 'n' Pop wetsuit/drysuit shop that can tailor a suit to your specifications and measurements. If you've seen approximations of Ultraman or Doraemon near the beach, chances are they have been here.

Jakotsu-yu

1-11-11 Asakusa, Taito-ku. ☎ ***03-3841-8645****. Closed Tuesdays. Nearest station:* ASAKUSA.

This is an Edo-period bath in a vibrant part of Old Tokyo, a long psychological distance from Shibuya at the other end of the Ginza Line. The well water here, the color of quick-brewed tea, is heated to a fierce forty-five degrees centigrade, submersion in which will in five seconds cause any tensed muscle to turn into tagliatelli. (This is the purpose of a real Japanese bath. Most baths these days are heated to a comparatively tepid forty-two degrees, which does not bring on the orgasmic shudder of release that a really hot bath does.) In these circumstances, Jakotsu-yu's commodious sauna for ¥400 is simply not worth it. The outside rotenburo, in a little pavilion hung with lanterns, is more soothing, and with the mizuburo (cold bath) outside right next to it there is no need to go back inside once you have unglued all your synapses by immersing them in the ruthless bath inside. Between dips, sit on a stool and lean up against the wooden railing while you contemplate, as if in a dream, the bath's rock garden and waterfall. The massage chairs are antique but no less effective for that. There are coin-operated washing machines in the changing rooms, so it is possible to undress, put your clothes in the washer, take your bath, then retrieve and don your newly washed duds without skipping a beat. There is no handy place to buy a can of beer from a vending machine because the area is so full of little drinking places. Consider paying a visit to The Hub, a jazz pub around the corner, or to Matsukaze, a wonderful izakaya one street over.

Asahi-yu

2-15-3 Hiyoshi, Kohoku-ku, Yokohama. ☎ ***045-563-1049****. Closed any day with a "7" in the date, unless that day is a Saturday or Sunday, in which case the bath will be closed the following Monday instead. Nearest station:* HIYOSHI *on the Toyoko Line.*

Asahi-yu is everything a modern public bath should be: a spacious old building, an immaculate sauna (¥350 extra), three comfortable hot tubs with variations on the jacuzzi, a salubrious cold bath, and a rotenburo in a rocky grotto, perfumed by a different herb each day. The mural on the back wall is of an Italian or possibly a Swiss lake. The front desk is welcoming, and for after-bath libations the sake shop on the corner stocks Bass Ale from England and the delicious Liberty Ale from San Francisco. The massage chair (¥100 for approximately five minutes) will work you over nicely. Normally the bath is not busy during the week, but if you hit it wrong, the Keio University Rugby Club, whose exceedingly muddy playing field is nearby, will have descended on the men's bath en masse to clean up after practice. They tend to be rowdy. In spite of Hiyoshi's being home to the Keio freshman/sophomore campus, the town has none of the atmospheric cheap restaurants, used bookstores, and art movie houses that would be expected of a university town. That's probably because Shibuya, romper room for undergraduates, is only twenty-two minutes away.

•••••••a landmark case, the Urawa District Court ruled against a company who fired a 38-year-old woman because she ••

The Tokyo Q Gang

Doc Agitprop. Former adrenaline junkie and champion athlete with a computer fetish, Doc was or is a research scientist, photographer, programmer, movie extra, stuntman, TV actor, writer, editor, scriptwriter, venture capitalist, gardener, painter, financial analyst, and architect. Also an acknowledged master of perception management.

Jason Atomic is at the moment resident in London. We expect him back any day now.

Kara Besher. A specialist in nineteenth- and twentieth-century Western paintings (and a former artists' model), Kara has been running her own consulting/art-brokerage firm and following contemporary art trends in Tokyo since 1985.

Jude Brand is, well, you know, Jude. She was TQ's Web martyr for several years and wrote the book on Tokyo nightlife.

Mark Dytham and **Astrid Klein** arrived in Tokyo fresh from the Royal College of Art's department of architecture. They said they would stay until they ran out of interesting things to see. Ten years later . . . they are still scouring Tokyo.

Tim Girdler is a Canadian who teaches at a Japanese kindergarten, where he's waiting for his toddlers to share in-the-know Tokyo info.

Kaz Hayashi is TQ's long-suffering contact at Sony Communications Network (So-net), without whom there would be no Tokyo Q.

Yums Hoist is an enigmatic quality food and drink scrounger, whose age, profession, and nationality all remain unknown—except he has never been seen unsauced.

Gilles Kennedy is a British writer based in Tokyo, who delights in her vulnerability in a house of strangers, waiting for the curtain to go up.

Ian Kennedy, son of Rick, began putting Tokyo Q on line in 1995, as a way to unwind after mending Unix boxes at Lehman Brothers. He is currently the point man for Dow Jones's Internet efforts in Japan.

Rick Kennedy can't remember how long he's lived in Tokyo, but he does recall working for Sony for twenty years. He's written three books about Tokyo.

Mike Kleindl has been lucky enough to live in Japan for nineteen years, and divides his time between pampering his wild yeast culture for "pain levain" and self-testing "le paradoxe français."

Steve McClure, *Billboard* magazine's Japan (one-man) bureau chief, has been fascinated with Japanese pop music ever since his aunt gave him a Japanese children's record as a souvenir of her trip to this country in the early '60s. A self-described sybarite and bon vivant, Steve can often be found at clubs and live houses blocking the view of those unlucky enough to be standing behind his ungainly, 191-centimeter-tall Canadian frame.

Jackie Mikami has alternated between Sydney and Tokyo for six years now. Translating and interpreting for bigwigs, she gets back to reality by covering Tokyo's endless and fabulous club scene.

Phillip Musgrave has been coming backward and forward to Japan (Tokyo every time) since 1985. He now lives right in the middle of Tokyo and isn't looking back yet.

N.B. reads eleven newspapers and newsletters in three languages to get material for Tokyo Q's "Last Week in Japan", which JP Morgan in New York has been printing out and distributing to all traders. TQ fans also feed him a lot of material. N.B. sells money for a major Japanese bank.

NikNak has been an active Tokyo concertgoer for about ten years and is unhappy that Club Cittá has added seats to the dance floor.

•••••• disrupted office harmony by refusing to serve tea. A Kobe youth who, threatened with reform school, had been ••

Stella Regalia, from New Jersey, mistakenly got on a plane she thought bound for Hong Kong fifteen years ago, which was actually bound for Tokyo, and she never left. She is a nationally ranked pole vaulter (13.67 feet) and brews her own sake.

Gwen Robinson, former TQ izakaya correspondent, covers Australia for the *Financial Times.*

Khristine Schaffner grew up on Long Island and studied political science at Swarthmore College. She now lives in Tokyo, where she is a corporate Website designer, co-leader of Japan Webgrrls, a writer/editor at a Japanese ISP, and HTML serf for Tokyo Q.

Izumi "Pina" Sekine. Longtime Turkish-Japanese resident of Tokyo and an all-round multilingual production person, is married to NikNak. She has been with Tokyo Q as the trusty assistant of the Webmasters for over a year, and is now living in Seattle where she'll continue to click around Tokyo Q to keep up with Tokyo goings-on.

Ken Straiton is an image person, resident in Tokyo for fifteen years, with a split personality—torn between commerce and art. Fills his spare time casting a delightedly cynical eye on Tokyo. Look for his new book on Japanese design, published by Weatherhill.

Robbie Swinnerton. For Kamakura-based freelance writer Robbie Swinnerton, the ultimate aim in life is to be paid to write about the things he loves. As izakaya columnist for Tokyo Q, restaurant critic for *The Japan Times*, and contributor to a weekly program about Asia for NHK's satellite TV, he believes that, to a considerable extent, he has achieved his goal.

Yuhei Takeuchi writes for the *Asahi Shinbun* and translates "Last week in Japan" into Japanese.

Tony Trollope sometimes wears a monocle. Something of a lad, he drives a battered vintage Morgan, British Racing Green, of course.

Alex Urbansky, born and bred in Tokyo and a graduate of Waseda, still doesn't know how to respond when people ask his obviously non-Japanese face, "Where are you from?" and refuse to believe him when he says, "Tokyo."

Andrew Watt is a thirty-year Tokyo resident, who is in love with Japanese popular graphics of the past and collects old magazines, books, postcards, matchbox labels—whatever he can find in Tokyo's used bookstores and flea markets.

Mikie Yaginuma keeps Tokyo Q organized by paying our bills and talking sweetly to people who want to run ads.

Dave Yarrington. Former brewer at Twenty Tank Brewery (San Francisco), Tommyknocker Brewery (Colorado), and the Commonwealth Brewery (Boston), Dave is currently working with Tokyo Brewing Company, brewing Tokyo Ale and helping set up their first brew pub.

Tim Young, intrepid izakaya photographer, teaches astrophysics at Todai.

••• contemplating taking his own life, threw a 6-year-old boy from the sixth floor of an apartment building to test, •••••

Index: Where to Buy

Antiques 18
Archery Equipment 56
Art Supplies 61
Bamboo Baskets 14
Bazookas 46
Butterflies 28
Combs 31
Dried Seaslug Roe 89
Fans 17
Finnish Bread 114
Fishing Gear 134
Goggles 51
Groceries 9
Japanese Clothes for Attending a Street Festival 12
Japanese Clothes for Lounging Around at Home (Samue) 11
Kaleidoscopes 123
Magic Tricks 39
Nightingale Droppings 32
Paper Lanterns 125
Pipes and Smiking Gear 132
Posters 72
Rock Concert Videos 43
Tenugui 131
Ukeleles 34
Wetsuits/Drysuits 137
Wrapping Materials 21

Index: Where to Eat

JAPANESE
Chicken and Yakitori 73
Country Cooking 75
General 76
Kaiseki and Ko-Ryori 79
Loach 81
Nabe Pot 81
Noodles (Soba, Udon, Ramen) 82
Oden 83
Okonomiyaki 83
Sushi and Sashimi 84
Temple Cooking 87
Tempura 89
Tofu 90
Tonkatsu 91
Unagi (Eel) 92
Yoshoku 93

FOREIGN
American 93
Chinese 95
Eclectic 97
French 99
Italian 107
Korean 112
Mexican 112
Natural Food 112
Spanish 113
Swedish 114
Thai 115
Turkish 116
Vietnamese 116

he said, if this was a good way to die. (The younger boy landed in a tree on the way down which broke his fall and

Image Credits

The publisher would like to thank the various people who provided images for this book. The candid snapshots scattered throughout the book were taken by Rick Kennedy. The vintage illustrations on the chapter opening pages were taken from the vast collection of Andrew Watt. Photographs for the "Art Scene" section on pages 60–64 are by Kara Besher. Photographs of police koban on pages 70–71 and vending machines on pages 102–3 were provided by Mark Dytham and Astrid Klein. Photographs of Tokyo cityscapes and alleyways on pages 126–27 are by Ken Straiton. Comments on these photos, plus an ever-changing array of images, can be found on Tokyo Q at www.tokyoq.com.

About Tokyo Q

What ties the wildly diverse group of people who put Tokyo Q together each week is their abiding fascination with the city. Most of us are graphic designers, architects, photographers, or journalists of one stripe or another. We've collectively traveled just about everywhere, but we always keep coming home to Tokyo.

Tokyo Q first went up on the Web five years ago. The first week we had 30 visitors, one from Chile and one from Iceland. We've now got something over 200,000 visitors a week from all over the place. Sony Communications Network (So-net) has sponsored us generously and with great good will for the past four years, allowing us to pay our contributors.

It seems natural to spin some of what we put up weekly on the Web into this little book. Stone Bridge Press plans to publish an updated Tokyo Q guide to the city every year.

Yoroshiku,

TOKYO Q
www.tokyoq.com

••• his shoulder, but he survived.) Twenty thousand fans filled Yokohama Stadium to watch a huge TV screen showing •••••

••••••the Yokohama BayStars whip the Hanshin Tigers in Kobe to take the Central League pennant for the first time in 38 years. One BayStars fan overcome with joy jumped into the Aratama River and drowned. A professor at Kinki University attempted to clone a mammoth. In Kawagoe, Saitama prefecture, a 30-year-old woman was changed into a man in Japan's first sex-change operation, a particularly problematical operation because at the moment there is no procedure to alter the sex of a person in the all-important family register. Residents of a small fishing village in Fukushima prefecture were found to be engaged in a thriving local industry of applying for passports, then selling them to illegal Chinese immigrants. The dodge was uncovered when Tokyo police found that an inordinate number of Chinese pickpockets had passports identifying them as natives of Fukushima. Police in Yamanashi prefecture reported finding since the beginning of the year the bodies of 58 people who had thrown themselves off a popular suicide jump. The number, a record, is made up mostly of middle-age men who, it was speculated, had run into financial difficulties because of the drepressed economy. After Prime Minister Obuchi said he was thinking of awarding Homerun King Mike McGuire a Japanese decoration, several newspapers suggested he must be senile. A man in Ebina was found to have accepted up to 90,000 yen each for adopting 193 Thai babies so they would have Japanese citizenship. Bridgestone Cycle unveiled a new model that, when you press a button on your pocket remote controller, your cycle is automatically unlocked and a built-in red light turns on to lead the owner to it in the jumble of bikes at the station. A farmer in Kyoto prefecture discoverd that crows are frightened by CDs dangling form a line so they glisten in the sun. Kimono makers sponsored a stroll by models down Omotesando (Tokyo's Champs Elysees, let us say) wearing kimono is creative ways, such as with a miniskirt and high heels, or with black stockings and garters. Two thieves commandeered a power shovel and used it to uproot two automatic teller machines containing 15 million yen and loading them into a getaway truck. A Frenchman scaled the 54-story Shinjuku Center Building and was arrested on the roof for his pains. After an Osaka woman had her purse containing 20,000 yen and her cellular phone stolen by a young man, police suggested she call her phone and tell whoever answers that she finds his voice attractive and arrange a meeting. She did and the police tagged along to make the arrest. Recycling organizations complained that the current wine boom has made it difficult to recycle glass because the glass used for wine bottles is inferior in quality to the glass used for sake bottles and the green color is less delicate. Kobe City organized a concert of 1,053 cellists to commemorate the 25th anniversary of the death of Pablo Casals. A man set fire to a shogi (Japanese chess) hall in Tokyo after failing to gain certification as a professional. In Yamaguchi prefecture, six plastic nabezuru cranes were put out as decoys in a field to entice more real cranes to spend the winter. A number of famous Shinto shrines announced that this year's lucky amulets will be biodegradable. A town in Saitama prefecture developed environmentally friendly concrete made of rice husks. The Environmental Agency said 94 percent of Japan's rivers are polluted. UNESCO declared a forest in Nara prefecture where no tree has been cut down since the year 841 a World Heritage Site. When a Kobe company advertised for young men to act as hosts at women's New Year's parties, pouring drinks and keeping the conversation going, 500 men applied. Kyodo News reported that there are now over 200 companies prepared to come to your house and for a fee clean it from top to bottom, relieving homeowners of this traditional year-end task. Twenty-five fire engines were called out to extinguish a fire in an old wooden building in Golden Gai, Tokyo, where the alleys are 3 meters wide at most. Toyota announced it had cross-bred camphor and jasmine trees to produce a new tree that can absorb 30 percent more automobile emissions than any other plant. 5,600 train lovers applied to take an exam to test their knowledge of railway operations. A maker of Japanese paper in Kofu announced the development of loudspeaker diaphragms made of banana-leaf fibers. Yoyogi Seminar, one of the nation's largest chain of cram schools, went bust, leaving over 150,000 students with no one to coach them on how to pass university entrance exams. Police collared the former president of a bankrupt electrical-component company for snatching 64 handbags from women from Hokkaido to Hiroshima over a 2-year period. It was estimated that 80 percent of high-school and university students have cellular phones. The government said it is considering introducing the jury system because it is more democratic. Nozomi, Japan's first exploratory spacecraft, set off for Mars. Check in next year with Tokyo Q to see what happens!•••••••••••••••